REMEMBER LITTLE ROCK

A VOLUME IN THE SERIES
Public History in Historical Perspective
Edited by Marla R. Miller

REMEMBER LITTLE ROCK

Erin Krutko Devlin

UNIVERSITY OF MASSACHUSETTS PRESS
Amherst and Boston

Copyright © 2017 by University of Massachusetts Press
All rights reserved
Printed in the United States of America

ISBN 978-1-62534-269-0 (paper); 268-3 (hardcover)

Designed by Sally Nichols
Set in Adobe Minion Pro
Printed and bound by Maple Press, Inc.

Cover design by Sally Nichols
Cover photo by Gary Crallé

Library of Congress Cataloging-in-Publication Data

Names: Devlin, Erin Krutko, author.
Title: Remember Little Rock / Erin Krutko Devlin.
Description: Amherst : University of Massachusetts Press, [2017] | Series: Public history in historical perspective | Includes bibliographical references and index.
Identifiers: LCCN 2016059939| ISBN 9781625342690 (pbk. : alk. paper) | ISBN 9781625342683 (hardcover : alk. paper)
Subjects: LCSH: School integration—Arkansas—Little Rock—History—20th century. | African American students—Arkansas—Little Rock—History—20th century. | Central High School (Little Rock, Ark—History. | Collective memory—Arkansas—Little Rock. | Little Rock (Ark—Race relations.
Classification: LCC LC214.23.L56 D48 2017 | DDC 379.2/630976773—dc23
LC record available at https://lccn.loc.gov/2016059939

British Library Cataloguing-in-Publication Data
A catalog record for this book is available from the British Library.

For Sean and my daughters Lillian and Olivia

CONTENTS

Acknowledgments ix

Introduction 1
1. Defining Successful Integration 13
2. Obscuring Effective Mechanisms of Change 43
3. Recasting Moderation and Resistance 71
4. Displacing Blame 111
5. Resisting Historical Erasure 149
Conclusion 179

Notes 191
Index 233

ACKNOWLEDGMENTS

As this project nears completion, I am humbled by the personal, professional, and intellectual debts that I have accrued along the way.

I would like to thank Charles McGovern, Kimberley Phillips Boehm, Grey Gundaker, and W. Fitzhugh Brundage for reading early drafts of this project so carefully. Their unflagging support and encouragement to think expansively molded this project from the outset. Charlie McGovern's advice has been indispensable throughout my graduate studies and early academic career. I work every day to pay his generosity forward with my own current and former students as they embark on new adventures. My colleagues in the American Studies Program at the College of William and Mary, and the history departments at Washington and Lee University, the Virginia Military Institute, the University of Wisconsin-Eau Claire, and the University of Mary Washington also helped sustain this project with their thoughtful feedback and encouragement. I would particularly like to acknowledge the collegial support of Andrew Sturtevant and Louisa Rice at UWEC for their insights as I reformulated aspects of this project. The students who enrolled in my public history courses while this book was in development have also challenged me to think in new ways about the selective appropriation of historical narratives and their representation in memorial space.

Other individuals were also generous with their experience and time, offering new perspectives on the public memory of the Little Rock school desegregation crisis. I was privileged to speak with two members of the Little Rock Nine—Minnijean Brown Trickey and Terrence Roberts—who were kind enough to share their stories and to reflect on how the history they shaped so directly has been told by others. The opportunity to learn and draw inspiration from their example was invaluable. I would also like to thank the public historians who spoke with me about the creation of the Central High Museum and Visitor Center and the Little Rock Central High School National Historic Site, particularly Johanna Miller Lewis, Laura Miller, and Superintendents Michael Maddell and Robin White. Members of the board of Central High Museum, Inc., including Rett Tucker, Ethel Ambrose, Skip Rutherford, and Ronnie Nichols, also graciously shared their insights about the visitor center's genesis.

As any historian or cultural studies scholar knows, this book would not have been possible without the helpful assistance of librarians and archivists who patiently directed me to important resources and manuscript collections. I would particularly like to thank the archivists at the Columbia Oral History Research Office, the Library of Congress, the National Archives, and Special Collections at the University of Arkansas Libraries in Fayetteville and Little Rock and the University of Wisconsin–Eau Claire. Their deep familiarity with the collections in their repositories, and the productive environment they have cultivated in their reading rooms, allowed me to piece together the story I have presented here.

I would also like to thank the University of Massachusetts Press for helping me put this book in the hands of readers. Director Mary Dougherty and series editor Marla Miller expressed early enthusiasm for the project, and I feel privileged to have this book included in the Public History in Historical Perspective series. The recommendations provided by the readers of the manuscript and the editorial board have made this a much stronger book. The careful copyediting of Eric Schramm has made it much easier to read.

Finally, my family and closest friends have offered the emotional support any author needs when trying to express complex ideas through the written word. I would like to thank both of my daughters for providing me with the inspiration to move this project toward completion, as well as their grandparents, Kathy Krutko, Ed and Natalie Devlin, and Paul Krutko and Ellya Jeffries for pitching in to enable me to meet important deadlines. "It takes a village" to raise a child and to write a book, but it takes a small city to do both at the same time. The teachers and staff at Children's House Montessori also enabled me to spend countless hours at my keyboard with the assurance that my eldest daughter was learning and expanding her young mind, too. And of course, I would like to thank my husband, Sean Devlin, who accompanied me on fruitful and fruitless research trips, sharing in every new discovery, patiently listening to every new line of argument, and supplying equal measures of enthusiasm and encouragement throughout this process. He has been a true partner in every sense of the word.

REMEMBER
LITTLE
ROCK

— INTRODUCTION —

Every year across the United States, school children are exposed to the history of the civil rights movement in their textbooks. After reading about the Supreme Court's sweeping *Brown v. Board of Education* (1954) decision, students take a brief detour to Little Rock, where the federal government's determination to enforce school desegregation was tested nationally. In the most common iteration of the story, President Dwight D. Eisenhower rose to the challenge, protecting the constitutional rights of the Little Rock Nine and repelling the forces of massive resistance by deploying members of the 101st Airborne to escort the black students into Central High School. The text may move on to other civil rights campaigns to end discrimination in public accommodations and secure voting rights, but it will likely never return again to the question of educational inequality and K-12 school desegregation. Instead, Little Rock serves as a symbol of the nation's commitment to eradicate this problem and its dedication to providing opportunity to all students regardless of color.

Students may be inspired by the temerity of the Little Rock Nine or take pride in the United States' commitment to the rule of law, but when they raise their heads from their textbooks most will find that their classroom continues to be shaped by the color line. A 2010 analysis of data provided by the US Department of Education revealed that nearly five million African American and Latino students in the United States continue to attend

FIGURE 1. Images of the 1957 Little Rock school desegregation crisis generated headlines around the world. Many emphasized President Eisenhower's deployment of the 101st Airborne and federal enforcement of the *Brown v. Board of Education* decision. (Getty Images)

intensely segregated schools (90–99 percent nonwhite) and three million attend what the study referred to as "apartheid" schools (99–100 percent nonwhite).[1] The United States has the dubious distinction of being the only developed country to *systematically* spend more on the education of wealthy children than poor children. This system perpetuates racial privilege and reinforces class-based hierarchies, leading some activists and scholars to conclude that beyond achieving the intent of *Brown v. Board of Education*, the nation still has not met the standard of *Plessy v. Ferguson*.[2]

Remember Little Rock investigates the chasm between the rhetoric of the "post-civil rights" era and the reality of persistent racial inequality in American education. It examines the public memory of the Little Rock school desegregation crisis, exploring how historical narratives related to this civil rights milestone have evolved in tension with ongoing debates about education, race, and public policy over the last sixty years. In federal courts of law, a triumphal narrative of racial progress, first crafted by the architects of passive resistance in the 1950s and 1960s, now functions as the foundation of "colorblind" jurisprudence. This celebratory narrative, which casts racial injustice as a relic of the past, has been designed and deployed to undercut the goals of mid-century civil rights advocates and has underwritten the release of school districts from court oversight despite tangible evidence of persistent racial inequality.

At the core of this book is an argument that illuminates why our public histories matter. The construction of popular historical narratives is a collective enterprise rooted in broader political, social, and cultural contexts; it is an active, ongoing process that continuously shapes and reshapes our understanding of the past in relation to the concerns of the present.[3] Narratives and arguments rehearsed in the memorial arena have a direct and evident impact on our cultural discourse. Public memory both constitutes and is constituted by the world we live in. On the contested terrain of public memory, dominant and politically powerful groups advance historical narratives to cultivate consent and legitimize the status quo, while those with less influence advance alternative or oppositional narratives in an effort to recast our collective understanding of the past and its relationship to current conditions.[4] As John Gillis has emphasized, "Identities and memories are not things we think *about,* they are things we think *with.*"[5]

A decade ago, in her seminal article "The Long Civil Rights Movement and the Political Uses of the Past," Jacquelyn Dowd Hall commented on the master narrative that dominates our public memory of the civil rights movement—in which the achievements of the 1950s and early 1960s are upheld and honored, while efforts to secure social and economic justice after the passage of 1964 Civil Rights Act and 1965 Voting Rights Act are dismissed or derided. Hall urged historians to carefully reconstruct and actively promote a different history of the mid-century black freedom struggle that was "harder to simplify, appropriate and contain."[6] The explosion of scholarship focused on the "long civil rights movement" has been dedicated to this task—complicating our periodization of the movement by extending its horizons back in time and toward the present, focusing on grassroots campaigns rather than those captured by television cameras, illuminating the contributions of female activists, highlighting the centrality of economic struggles for equality, and generally connecting efforts to "make use" of the reforms embodied in civil rights legislation with the efforts to secure those changes in the first place.[7]

This is important, vital, and vibrant work, but it is equally important to turn our gaze to the construction of the triumphal narrative academic scholars seek to supplant—to reveal its roots, the individuals and institutions that have promoted it, and the ends to which it has been deployed. Historians can challenge the dominance of the narrative of progress and the political project it represents, not just by forging alternative or even oppositional histories, but by deconstructing its growing influence over American public memory. As Michel-Rolph Trouillot noted in *Silencing the Past*, "History is the fruit of power, but power itself is never so transparent that its analysis becomes superfluous. The ultimate mark of power may be its invisibility; the ultimate challenge, the exposition of its roots."[8] Analyzing how the triumphal narrative of progress rose to prominence, and demystifying its hold on the nation's collective conscience, creates the space for broader, more inclusive, and more complicated histories of the civil rights movement.

The dominant memory of the civil rights movement is marked by significant narrative gaps that underscore the great distance between popular histories and the contradictions, complexities, and continuities that have emerged in civil rights historiography. In the public memory of the black freedom struggle, there is a remarkable degree of consensus about which civil rights campaigns were significant and deserve to be commemorated, what the movement meant, and who its protagonists were. Chronologically, the dominant version of the civil rights story begins with the National Association for the Advancement of Colored People's (NAACP) campaign to integrate schools, the Supreme Court's *Brown v. Board of Education* decision in 1954, and its implementation order known as *Brown II* in 1955. When integration did not proceed "with all deliberate speed," civil rights activists demanded change through nonviolent civil disobedience. In this narrative, spectacular, confrontational campaigns orchestrated by the Southern Christian Leadership Conference (SCLC) and the Student Nonviolent Coordinating Committee (SNCC) attracted sympathetic media coverage that moved the nation and placed pressure on political leaders. Civil rights activism resulted in the passage of the 1964 Civil Rights Act and the 1965 Voting Rights Act. With a stroke of the pen, this legislation (in public memory, at least) put an end to segregation, political disenfranchisement, and overt racism in the South.[9] In most public accounts, noteworthy campaigns were led by national civil rights organizations and their charismatic leaders, particularly Martin Luther King Jr. Indeed, a selective vision of King's image, philosophy, and words occupies center stage in popular memory, overshadowing local leaders, grassroots mobilization, friction among civil rights organizations, and philosophical differences over the means and ends of black liberation.[10]

In recent years, historians have problematized the marginalization of grassroots mobilization over national leadership, unknown local struggles over media-savvy national campaigns, and women's participation in our public discourse. The exclusion of these events and social actors limits our understanding of the roles that ordinary people played in the movement and the strength of their commitment toward changing their own communities. Scholars have also noted the lack of attention to struggles against economic inequality and social injustice, Northern and urban struggles against de facto segregation, and black nationalism. However, attempts to move beyond token integration or efforts to dismantle anything other than de jure barriers to equality are marginalized in public memory—the result being a selective vision of the movement that excludes consideration of some of the nation's most enduring racial problems and concerns. It is precisely these elisions that foster the illusion that the struggle for black freedom is complete. Although many activists have stressed the continuity between the "struggles to gain political rights for southern blacks and the struggles to exercise them in productive ways," these connections are rarely explored in the nation's commemorative spaces. Rather, this selective history has been preserved and reproduced in documentaries, civil rights museums, the mass media, and public ceremonies.[11]

Remember Little Rock examines the construction of "Won Cause" mythology[12] in relation to school desegregation. Second only to the *Brown v. Board of Education* decision, Little Rock occupies center stage in the public memory of civil rights struggles for equal education. Largely defined as a constitutional crisis precipitated by Governor Orval Faubus's interference with the implementation of a federal court order, the events of 1957 stand symbolically for federal enforcement of *Brown*. Like so many popular narratives related to civil rights, this symbolism obscures more than it illuminates. *Remember Little Rock* examines how the federal government, publishers, television executives, travel and tourism bureaus, civic leaders, as well as school desegregation litigants and their attorneys, have promoted this breathtakingly constrained perspective of the crisis over the course of nearly sixty years. In doing so, it situates the construction of the public memory of the crisis in historical context and allows us to trace the development of its contours over time. It illuminates the concrete connections between the architects of passive resistance in the late 1950s and their "colorblind" counterparts at the turn of the twenty-first century.

Little Rock's celebration as a civil rights milestone in the dominant narrative of the movement has obscured the simmering undercurrent of sustained resistance and the clash of memory that shaped both public remembrance and the formation of the school district's desegregation policies from the outset. The US government and the Eisenhower administration framed the events that unfolded at Central High School as a constitutional crisis precipitated by Governor Faubus's decision to call out the National Guard to block the admission of the Little Rock Nine in defiance of a court-ordered integration plan. For the benefit of domestic and international audiences, the Eisenhower administration argued that this conflict of state and federal power was resolved when the president utilized the 101st Airborne to clear crowds of white segregationists away from the school grounds and to escort the Little Rock Nine to classes.[13] While this action was represented and is frequently recalled as a vindication of African American civil rights and the rule of law, other actors immediately involved in the crisis framed these events differently. Advocates of massive resistance, steeped in Southern "Lost Cause" mythology, defined Eisenhower's intervention as a second Reconstruction—yet another example of federal interference and "racial engineering." For these "unreconstructed southerners," as Tony Horowitz has called them, the victories of the civil rights movement were the ultimate betrayal of Southern heritage and white privilege.[14] In this context, the Supreme Court's *Brown v. Board of Education* decision was not heralded and celebrated, but derisively referred to as "Black Monday," and Eisenhower's deployment of the 101st Airborne to enforce that decision in Little Rock was viewed as an unjustified federal occupation. The Capital Citizens' Council, for example, emblazoned the slogan "Remember Little Rock" on its segregationist literature and warned other Southern communities to dedicate themselves to massive resistance lest they also experience forced integration. Indeed, in Little Rock itself, voters elected to close all city high schools during the 1958–59 school year rather than readmit black students to Central High. The 1957 crisis and the "lost year" that followed have been carefully analyzed by scholars and parsed in a variety of public forums.[15] Yet the focus on these events has obscured a decades' long struggle to secure meaningful access to educational opportunity in the city.

As a Southern and urban school district, Little Rock experienced virtually every phase of school desegregation litigation as it evolved over the second half of the twentieth century—pupil placement and freedom-of-choice plans; neighborhood schools and busing; limited interdistrict desegregation; magnets, incentive schools, compensatory education plans, and charters; and its most recent reincarnation as a unitary school district in 2009. Indeed, Little Rock is just one of many school districts that have been declared unitary in recent years. This shift in legal status carries enormous import, not just for Arkansas's capital but for districts across the country. In declaring the school district in Little Rock unitary, the courts determined that administrators had eliminated the dual school system composed of segregated black and white schools that made it famous in 1957. A declaration of unitary status requires a finding that the school system in question has eliminated the vestiges—the residue—of the discrimination and segregation that were hallmarks of the Jim Crow era. As a symbol of the triumphal narrative of progress, a unitary school district is no longer subject to court oversight. Yet, like so many other school districts around the nation, Little Rock continues to be afflicted by academic tracking, disparities in discipline and graduation rates, achievement gaps on standardized test scores, and "black" and "white" schools in racially identifiable neighborhoods. Despite these conditions and their historical roots, a declaration of unitary status is a formal finding that these problems can no longer be attributed to the legacy of discrimination in Little Rock. The implication is that these conditions are related to *other* factors outside of the school system's control, and the Little Rock school district can no longer be held responsible for redressing them.

The historical arguments advanced in Little Rock to rationalize and justify

FIGURE 2. The Association of Citizens' Councils, a federation of white supremacist organizations, distributed this image of a soldier prodding two white high school students in the back as an iconic representation of "forced integration" and "brotherhood by bayonet." The Citizens' Council used literature stamped with this slogan to encourage other communities throughout the South to rally behind the cause of massive resistance. The council's call to "Remember Little Rock" as early as 1958 demonstrates that the public memory of the crisis was contested from the outset and was claimed by civil rights advocates as well as their opponents. (Citizens' Councils of America Literature [MS C49], University of Arkansas Libraries, Fayetteville)

token integration, local control, and limited federal intervention, and to rollback and undermine court-ordered and voluntarily adopted mechanisms of school integration in Arkansas, illuminate and inform broader questions about the relationship between public memory and ongoing debates about race, education, and public policy. It is essential to not only be attentive to the construction of public memory, but also its practical applications. As Renee C. Romano has observed in her examination of reopened civil rights cases, courts of law have become "one of the key arenas in which the American public is asked, even encouraged, to engage with the past." As courts weigh the impact of racial injustice, their decisions draw directly on the public memory of the mid-century black freedom struggle, popular perceptions of civil rights activism, and the scope of white resistance. More importantly, legal decisions become binding precedents that transform contested histories into fixed findings of fact with concrete consequences for litigants and American society more broadly.[16] This process has been particularly evident in school desegregation litigation in the second half of the twentieth century.

A central tenet and core argument of those who have endeavored to escape court oversight has been a celebration not of the civil rights movement's history, but the civil rights movement *as history*. They have declared that the civil rights movement, and the resistance that accompanied it, is an epoch of the distant past. From this perspective, further efforts to redress discrimination (which purportedly does not exist) do not help to even the playing field, but instead place white students at an unfair disadvantage, cast a questionable light on the accomplishments of black pupils, and wrest control of local school decisions away from educational authorities. *Despite the tangible evidence of inequality on the ground,* this public history of the movement has buttressed the federal courts' turn away from intervention in local school affairs and the spate of unitary status decisions that have swept the nation.

The triumphal narrative of progress that has underwritten Supreme Court jurisprudence since the early 1990s and the release of school districts from federal court oversight is founded on several central principles: (1) defining desegregation as narrowly as possible; (2) advancing the argument that the passage of time itself is sufficient to erode the legacy of centuries of state-sponsored discrimination; (3) presenting demonstrably ineffective policies as model desegregation procedures; and (4) advancing the argument that persistent inequities are the product of individual deficiencies rather than structural disparities. The first four chapters of *Remember Little Rock* explore the historical development of each of these central tenets, their articulation in historical narratives about the 1957–59 school desegregation crisis, and their application in Arkansas's capital.

Although this book takes its title from the slogan the Capital Citizens' Council used as a rallying cry for massive resistance, it was not this constituency that constructed a "Won Cause" mythology with regard to school desegregation. Rather, this memorial project was advanced by the forces of *passive* resistance who sought to minimize desegregation through the use of selective pupil placement, student transfers, screening mechanisms, and administrative policies. In Little Rock, school administrators and civic leaders who defined themselves as racial moderates advanced these plans as a legal alternative to outright defiance of the Supreme Court's *Brown* mandate. These historical actors advanced tokenism and gradualism as the most reasonable and pragmatic approach to school desegregation, and argued that more sweeping change jeopardized white support of public education.

In a defense of white privilege, moderates sought to preserve as much of the architecture of the city's dual system of white and black schools as possible. A key component of their effort to frame their policies as a "good faith" effort to comply with the *Brown v. Board of Education* decision was their effort to distance themselves from their more strident segregationist counterparts. Early retrospective accounts of the Little Rock school desegregation crisis, like Superintendent of Schools Virgil Blossom's memoir *It HAS Happened Here* (1959), sought to define desegregation within the parameters of tokenism and gradualism, and to obscure the personal, political, and philosophical connections between the passive resistance adopted by school administrators and the rhetoric of massive resistance that animated the mobs outside Central High. In doing so, moderates sought to define desegregation as narrowly as possible and frame their own actions during the crisis as racially progressive and socially responsible.

This historical narrative, in conjunction with the pupil placement procedures and freedom-of-choice plans crafted by the architects of passive resistance, successfully delayed systemic integration in Southern school systems for nearly a decade after the *Brown v. Board of Education* decision. However, in the absence of significant or sustained progress, the federal courts struck down the use of these procedures in the late 1960s and demanded the development of student assignment plans that were demonstrably effective and dismantled dual school systems comprising white and black schools. In the early 1970s, the courts approved the use of student transportation, noncontiguous attendance zones, and other remedies that were designed to counteract the impact of residential segregation. They also authorized these remedies in Northern and Western school districts that were found guilty of de jure violations.

Although the courts decisively rejected tokenism and gradualism during this period, the arguments in favor of this position were nurtured in public discourse and incubated cultural memory. During the controversy surrounding busing, for example, new attacks on black students and school integration efforts in cities like Boston were measured against the Little Rock desegregation crisis. Despite the application of legal precedent from Little Rock in the Boston transportation case, Northern antibusing organizations sought to disassociate themselves from the legacy of segregationist resistance geographically and temporally by promoting the fiction of de facto discrimination. Antibusing advocates in the mid-1970s sought to frame the civil rights movement as "history"—if the black freedom struggle could be located in the historical past, further federal action and court intervention was not only unnecessary but also potentially destructive.

Notably, as antibusing advocates and civic leaders chronicled the changes that had occurred in American society over the preceding two decades, they constructed a historical narrative that was written in the passive voice. In this narrative, the changes that had been wrought in Southern society were not wrought by civil rights activism, persistent litigation, court-ordered remedies, or federal enforcement, but were the product of the passage of time itself and an amorphous shift in American racial attitudes and perceptions. This narrative of passive progress divorced the *actions* of African American civil rights activists from the fruits of their labor. With their contributions obscured, filmmakers and other representatives of the culture industries looked favorably on retrospective accounts of the civil rights movement that presented white moderates as the midwives of lasting change in Little Rock and elsewhere. In this context, white moderates were repositioned as allies rather than opponents of the mid-century black freedom struggle, and African American activists were marginalized in popular accounts of the movement.

This public memory of desegregation coincided with a turn away from the systemic remedies promoted by civil rights organizations and a resurgence of the policies white moderates crafted in the 1950s and 1960s. Mechanisms of change that produced substantial and measurable integration in Southern and urban school districts, like busing, were not celebrated as solutions but redefined as "problems" that precipitated white flight and disinvestment in public education. Instead of being viewed as another form of resistance to integration, white flight was naturalized and accommodated as federal courts looked favorably on the arguments of school districts that sought to escape from or reshape court oversight. In this context, school districts resurrected arguments in favor of gradual change, local control of school desegregation, residential school attendance, the integration of "exceptional" students into "special" programs, and the flexible application of federal law. The federal courts upheld claims that school districts could only be held accountable for doing what was *practicable* to address racial segregation, and the public embrace of racial "moderation" obscured the fact that many of the voluntary "integration" programs promoted during this period had been designed to limit, not encourage, the dissolution of dual school systems two decades earlier.

The effort to historicize, contain, and appropriate the legacy of the civil rights movement also underwrote the claim that persistent racial inequities in American society and education were not the product of institutionalized racism. In the early 1990s, the federal courts affirmed arguments that "racial imbalances" in a school district were less likely to represent "vestiges of a constitutional violation" *as the years passed* and that time itself should be taken into consideration when considering petitions for release from oversight. The majority of the justices agreed that discrepancies in student achievement could be attributed to "external factors" rather than racial discrimination.[17] Increasingly, in Little Rock and elsewhere, civic leaders and school officials asserted that remaining inequities were the product of problems within the black community generated by a purported "culture of poverty" rather than administrative procedures or educational practices. These arguments and others have served as the foundation of petitions for release from court oversight in school districts across the nation. At the turn of the twentieth century, the triumphal narrative of passive progress has been reified into Supreme Court jurisprudence—this narrative, robbed of any sense of historical contingency, agency, or critical inquiry, has had a tremendous impact on the contours of our educational system.

However, although *Remember Little Rock* traces the ascendance of the triumphal narrative of passive progress in public memory and federal courts of law, it also illuminates the persistent efforts of civil rights advocates and community activists, including the Little Rock Nine, to advance alternative histories in support of ongoing efforts to secure educational equity and opportunity. Those in Little Rock who have a vested interest in the desegregation of the city's schools, and the litigation that was designed to achieve it, have not observed the evolution of the public memory of the Little Rock school desegregation crisis silently. In newspaper articles, memoirs, public forums, and commemorative ceremonies, civil rights activists and their allies have repeatedly contested efforts to cast Little Rock's school desegregation drama as a distant relic of the past that has no bearing on the concerns of the present. This sustained resistance demonstrates that the public memory of the civil rights movement is not simply subject to manipulation and appropriation, but also can be mobilized to nurture oppositional narratives that empower movements for social change.

— CHAPTER ONE —

Defining Successful Integration

During the 1957–58 school year, segregationist students inside Little Rock Central High School continued their campaign to halt the progress of school desegregation long after protestors, soldiers from the 101st Airborne, and representatives of the press disappeared from the lawn outside of the building. As part of their campaign of harassment, they distributed small printed cards that derided members of the Little Rock Nine, the school administration, and the NAACP. With the support of adult organizations like the Capital Citizens' Council and the Mothers League of Central High School, students passed out materials that accused Superintendent of Schools Virgil T. Blossom of entering into a conspiracy with the president of the NAACP's Arkansas State Conference, Daisy Bates, to impose integration on the residents of Little Rock. The Capital Citizens' Council distributed literature insinuating Bates had been given "free access" to Central High School and had been provided with authority as an "unofficial 'principal'" to "cross-examine" white students resisting desegregation during disciplinary procedures. "Who is running Central High School?" they asked. "Blossom or Bates . . . or Both!"[1] Even the "permit" cards circulated by segregationist students sanctioning the abuse of the Little Rock

> **PERMIT**
>
> **GOOD ONLY UNTIL MAY 29, 1958**
>
> BEARER MAY KICK RUMPS OF EACH CHS NEGRO ONCE PER DAY UNTIL ABOVE EXPIRATION DATE.
>
> LAST CHANCE, BOYS. DO NOT USE SPIKED SHOES.
>
> SIGNED: **DAISEY BLOSSOM**

FIGURE 3. Segregationist students at Little Rock Central High School distributed small printed cards like this one in order to encourage the harassment of the Little Rock Nine throughout the 1957–58 school year. On this card, the conflation of NAACP Arkansas State Conference president Daisy Bates's name with that of Superintendent of Schools Virgil T. Blossom was designed to suggest that civil rights leaders and school officials were conspiring to impose desegregation on the city of Little Rock. (Image 127769, Wisconsin Historical Society)

Nine gestured to this supposed conspiracy by stating that the authorization for such action came from "Daisey Blossom."[2]

Although the forces of massive resistance attempted to cast Blossom and Bates as collaborators, these two central protagonists clashed repeatedly over school policies and admission procedures in the months leading up to the Little Rock school desegregation crisis, not only in informal meetings but also through their legal representatives in courts of law. While Blossom advanced his token integration plan as a moderate and measured response to the *Brown* decision that could be implemented without sustained damage to the system of public education, Bates and the NAACP argued that tokenism continued to deny thousands of African American school children their constitutional rights and was a smokescreen designed to preserve the dual system of education in Arkansas's capital. Both the Little Rock school district and the NAACP made these arguments in federal court. The courts' determination that the Blossom Plan marked a reasonable start to integration put in motion the selective screening procedures that ultimately winnowed the number of African American students entering Central High School in the fall of 1957 down to nine. But crucially, these same questions would *continue to be litigated* in the aftermath of the school desegregation crisis, not only in federal courts of law but also in the field of public memory. Blossom and Bates published two of the first retrospective accounts of the crisis. Their books were written with an eye toward constructing a public memory that would shape the trajectory of school desegregation litigation in the 1960s as courts struggled to define the parameters of successful integration.

Blossom's *It HAS Happened Here* (1959) and Bates's *The Long Shadow of Little Rock* (1962) revealed that they were far from co-conspirators during the events leading up to the school desegregation crisis. When Bates's memoir was published, the *Arkansas Gazette* acknowledged the persistence of these rumors in the state capital but suggested it was time to put them to rest. "There is a popular belief that Virgil Blossom, the Little Rock school superintendent during that time, conspired with Mrs. Bates to integrate the Little Rock schools," observed reviewer Roy Reed. "Mrs. Bates' book does not leave that impression . . . Overall, she seems to have as little use for Blossom as for most of the other white principals in the crisis."[3] Indeed, in many respects Bates's memoir was written in direct counterpoint to Blossom's own retrospective account, in which he worked diligently to distance the overt opposition of massive resistance from what the historian John A. Kirk has described as his strategy of minimal compliance.[4] In contrast, Bates sought to collapse the distinction between these courses of action. Although she was not privy to the backroom deals brokered between Faubus, Blossom, and the school board, she highlighted the rhetoric of white supremacy and the presumption of white privilege that undergirded both of these approaches to resisting school desegregation. She described Blossom's strategy of minimal compliance not as a model integration strategy assured of success, but as a devious means of evading the mandate of *Brown* and preserving segregated education. In her account, massive resistance to school integration was not imposed on Little Rock by "outsiders." Instead, the 1957–59 school desegregation crisis was the predictable byproduct of Blossom's own public rhetoric and the efforts of the school board to minimize and delay the implementation of desegregation.[5]

At a fundamental level, these two memoirs advanced competing arguments related to how successful integration should be defined not only in the past, but also in the immediate present. While both the Little Rock school district and the NAACP advanced their claims through the courts, Blossom and Bates advanced arguments in support of the litigants through their retrospective accounts. What did the *Brown* decision require? Did the Little Rock Nine represent successful tokenism or the promise of deeper systemic transformation? What were the responsibilities of the federal courts, civil rights organizations, local school boards, national and state political leaders, and citizens in relation to the transformation gripping Southern schools? Both authors believed that their answers to these questions, and their proposed strategies of change, still spoke directly to the needs of their community and the nation at large. Both sought to relitigate the arguments advanced in the courts in hopes of securing broader public acceptance of their actions during the school desegregation crisis, while furthering their goals and bolstering their professional reputations in its immediate aftermath.

Defining the *Brown* decision as narrowly as possible was a central strategy of passive resistance to school integration in the late 1950s and early 1960s. Indeed, despite Little Rock's iconic status as a site of massive resistance, under the leadership of Superintendent Virgil Blossom, the city was at the vanguard of developing administrative procedures and legal arguments that token integration satisfied the Supreme Court's requirements in *Brown I* and *Brown II*.[6] In the mid-1950s, Blossom had staked his professional reputation on the strategy of minimal compliance. Following the Court's implementation order in *Brown II*, the superintendent developed the "Blossom Plan," an approach designed to capitalize on residential segregation in Little Rock and reduce the number of African American students transferred into the city's white schools. Blossom argued that this approach would help preserve support for public education in the white community while fulfilling the requirements of federal courts of law. If implemented successfully, the superintendent believed his plan might serve as a model for the nation and provide a viable strategy for Southern school districts struggling to reconcile themselves to *Brown*. Blossom certainly hoped that the public visibility of his plan would help propel his career to greater heights. Years later, he reflected, "My career, my whole interest, were bound up in that hope of future progress."[7]

The 1957–59 crisis derailed these ambitions. Across the political spectrum, few viewed Little Rock as a successful model of school desegregation. Blossom, however, was unwilling to abandon this project and determined to rehabilitate his professional reputation in the wake of the crisis. Indeed, he had little choice in the matter. During the 1958–59 school year, the Little Rock school district released Blossom and bought out the remainder of his contract. Nationally, the superintendent faced criticism as well; Blossom admitted that he received a lukewarm reception at the meeting of the American Association of School Administrators in St. Louis at the end of the 1957–58 school year in the wake of reports that he had expelled one of the Little Rock Nine for responding to repeated provocation from white students.[8] In the market for a new job, Blossom was determined to defend the plan of action he had developed for Arkansas's capital city and the disciplinary procedures he had instituted inside Central High.

In his memoir, first serialized in the *Saturday Evening Post,* the superintendent cast himself as a moderate and painted minimal compliance as a reasonable and lawful alternative to massive resistance as well as immediate integration. In his view, the crisis in the fall of 1957 was the product of nefarious "outside" influences who worked vigorously to discredit him and to derail his carefully wrought plans, precisely because they promised to be so successful: "They decided they must stop our plan just because it was so reasonable and initially involved so few Negro students that it had every chance of success."[9] The superintendent's memoir was designed to demonstrate that it was the inability of the school district to adhere to his moderate course that precipitated the crisis in Little Rock, not weaknesses in the Blossom Plan itself. Moreover, Blossom contended that even in the aftermath of the crisis and Little Rock's "lost year," when all of the city's high schools were closed in defiance of federal court orders, his approach remained the only viable strategy tailored to the needs of Southern white communities that would pass constitutional muster.

Blossom positioned his memoir as a primer that would enable other school districts to avoid the stumbling blocks that had pitched Little Rock headlong into a constitutional crisis.[10] According to Blossom, the catastrophic consequences of massive resistance and "forced" integration "by bayonet" demonstrated not only the superiority of his original plan but also justified the school board's perpetuation of this strategy through pupil placement laws and freedom-of-choice plans well into the 1960s. "One thing is obvious," Blossom noted, "if the South does not plan the future of its system of public education in line with the mainstream of progress, then the federal government will do it for us."[11] By provoking the direct intervention of the federal government, overt resistance might result in more integration than plans like his own that were designed to minimize *Brown's* impact. With his guidance, Little Rock had developed a plan rooted in minimal compliance that had survived the ups and downs of the school crisis. As the nation moved into its second decade of school desegregation in the 1960s, Blossom argued that the city was in a good position to build on the foundations of his plan and implement pupil placement provisions approved by the Supreme Court that would allow school boards to continue to minimize African American transfers into white schools. Although written in racially neutral language, Blossom understood that transfer policies could be used to maintain a "high degree of segregation" in the name of preserving "educational standards."[12] Indeed, the historian John A. Kirk has argued that it was precisely the "low-key and surreptitious approach to school desegregation" adopted by the architects of passive resistance in Little Rock that made their strategies "far more effective in undermining the *Brown* decision in the long run."[13]

Little Rock's superintendent acknowledged that the plan he developed for the Little Rock school district in the late 1960s "represented minimum integration," but defended his approach on the grounds that circumventing systemic desegregation "was definitely what the majority of white residents wanted."[14] Blossom's primary concern while developing his proposed course of action was that it be accepted by the majority of white Little Rock citizens; it was in this direction that his social relationships and his prospects for advancement lay. In contrast, the approval of Little Rock's black community about the district's approach to school desegregation was a low priority. Even overt opposition from civil rights leaders seemed little more than an inconvenience and did little to disrupt Blossom's confidence that he, or other officials in his position, could command the co-operation of local residents and maintain control over the speed and pace of integration in the Little Rock school district. Blossom's preoccupation with white public opinion shaped his initial response to the *Brown* decision in 1954, and it was equally evident in his memoir. The superintendent argued that school districts could not develop school desegregation plans without consideration for their white patrons. In Southern communities where voter registration procedures disenfranchised the majority of African American residents, Blossom clearly felt that the future of the school system rested in the hands of white citizens who turned out for school board elections, supported or rejected school bonds, and enrolled their children in the public schools; if school districts did not take preemptive measures to minimize *Brown*'s impact, white public support for the school system itself would be in jeopardy.[15]

Consequently, Blossom highlighted the strategies he had adopted to appease this constituency as a model for other school districts interested in adopting his approach. As superintendent of Little Rock schools, Blossom introduced a phased plan designed to limit the initial impact of desegregation to high schools, with middle and elementary schools to follow at a later date. The superintendent reported that the benefit of starting with older students was that their understanding of Southern social mores and racial etiquette was more fully developed than that of their younger peers.[16] Moreover, the architecture of the Blossom Plan was built on the bedrock of geographic segregation in the city. For over a decade, the city's public housing authority had been razing African American housing in Little Rock's central core and relocating black families to segregated public housing units on the east side of the city. Simultaneously, as development in the city of Little Rock spread to the west, affluent white neighborhoods collectively known as the "country club" sector or "silk-stocking district" emerged.[17] Under Blossom's plan, Little Rock would not proceed with any plan of desegregation until two new high schools were constructed that would service these areas. Horace Mann High School was designated as a "Negro" high school on the east side of the city, while Hall High would serve the affluent white developments on the west side. As a result, the "first impact" of integration would be concentrated on Central High School.[18] School districts following Blossom's model might also consider building new school plants in highly segregated neighborhoods or gerrymandering school attendance zones to achieve the same effect.

Blossom was careful to note, however, that his plan did not rely on geographic attendance zones alone to minimize integration. Both white and black students resided in all three zones. Consequently, the school board developed a system of "voluntary transfers" and screening procedures to address this issue. By default, African American students would continue to attend school at Horace Mann unless they expressed interest in attending Central. In this regard, Blossom's transfer system was built on Little Rock's long legacy of maintaining a dual system of racially defined schools. The superintendent conceded that 80 of the 526 African American students who resided in Central's attendance zone volunteered to integrate the high school in 1957, but in his memoir he provided insight into how he reduced the number of prospective registrants even further. First, Blossom asked African American junior high and high school principals to counsel the students and their parents about the challenges they would face as school desegregation pioneers. In his instructions to the principals, Blossom commanded, "It should be your purpose to guide those who are not equipped *away from participation* in the transition program." Student records were also scrutinized in an effort to reduce or eliminate prospective students on the grounds of their "mental ability, achievement record, school citizenship record and health record," and African American pupils were told that they would not be able to participate in sports or other extracurricular activities at the integrated school. According to Blossom, the school district adopted these screening procedures to reduce community resistance and reassure white parents that "educational standards" would not be impaired by large numbers of purportedly underprepared African American students entering Little Rock Central High.[19]

Blossom acknowledged that the majority of white residents in the city were segregationists, but he insisted that they were "law-abiding" citizens who favored and supported this "reasonable" approach. Throughout his text, the superintendent was careful to try to create distance between those who embraced his strategy of minimal compliance and the mobs that attracted international attention in the fall of 1957.[20] Blossom's book was a strategic construct designed to demonstrate that a policy of minimal compliance, gradual implementation, and tokenism was the best course forward for Little Rock and Southern school districts more generally. A key part of this project was distancing the "legal" and "lawful" path of resistance to *Brown*—tokenism and minimal compliance—from massive resistance. Blossom went to great lengths to try to obscure the connections—both personal and philosophical—between these two camps in an effort to present minimal compliance as an "integration" strategy that would satisfy the requirements of federal judges, when in fact it had been designed and presented to residents in Little Rock as a means of preserving segregation and a dual system of education for the majority of the city's white and black pupils. If the massive resistance movement had sought to frame the Little Rock school desegregation crisis as a second Reconstruction, Blossom understood that passive resistance required an alternative memorial strategy—not one that cast the 1957–59 Little Rock school desegregation crisis as a call to arms—but one that used it as a careful foil.

Blossom was determined not only to present his school desegregation plan as a "sane" approach to school desegregation but also to displace responsibility for the administrative chaos inside and outside Central High School onto the shoulders of other historical actors. In his memoir, the superintendent recalled that "all hands" were raised against the successful execution of his plan. Beset by extremist civil rights organizations and white supremacists, neither state nor federal officials came to the school administration's aid. "Little Rock did not bring on disaster," Blossom argued. "Disaster was deliberately thrust upon a majority of progressive and law-abiding citizens by extremists and outsiders seeking to serve their own ends."[21] In his effort to restore his professional reputation, Blossom adroitly sidestepped any responsibility he might have had to lead his community, to speak publicly and enthusiastically about the merits of his own plan, to act to ensure the successful implementation of his own policies and procedures, to maintain discipline and protect the Little Rock Nine in the halls of Central High School, or to ensure that illegal acts were punished.

The first direct challenge to the Blossom Plan came from the NAACP. Blossom insisted that 95 percent of the city's black population supported his "go-slow" approach out of fear that more rapid action might lead to the collapse of public education, concern about potential violence or economic retaliation, or because of their own affinity for Southern "tradition." However, Blossom lamented, "Negro extremists were unsatisfied."[22] Certainly, the school district's deliberate action to reduce the number of African American students eligible to attend Central High School had eroded the black community's confidence that the school board was operating in good faith. Responding to an appeal from black parents in the school district, the state chairman of the NAACP Legal Defense Committee, Wiley Branton, and the regional attorney for the NAACP, U. Simpson Tate, filed suit in federal court. In a direct challenge to the constitutionality of the Blossom Plan, the petition called for the immediate integration of all Little Rock schools in grades 1–12.[23] In his memoir, Blossom conceded that the families involved and some others who supported the test case "were citizens of Little Rock" but insisted that the suit was "being supported, if it had not been initiated by outsiders."[24] In depositions taken in the case from local NAACP leaders Daisy Bates and J. C. Crenshaw, school district attorneys sought evidence that the Little Rock branch was taking its orders directly from the national office in New York.[25]

Ultimately, the NAACP's challenge to the Blossom Plan failed and the courts upheld the superintendent's model as a good-faith effort to proceed with school desegregation with "all deliberate speed." In his memoir, Blossom was careful to note that the NAACP did not appeal this decision all the way to the Supreme Court and suggested that the civil rights organization's decision implicitly recognized the constitutional validity of his approach. "The suit was then dropped without explanation," he recalled, "but it seemed likely that the NAACP legal staff came to the conclusion that the Supreme Court also might uphold our plan—and thus establish a legal pattern of gradual integration everywhere."[26] Although the test suit ultimately did not result in any changes to the Blossom Plan, the NAACP did gain some important ground. For the first time, school officials were required to put their plan in writing. More importantly, the district was now under court order to integrate in the fall of 1957.[27] If they failed to follow through with their promises, they could be held in contempt of court.

This lack of flexibility would later present challenges for the school board, but in the months leading up the opening of the 1957 school year Blossom suggested that the test suit was problematic for an entirely different reason. The NAACP's legal action "attracted undesirable attention" from white segregationists.[28] Subsequently, the Blossom Plan became a target for the forces of massive resistance who denied the authority of the Supreme Court to "create law" and who argued for the perpetuation of segregation through the rhetoric of state's rights and white supremacy. Like the NAACP, the superintendent recalled, "their strategy was to prevent at any cost a demonstration that school integration could be accomplished gradually and successfully."[29] By holding the line in Little Rock and refusing to acknowledge the superiority of his model, Blossom suggested that segregationist organizations like the regional affiliates of the White Citizens' Council hoped they would strengthen their efforts to promote massive resistance to school desegregation in other communities.[30] This coalition of "die-hard segregationists" unleashed a "ruthless, whirlwind campaign of bigotry, of political pressure, of economic boycott and mob violence" designed and "artfully combined" to turn the "optimum situation into a disaster."[31] Although Blossom frequently referred to the crowds of protestors gathered outside Central High as a "mob," he did not characterize their actions as spontaneous. Instead, this "extremist minority" was an active and organized force that worked diligently to create a climate of hysteria. Their advocacy of massive resistance created uncertainty, fear, and confusion among Little Rock's white population. Blossom characterized himself as the primary "target" of segregationist propaganda and recounted a systematic campaign of harassment designed to intimidate him and other members of the board into abandoning the Blossom Plan.[32]

Throughout his memoir, however, Blossom insisted that the impetus behind efforts to derail his plan in favor of massive resistance came from outside Little Rock. This argument bolstered the superintendent's claim that he had diligently cultivated community support for his approach and had persuaded "ardent segregationists" on the local level that his strategy was the "best they could get."[33] Indeed, Blossom's efforts to shield the citizens of Little Rock in his text attracted the attention of his editor, who cautioned him about putting "*all* of the blame for defiance on outsiders," and subsequently inserted qualifiers like "majority," "mainly," and "mostly" in the final draft of the book.[34] Nevertheless, in a review of the manuscript, even the Little Rock school board's attorney, Archie House, took issue with his colleague's characterization of the city's citizenry. "When I first read the manuscript I noticed your emphasis on the 'outside influence' which was exerted on L[ittle] R[ock] residents," House observed. The attorney was not as quick to absolve local citizens of responsibility for the events that unfolded inside and outside Central High. "There was something in L[ittle] R[ock] residents beneath the surface which made them susceptible to such demagoguery, and they fundamentally were at fault," he wrote. House insisted that the city was beset by "ignorance and prejudice" and it was not quite right to suggest that it was a "case of a little lamb losing its way."[35]

This framing of the crisis, however, was central to Blossom's text and his image of himself as a moderate man beset on all sides by extremists and fanatics. The title of his memoir, *It HAS Happened Here*, echoed Sinclair Lewis's satirical 1935 novel *It Can't Happen Here*, a cautionary tale about the dangers of demagoguery and the burgeoning threat of fascism. While many Americans dismissed such concerns with the casual aside that "it can't happen here," Blossom's title suggested that under the influence of political leaders trumpeting the cause of massive resistance, it already had. The campaign of opposition unleashed against his school desegregation plan created a climate that stifled political debate and productive decision making. By the end of 1958, moderates and civic leaders had been effectively silenced through a campaign of intimidation, state legislators had turned over "unprecedented powers" to the executive, and the State Sovereignty

Commission and state police regularly questioned and observed those who opposed the governor's politics.[36] This windstorm of controversy had also swept away Blossom's hopes of demonstrating the efficacy of minimal compliance.

Blossom and many other moderates in Little Rock contended that the crowds would not have gathered outside Central High if they had not been encouraged by Governor Faubus and assured that the "power of the state" supported their actions. In Blossom's book, Faubus might be said to have been cast in the role of Sinclair Lewis's President Berzelius Windrip, a folksy political leader who capitalizes on public anxiety to establish a totalitarian state in the name of preserving American tradition and patriotism.[37] The governor justified his intervention in Little Rock in the name of preserving law and order and protecting public safety. Publicly and even under oath, the superintendent challenged this claim and denied any knowledge of planned violence in the weeks leading up to the opening of Little Rock's 1957–58 academic year. Although his memoir revealed his mounting concern over the threats to himself and his own family and his frantic appeals to the governor to issue a public statement supporting the implementation of the court-ordered Blossom Plan, the superintendent sought to minimize this inconsistency between his sworn testimony and his retrospective account by suggesting that any threat of impending violence could have been quashed with a "single gesture of firm and courageous leadership on behalf of law and order."[38] Blossom rebuked Faubus for not following this course of action, and he accused the governor of encouraging the forces of massive resistance by calling out the National Guard and publicly stating that the schools could continue to be operated on a segregated basis until the conflict between state and federal law was resolved. Blossom argued that this action persuaded Little Rock's citizens, including those who had previously accepted minimal integration, that they might avoid it all together.[39]

Blossom's narrative painted Faubus as a weak-kneed politician who wanted to displace responsibility for the enforcement of federal court orders onto others. Indeed, Blossom accused Faubus of manufacturing some of the threats made against school officials such as himself in order to persuade them to abandon their planned course of action.[40] In *It HAS Happened Here*, Governor Faubus is depicted as having failed to demonstrate "courageous leadership" and instead acted to preserve his own political interests in order to court favorable public opinion. More pointedly, Blossom's contention that the implementation of the Blossom Plan was "no longer a local, school administrative problem" but instead had become a "state political" issue conveniently absolved the superintendent himself of any responsibility for the events that followed.[41]

It HAS Happened Here also castigated the federal government for failing to support school administrators through civil, rather than military, action. The superintendent wrote that Governor Faubus would have welcomed "vigorous enforcement action" by federal officials, and he noted that the Department of Justice refused to supply US marshals to protect Central High School in advance of the start of the school year. The superintendent also suggested that this reluctance was motivated by the Eisenhower administration's desire to force local and state officials to absorb the political heat generated from enforcing the *Brown* decision. Instead of engaging in preemptive action, the federal government waited until the crisis had already fully developed and then deployed overwhelming force. Blossom felt that the deployment of military troops to the city of Little Rock only exacerbated tension in the city and increased resistance to the court-ordered integration plan. Public resentment of "forced" integration jeopardized the successful implementation of even minimal plans based on tokenism and gradualism. "If the use of armed force in the controversy over the integration of Central High proved anything," Blossom contended, "it was that America's civil rights problem cannot be solved with bayonets." After the Little Rock Nine were escorted into the school, "Central High was integrated," Blossom recalled, "and our troubles *began*."[42] Blossom maintained that military intervention hardened public opinion and moved the struggle over school desegregation inside the halls of Central. Ardent segregationists appealed to Little Rock residents to close the school down entirely rather than permitting it to be operated under "armed guard."[43]

Blossom also criticized the Department of Justice for failing to file injunctions or charges against those that had gathered outside the school to prevent token desegregation. For their part, federal officials contended that the Little Rock school board should have undertaken this action itself in order to ensure the successful implementation of the Blossom Plan. Blossom dismissed this position in his memoir. School officials, he argued, should not be asked to "assume the untenable position of seeking court restraint of their neighbors." If they were expected to do so, few "moderate and able citizens" would agree to assume these positions of public responsibility.[44]

Indeed, rather than filing injunctions against ardent segregationists who sought to derail the Blossom Plan, school officials attempted to redirect public complaints about the district's approach to the federal courts. As public controversy surrounding the implementation of the Blossom Plan mounted in the summer of 1957 and the tide of public opinion turned against them, school administrators and board members retreated behind the legal cover provided by federal court orders. In public statements, the school board publicly reiterated that it did not support the principle of integration but was compelled to obey the mandate laid out in *Brown*. Moreover, the board explained that the passage of state segregation laws did not inoculate them from their legal obligation to implement what was now—in the wake of the NAACP's test suit—a "court-ordered" integration plan. "In our opinion," the board asserted, "the language is unmistakable [in the Constitution] and those who say that state laws permitting segregation are supreme simply refuse to read that which is plainly written." However, as Blossom noted in his memoir, the board "*invited* the segregationists to file a suit in federal court in order to obtain a definite judicial decision."[45]

A number of observers have suggested that the school board did more than invite others to file suits against the plan, but actually colluded with Governor Faubus and the forces of massive resistance in order to ensure that challenges to the Blossom Plan would be filed and integration would be delayed. Blossom only gestured to these developments obliquely in his retrospective account.[46] However, in her study of the Little Rock school desegregation crisis *Turn Away Thy Son,* Virgil Blossom's niece, the historian Elizabeth Jacoway, has concluded that at least Blossom and school board member Wayne Upton were directly involved in the preparation of what became known as the Thomason suit, a legal petition designed to temporarily delay the implementation of the Blossom Plan in order to provide time for state segregation laws to be declared invalid.[47] Although the degree of collusion between Faubus, Blossom, and the school board has been the subject of substantial speculation and debate,[48] the board's direct or indirect participation in such suits is hardly surprising. School board members repeatedly reiterated their opposition to integration. In cooperation with Blossom, they had devised an "integration" plan designed to keep the number of African American students attending "white" schools as low as possible. Their repeated efforts to reduce the number of qualified black pupils through the introduction of "voluntary transfer" mechanisms and screening procedures had prompted the NAACP to file suit precisely because they believed the school district's implementation timeline was too vague. Although the federal court supported the architecture of the Blossom Plan, it retained jurisdiction over the case, which meant that the implementation of the plan was no longer voluntary. The Thomason suit calling for further delay was entirely in keeping with the board's broader strategy of gradualism and their efforts to retain control over the timing and pace of school desegregation while avoiding public disapprobation.

Indeed, after Governor Faubus called out the National Guard, the school board itself filed a petition after the first week of classes asking for a temporary delay in the implementation of the Blossom Plan. Before the court, the district painted a picture of a school board caught in the middle of extremist forces. District officials alone labored to implement their plan with no support from the community at large, with the active opposition of segregationist groups who enjoyed the support of state officials like Governor Faubus, with the proliferation of pro-segregation legislation that sought to circumvent the *Brown* decision, and in the absence of coordinated support from the federal government. The petition lamented, "The District now finds itself in a most difficult position in providing satisfactory education for its pupils. It has the responsibility of operating under a phase Plan of Integration as directed by this Court, and yet it has no power to prevent interference with the operations of its schools under the terms of the Plan."[49] As the superintendent wrote, "The Board's position said that tension was developing inside the school, that parents were forming antagonistic groups, that education was impossible and that the court was requested temporarily to stay its order for integration until calm could be restored to a point where intelligence could be substituted for emotional agitation 'for the good of all pupils.'"[50] Federal judge Ronald N. Davies dismissed this argument as "anemic" and chastised school officials for failing to adhere to "the duty of the petitioners to adhere with resolution to its own approved plan of gradual integration in the Little Rock Public Schools." Even years later, Blossom's outrage at this decision was palpable. "The federal court," he wrote, "had denounced us in a humiliating fashion. By failing to show any human understanding of our problem, the court had publicly slapped those who attempted to uphold the law while those who sought to overthrow the law were able to demonstrate and agitate freely."[51] However, Judge Davies concluded that the board's desperate maneuvers to escape their obligation to implement the Blossom Plan revealed that there was little to no distance between the position of those who claimed to be "upholding" the law in his courtroom and those who sought to "overthrow" it.

In contrast, Blossom's memoir was designed to shore up his claim, and the claim of his successors in the Little Rock school district, that the strategy of minimal compliance outlined in his plan was distinct from massive resistance and provided a pathway that would allow Southern school districts to legally and lawfully continue to retain dual school systems with only minimal disruption to "local cultural patterns." In his text, the superintendent carefully defended the gradualism and tokenism represented by the Blossom Plan and insisted that the course of action he proposed satisfied the requirements of the *Brown* decision. His memoir drew liberally from court testimony and legal briefs produced in ongoing school litigation in Little Rock, and his historical account of the events of the 1957–58 school year provided the school board with the framework needed to support the legal posture it adopted in the 1960s that (in the absence of political obstruction and the turmoil produced by federal military intervention) the school district was now proceeding with "all deliberate speed" toward school integration.

From the perspective of other historical actors like Daisy Bates, however, successful integration required systemic change and an end to the city's dual school system with its racially identified black and white schools. Even with token numbers of African American pupils attending Central High School, Bates understood that the Blossom Plan did not intend to create a single integrated school system, but instead sought to preserve segregated education to the extent possible. Moreover, as Bates completed her work on her book *The Long Shadow of Little Rock,* she believed the superintendent's efforts to promote his approach to school desegregation through his memoir needed to be confronted directly.

Five years after the onset of the 1957–59 school desegregation crisis, the Little Rock school district was still utilizing the architecture of Blossom's original plan to minimize the impact of *Brown*. As Bates's book went to press, only seventy-eight African American students were attending the city's white junior and senior high schools. During the 1963–1964 school year, that number climbed to 118 in a school district with approximately 16,000 white students and 7,000 black students. No white students attended any of the city's traditionally black schools.[52] Indeed, some of the primary features of the original Blossom Plan were enhanced in 1959, when Arkansas adopted a pupil placement law modeled on a statute in Alabama that had survived Supreme Court review.[53] The pupil placement law formalized the procedures under which students requested transfers, and continued to provide the school board with considerable power over student assignment, allowing school officials to consider criteria like the "qualifications, motivations, aptitudes, and characteristics" of individual pupils. This statute, like others across the South, was written in race-neutral language, and the federal courts found that it was constitutional "upon its face." The Little Rock school board could utilize pupil placement criteria as long as they were not applied "in an artificial manner and for the purpose of continuing segregation."[54] Despite this admonition, the city's commitment to the approach formulated by Superintendent Blossom led district officials to continue to manipulate these criteria in order to preserve Little Rock's dual school system well into the 1960s.

For example, when the city's high schools reopened in 1959, students applying for transfer were required to fill out a seventeen-section questionnaire with their parent or guardian and to submit to an oral examination. In the early 1960s, these applications were weighed individually by the school board, and requests could be denied for any number of reasons.[55] Students who adopted an attitude of "sticking up for one's rights" or admitted to conferring with local civil rights leaders were dismissed on the grounds that they had been unduly influenced by outside forces.[56] The most liberal member of the board, Ted Lamb, publicly accused his colleagues of using this procedure as a "devious means" by which they hoped to "out-trick, out-maneuver and defy the federal government."[57] In 1959, forty-nine students (thirty-two white and seventeen black) appealed their assignment through procedures outlined by the board. All of the African American students, but only three of the white students, were subjected to psychological and intelligence testing and home visits from social workers.[58] Three-quarters of the white applications were approved, while more than four-fifths of the applications from black students were denied. Only three additional African American students were assigned to Central High as a result of this process by the beginning of the 1959–60 school year. The racial disparity in the board's treatment of transfer requests was particularly evident when considering that *all* of the white students seeking reassignment were applying to attend schools *outside* their attendance zone, while *all but one* of the black students seeking reassignment were attempting to attend schools *within* their residential neighborhoods.[59] In 1963, as Bates promoted her memoir, *New York Times* reporter Gertrude Samuels visited the city and concluded that the city's integration plan was little more than "tokenism plus." Samuels concluded that the school board had taken a "negative and resistant" approach to school integration, "doing as little as humanly possible" to comply with court orders. She found that the limited changes that had taken place were the result of sustained pressure from the black community.[60]

Bates echoed these sentiments in her memoir and situated them in historical context, connecting the evasive procedures of the board in the mid-1960s to the district's initial response to the *Brown* decision. She pointedly underscored the difference between the school district's understanding of "good faith" compliance and the NAACP's approach. "To the nation's Negroes the Supreme Court decision meant that the time for delay, evasion, or procrastination was past," Bates wrote.[61] Bates characterized her meetings with the superintendent in the months leading up to the 1957–59 school desegregation crisis as cordial but adversarial; she suspected that the superintendent met with her primarily out of a desire to diffuse the threat of an NAACP challenge to his plan. "For this reason he was always willing to discuss the plan with NAACP officials and try to convince them of his sincerity," she wrote. However, as the school desegregation plan evolved and as the number of black students selected to integrate the schools became smaller and smaller, Bates informed the superintendent that an increasing number of people in the black community felt that Blossom was offering them little more than "double talk."[62] The board's proposed school integration plan was "vague and indecisive," Bates observed. School officials seemed "more interested in appeasing the segregationists by advocating that only a limited number of Negroes be admitted than in complying with the Supreme Court's decision." Moreover, school officials neglected to put the outlines of their plan in writing, and the only assurance black parents had that its proposal would ever be put into effect was the word of the superintendent. This was not enough. "Years of bitter and tragic experience had taught the Negro that the word of the Southern white man meant very little when it came to granting the Negro his constitutional rights," Bates wrote.[63] In a recorded deposition, she reported that her conversations with school officials had always been "courteous" and "polite." The civil tone of these exchanges, however, was no indication that district officials and the NAACP were working together cooperatively to integrate the schools. "We were friendly about it," Bates noted, "but the fact still remains that the children are being denied today in Little Rock the right to attend the school nearest their home."[64]

In her memoir Bates positioned Blossom as one of the insiders who helped to foster the school desegregation crisis. His policy of minimal compliance, his efforts to winnow out more and more prospective African American registrants, and the public rhetoric he used to sell the Blossom Plan to white audiences created a climate where many residents of the city seemed to believe that the number of black students admitted to Central High could be whittled away to none. Instead of counting heads to maximize the number of children that might *benefit* from school desegregation, the school superintendent worked assiduously to maximize the number of pupils who could be *eliminated*. Instead of concerning himself with the educational rights of all patrons in his district, he courted middle-class white parents with political and economic influence in the capital city. "So it happened that as we were counting the number of school districts in the state, Superintendent Blossom was counting heads in the Little Rock School District," Bates wrote.

> He used a large city map with red thumb tacks to indicate white children and blue thumb tacks to indicate Negro children. Lines for attendance areas were drawn and re-drawn, counts were made and then made again in a desperate effort to include a very low minimum number of Negro children in attendance areas of white schools. When the counts were finished and the numbers were unsatisfactory, shouts could be heard from the school board office, "Too many, too many, count again!" Then would be made another count—another line on the map.[65]

Bates understood that the Blossom Plan was built on the bedrock of geographic segregation in the city, and may have anticipated that gerrymandered school attendance zones would only continue to encourage and exacerbate the growth of affluent and predominantly white housing in western Little Rock.

However, like Blossom, Bates was also careful to note that the superintendent introduced additional screening mechanisms to reduce the number of eligible students even further. As the school district's plan evolved, these additional procedures raised doubts even among those who initially celebrated Blossom's repeated commitment to comply with the law. From Bates' perspective, the introduction of screening procedures did not have the effect of reducing community resistance as Blossom claimed, but rather heightening it. Each time Blossom spoke to African American audiences, Bates recalled, his plan became more "confusing." The superintendent spoke of attendance areas and hundreds of African American pupils who lived within Central's attendance zone, but then indicated that only a handful would be admitted during his plan's inaugural year. "Why is he spending all this time developing attendance areas," a black parent asked, "if they are going to admit such a small number, unless it is to try to convince the Negroes of his good faith?" Bates and other members of the black community became increasingly convinced that Blossom and the school board were proceeding in bad faith, and as a result the local NAACP decided to resort to court action in order to press the issue.[66]

Despite the formal finding of the courts that the Blossom Plan represented a "good faith" effort to comply with federal law in 1957, Bates remained unpersuaded five years later. From her perspective, the public pronouncements with which Blossom sold his plan to white audiences told a different story. In her public speeches and in her book, Bates asserted that the reluctance of school officials to embrace the spirit of the *Brown* decision cultivated a climate that led white school patrons to believe that the district had no obligation to eliminate its dual school system and that the "best" desegregation plan for the district was one that operated as efficiently as possible to keep African American students out of "white" schools. According to notes in Bates's file, "At no time in Little Rock has there been a serious discussion among persons of leadership concerning the possibility of implementing or accepting the United States Supreme Court's 1954 school decision that racially 'separate educational facilities are inherently unequal.'"

> No thought was ever given by the Little Rock school board to the possibility of eliminating a dual school system for the two races and the integrating of all pupils regardless of race into a single nondiscriminatory educational program. From the beginning of its attempt to cope with the Supreme Court school decision the Little Rock school board translated the law into terms of how many, if any, Negro pupils would be required by the federal government to enter the corridors and classrooms of white schools.

Indeed, Blossom sold his "integration" plan to white audiences with the "confident air of a high pressure salesman." With charts, maps, and statistics he demonstrated that it was designed to minimize desegregation. He reassured white school patrons by drawing attendance zones that mirrored patterns of geographic segregation in the city, by introducing screening procedures, by creating transfer regulations designed to allow white school patrons to flee from integrated institutions, and by retaining all-white or all-black faculty at historically white or black facilities in the school district.[67]

In doing so, Bates believed, the school superintendent set the tone for the way school district patrons would think about the district's constitutional obligations. In more than 250 public meetings, "the school problem" had been situated in "the context of maximum avoidance of racial mixing." As the number of African American pupils who were eligible to integrate Central High dwindled, "devout segregationists insisted . . . there was no reason why it could not be further cut down to none." When the Capital Citizens' Council and Governor Faubus rose up in defiance of the Blossom Plan, "the Little Rock school board was in no position to protest. Nor did it do so." As noted, the board appeared in court to ask for a temporary stay of integration just days after Faubus called out the National Guard. Bates argued that the board's petition was rooted in its belief that "no Negro pupils at Central was better than nine."[68] From her perspective, here was further proof that the 1957–59 school desegregation crisis had not been thrust upon the city of Little Rock by outsiders, but rather had been cultivated from within.

In September 1957, the school board's first petition for a temporary stay of integration was dismissed, but NAACP officials suspected that the school district never abandoned their plan to pursue this course of action. The civil rights organization would later argue in court that school officials deliberately sought to shore up their case for a delay by creating an environment that fostered chaos within Central High throughout the 1957–58 school year. They did so by deciding to discipline only those students involved in incidents of harassment witnessed and reported by an adult, by failing to coordinate responsibility for identifying and disciplining offenders with representatives of the US Army and National Guard, by refusing to expel known segregationist ringleaders, and by abdicating any responsibility for preventing external forces from interfering in the implementation of their integration plan through injunction procedures.[69] Although school officials like Blossom repeatedly painted themselves as "victims" of segregationist harassment and verbal abuse, advocates for the African American students were incredulous that officials took "no firm action" to eliminate or reduce interference with administrative policies. "Caught in their own web of maximum avoidance of the law," one observer noted, "they were prey to any segregationists who insisted that by systematic harassment they could either reduce the number of Negroes at Central High or prove that desegregation in any form at Little Rock would not work."[70] When Minnijean Brown was expelled after responding to repeated provocation, the school board "put its stamp of approval on the segregationist strategy of terror."[71]

In her memoir, Bates connected the crisis to the long legacy of racial segregation and discrimination in Arkansas's capital. Although the civil rights leader admitted that she was taken by surprise by the violence that erupted in the fall of 1957 because of the lack of "surface friction" in the city, she insisted that the Little Rock school crisis came not "from the sky but from within." In a draft of her manuscript, Bates observed, "Most cities have their cesspools of racial hatred lying dormant under a thin layer of respectability. The people who foster these pockets of hatred and keep them alive and deadly are unwilling (perhaps unable) to accept the fact of a changing world." Bates contended that Blossom and others who promoted the idea that Little Rock was little more than a neutral battlefield, where outside forces sought a "fight to the finish" on the issue of integration, failed to see or were unwilling to acknowledge the "slime at the bottom of the pool." The activities of the Citizens' Council were not "isolated incidents" but rather were connected to a long history of racial violence and intimidation in Arkansas. Organized white supremacist groups were not an aberration but a fixture of life in the new South as well as the old. "With all due respect to Mr. Blossom," she wrote, "the 'trouble' that hit Little Rock was not just 'thrust upon us by outsiders.'"[72]

Moreover, Little Rock's commitment to segregation and the preservation of white privilege was evident in its perpetuation of Blossom's policy of minimal compliance after the city's high schools reopened in 1959. In its assessment of conditions in Arkansas in August 1959, the Southern Regional Council (SRC) believed that conditions in Little Rock had improved over the preceding two years and that city officials were better prepared to implement and enforce the integration plan than they had been in 1957. The organization believed that "disenchantment" with the course of massive resistance had emerged in the city of Little Rock during the school closures, and that the recall of segregationists on the school board provided evidence of "popular unwillingness" to continue to defy the Supreme Court. However, the SRC concluded this shift in public opinion was not motivated by a reconsideration of the merits of school desegregation, but rather was undergirded by a general distaste for the "notoriety" that accompanied overt resistance to school integration, the intransigence of the federal courts, and concerns about damage to the local economy and the prospects of the city's young people.[73] Many white residents in the city also concluded that they could continue to minimize desegregation through the mechanisms established in Blossom's plan and the formalized transfer procedures adopted under the Pupil Placement Act.[74]

In light of these conditions, Bates concluded her memoir with a call to action. One hundred years after the Emancipation Proclamation, the nation continued to segregate and discriminate against African American citizens; the promise of racial equality remained unfulfilled in Little Rock and elsewhere. Bates contended that the 1957–59 Little Rock school desegregation crisis provided a "spark" that continued to inspire young people across the nation to commit themselves to the cause of civil rights. The spirited resistance that motivated the sit-ins and Freedom Rides of the early 1960s signaled that the time was ripe for a "social revolution." Yet Bates cautioned that the slow pace of progress and the half-hearted commitments of the nation's political leaders were fostering "disillusionment" and breeding "contempt and hostility" that contributed to the growth of black nationalist organizations with platforms far different from those of the NAACP. In an interview a few years later, Bates warned that she was "as harmless as a popcorn popper" compared to more militant activists like Stokely Carmichael.[75] Despite her own efforts, Bates expressed dismay at the low number of African American students permitted to attend classes in Little Rock's predominantly white schools. The gradualism and delay that were hallmarks of the Blossom Plan, and that continued to infuse the school board's pupil placement procedures, were purposefully designed to thwart meaningful integration by preserving the city's dual system of racially identifiable schools.[76]

The portions of Bates's text that looked to the future rather than to the past provoked substantial commentary in the press. In her foreword written for the book, former First Lady Eleanor Roosevelt expressed her wish that Bates had been able to "keep from giving us some of the sense of her bitterness and fear in the end of her book." However, for Bates, these persistent concerns underlay her motivation to write the memoir in the first place. John Kirk has noted that Bates's memoir focused almost entirely on "events in the public realm" and her "public persona [was] . . . privileged over her personal life" in the text.⁷⁷ Bates did not write her book to provide readers with substantial insight into the personal motivations that drove her activism, but to inspire further action in what she described as a "crusade for equality."⁷⁸ The memoir was designed to cultivate what Genevieve Fabre has referred to as "memory for the future"—a historical narrative written "in anticipation of action to come" in order to force change and invent a more viable future. Fabre argues that African American commemorative traditions often adopt a "subjunctive" tone, focusing on what should have happened and what ought to happen as much as on what did happen.⁷⁹

In the early 1960s, Bates no longer served as president of the NAACP's Arkansas State Conference, but she continued to serve as a spokesperson and representative of the organization's national board. In this respect, Bates used her retrospective account of the Little Rock school desegregation crisis as a vehicle for promoting the work of the nation's oldest civil rights organization and its efforts to secure meaningful school desegregation throughout the nation. Bates argued that the NAACP's challenge to the Blossom Plan was not an aberration and was no more the product of outside influence than massive resistance. Although writers like Superintendent Virgil Blossom underscored Little Rock's reputation for "progressive" race relations in support of their more pointed claim that the mobs that had been captured on film outside of Central High School were from elsewhere, Bates dismissed these characterizations of the city's race relations. If Arkansas's capital had gained a reputation as a "liberal southern city" before the school desegregation crisis, it was only because of the grudging concessions forced upon it by active and organized citizens. "It was not a changed Little Rock," Bates maintained, "but a new Negro who had appeared on the surface."⁸⁰ Any relaxation of Southern racial mores in the city was not a gracious gesture of goodwill on the behalf of the city's white population, but the product of the collective action of small, integrated organizations that had pushed for change and exerted "political and economic pressure against violations of fundamental rights guaranteed to all Americans under the Constitution."⁸¹

Bates believed that leaders like Blossom fundamentally misunderstood or failed to acknowledge this spirit of resistance in the past and continued to underestimate the determination of the black community in the present. In her memoir, Bates asserted that this refusal to acknowledge the forces driving change led school board attorneys and white supremacist organizations to the mistaken conclusion that school desegregation litigation in Little

Rock was initiated in the NAACP's New York headquarters. The suit's genesis, Bates recalled, came from frustrated African American parents in Little Rock who were troubled by the vague outlines of the district's desegregation plan. These parents "appealed *to*" local civil rights leaders to represent them in the initial suit of *Aaron v. Cooper*. The lawsuit, Bates maintained, started at the grassroots.[82] The civil rights organization responded and reacted to the shifting ground of Blossom's own proposal and the threat it posed to the constitutional rights of black children in the school district.

Likewise, Bates observed, segregationist literature denied the agency and self-determination of the Little Rock Nine by suggesting that they had been handpicked by the NAACP to enter Central High. Throughout the crisis, the NAACP vigorously denied persistent claims that the students were not residents of Little Rock but had been "imported" and were being paid to endure harassment that no "normal" teenager would voluntarily subject themselves to.[83] Bates believed that the idea that she and the students were no more than "pawns" gained traction because segregationists, and the news media they courted, did not comprehend the new spirit of resistance that was emerging in the South. She told audiences around the country that the children and their parents were repeatedly quizzed by reporters and asked "the same question a hundred times in as many different ways": Why would they allow themselves to be "used" in this way?[84] As the NAACP asserted at the time, this question revealed a complete "lack of understanding" on the part of reporters and segregationists: "Negro parents have the same high hopes and aspirations for their children that other parents have. And they know that these aspirations have their best chance of fulfillment if their children can be exposed to the best possible education."[85] The more reporters looked for signs of subterfuge, Bates reported, the more the courage of the children and their families became apparent. The students were not "pawns" but brave pioneers who willingly shouldered the weighty responsibility of desegregating Central High. "It was the children themselves . . . who quietly and determinedly 'pushed' until they got certificates of admission," she contended.[86] The Little Rock Nine and their parents were "serving notice on America that we are a determined people, willing to pay the price that our children might enjoy true Democracy."[87] Ultimately, Bates concluded that the school board could have randomly selected any nine children in Little Rock and they also would have disproved the stereotype of the "'contented' Negro" and emerged as leaders in the fight against second-class citizenship.[88] If white

Americans refused to recognize this determination, that refusal said more about them than it did about the African American students.

The final pages of *The Long Shadow of Little Rock* were not marked by bitterness and disillusionment as some reviewers claimed, but rather were intended to advance the author's argument that the struggle for equal educational opportunity was far from over.[89] Despite Bates's efforts, by the early 1960s the NAACP's strength in Arkansas had been severely compromised. As she worked on her memoir in New York, local branches throughout the state were crippled by state legislation that threatened to expose their membership lists. However, in this vacuum, other community organizations stepped to the fore. During this period, Little Rock's Negro Council on Community Affairs (COCA) functioned as an umbrella organization designed to help coordinate civil rights activity in the city. At its founding, COCA was composed of two representatives from each black community organization in the city of Little Rock with the notable exception of the NAACP, which continued to define its own priorities. Both Bates and her husband struggled to reconcile themselves to the emergence of these new groups, but they did share common concerns about the "painfully slow" pace of progress in Little Rock. When their goals coincided, COCA and the NAACP worked together cooperatively.[90]

In August 1963, COCA formally filed a complaint with the school board, noting that at the present rate of progress it would take "450 years to completely desegregate our school system." The organization urged the board to abandon its pupil placement procedures and assign students to schools solely on the basis of geographic residence. COCA accused school officials of continuing to apply selective criteria in a discriminatory matter, and served notice that it had not escaped their attention that these practices continued in direct violation of federal court orders. If the school board harbored the hope that "racial harmony" would emerge in the city without moving "swiftly toward the noble objective of a better education for all children free from the eroding effects of segregation," they were mistaken. COCA asserted, "There is no reason to encourage the belief that Negroes will relent in their natural aspirations for full and complete citizenship rights." While the board might have perpetuated the architecture of the Blossom Plan and adopted its pupil placement criteria in order to minimize white resistance to desegregating the city's schools, the civil rights organization's perspective was different. "Peace is not to be desired over justice," the group warned.[91]

The school board rejected this appeal and informed COCA that it operated well within its bounds when it assigned students to schools according to its own criteria. Board members and school district attorneys contended that reliance on geographic attendance zones alone would produce "compulsory integration," an outcome that they believed was not mandated by the *Brown v. Board of Education* decision or desired by white or black pupils in the district. School board members also argued that the low number of African American students attending classes in Little Rock's formerly all-white institutions was the result of the low number of black pupils who appealed for reassignment rather than institutional discrimination. "As you know," the board replied, "the proper measure of progress in desegregation is not the number that have exercised a right to attend a school with another race, but the number to whom this right is available."[92]

This exchange between COCA and the Little Rock school board in 1963 revealed how little the controversy surrounding school desegregation in the city had changed over the intervening years. Both Virgil Blossom and Daisy Bates believed their retrospective accounts would be of use to those embroiled in these persistent arguments. The school board remained committed to the foundation laid by Blossom and the processes he defended in his memoir. In an effort to minimize the impact of school desegregation and preserve Little Rock's dual system of white and black schools, Little Rock school officials continued to define "successful integration" as narrowly as possible. Systemic change was not required; instead, school districts could reasonably set their goals much lower. Not only did the board continue to preserve the architecture of the Blossom Plan and the mechanisms it created to minimize the impact of the *Brown* decision, but school officials also retained his confidence that they could continue to exercise their prerogative to control the pace of school desegregation in the district without interference from "outside" organizations. The logic of white supremacy undergirded their actions and colored their consideration of African American requests for reassignment, yet they continued to justify their procedures by distancing themselves from "extremists" who advocated the course of massive resistance.

Like Bates, COCA continued to challenge the claim that the school board intended to comply with constitutional law through its adherence to pupil placement procedures. The preservation of segregation in the district undermined the constitutional rights of black students. The tokenism and gradualism of the school board were not model administrative procedures. Rather, they exposed black students to the threat of violence, produced a climate of crippling isolation, and emboldened white segregationist students and their adult allies. In the eyes of the city's civil rights community, advocates of passive resistance worked from inside the system to perpetuate white privilege. COCA's petition to the board made clear that, in the absence of racial justice, the Little Rock Nine merely represented the vanguard of an ongoing effort to secure more substantive change.

Nevertheless, after a decade of school desegregation, civil rights organizations seemed to have gained little traction. In 1964, nearly 99 percent of black pupils in the eleven states of the former Confederacy attended historically black schools.[93] In Little Rock and elsewhere, school boards minimized the impact of desegregation through pupil placement statutes and other mechanisms. Yet in the absence of significant progress toward dismantling segregated school systems, federal courts viewed such assignment procedures with increasing suspicion. As a result of persistent civil rights litigation and the direct action campaigns of the early 1960s, school districts also faced fiscal consequences for refusing to comply with federal law in the wake of the passage of the 1964 Civil Rights Act and the 1965 Elementary and Secondary School Education Act. For the first time, the federal government threatened to withhold funds from school districts that maintained segregation.

In the context of these developments, the Little Rock school board's attorneys advised the district to revise its student assignment policies. However, the minimal changes instituted by the district failed to satisfy the city's civil rights community. In the fall of 1964, Delores Clark, a new Little Rock resident, was instructed over the telephone to enroll her children at a white school. When she appeared in person to register, her children were denied placement and enrolled in a black school. Clark filed suit, challenging the district's procedures, in a case that became known as *Clark v. Board of Education*. Under legal pressure from African American plaintiffs, and with the release of specific school desegregation guidelines from the Department of Health, Education and Welfare (HEW), Little Rock adopted a "freedom-of-choice" plan in April 1965. Under the new plan, student school choices would be honored except in cases of overcrowding. Nevertheless, even with these new provisions, nearly 7,200 black children in the school district continued to attend historically black schools.[94] Thelma Mothershed, one of the Little Rock Nine, publicly expressed her doubt that many of the city's black families would exercise their choice due to fear that their children would be harassed in virtually all-white schools.[95] In federal courts, Clark and her lawyers challenged the constitutionality of the district's freedom-of-choice plan, arguing that the district's approach failed to fulfill the constitutional mandate outlined in *Brown*. At best, civil rights advocates argued, freedom-of-choice procedures could be considered part of an effective *transition* to an integrated system, but in and of themselves they could not dismantle the city's system of dual education.[96]

In May 1968, the Supreme Court struck down the use of freedom-of-choice plans like the one in Little Rock. In *Green v. New Kent County,* the Supreme Court held that school districts were required to take affirmative steps toward establishing unitary and nondiscriminatory school systems. If a plan failed to eliminate segregation "root and branch," it was not sufficient. Moving forward, the constitutionality of desegregation plans would be measured by their efficacy in relation to other alternatives that promised "speedier and more effective conversion" to unitary status. The Court noted that *Brown* placed the burden for making this transition on school boards, not on students and their parents by using tactics like freedom-of-choice provisions. Further delay under the guise of "deliberate speed" was intolerable. "The burden on a school board today is to come forward with a plan that promises realistically to work, and promises realistically to work *now*," the Court declared.[97] In the wake of this decision, federal courts would push local school districts to adopt procedures that went far beyond the strategies that had governed their student assignment policies for well over a decade. In Little Rock, the plaintiffs in the *Clark* litigation petitioned the Eastern District Court of Arkansas for further relief, challenging not only freedom-of-choice procedures but also the gerrymandered geographic attendance zones the school board proposed to replace them with.[98]

Green v. New Kent County directly refuted Blossom's argument that tokenism satisfied the requirements of the *Brown* decision and vindicated Bates's call for systemic and sweeping change. Bates's contribution to the struggle for equal educational opportunity continued to be recognized in recurrent Daisy Bates Educational Summits and Institutes organized by the NAACP at the turn of the twenty-first century, and her home in Little Rock has been recognized as a National Historical Landmark. However, the arguments presented by advocates of passive resistance also continue to resonate in public discourse nearly sixty years later. Karen Anderson has noted that the use of pupil placement laws as a means of minimizing change played a crucial role in the development of "race neutral" legal strategies and laid the foundation for the "colorblind" jurisprudence of the post-civil rights era. The use of pupil placement laws in Little Rock and elsewhere that were "suffused with racist assumptions and designed to sustain white supremacy," Anderson contends, "reveal with particular clarity the racial roots of 'race-blind' legal theory and institutional practices in the postwar era."[99] Indeed, many of Blossom's claims in his text, particularly his argument that systemic desegregation erodes broad-based white support for public education, have been actively deployed to justify a turn away from systemic strategies in favor of "voluntary" integration mechanisms like magnet and charter schools. Careful attention to the way the public memory of the Little Rock school desegregation crisis was shaped and reshaped in the intervening decades illuminates how these arguments gained traction even when they fell out of favor in the late 1960s and 1970s in federal courts of law.

— CHAPTER TWO —
Obscuring Effective Mechanisms of Change

Under pressure from black plaintiffs in the wake of the *Green* decision, the Little Rock school district was ordered to replace its selective pupil placement procedures and dismantle its system of dual education.[1] Shortly thereafter in public hearings held in Washington in 1971, Arkansas senator John L. McClellan publicly protested against what he perceived to be a "double standard in America today." McClellan questioned Attorney General John H. Mitchell closely on his department's disinterest in investigating Northern school districts like Boston, which adopted "open enrollment" plans that allowed students to transfer out of their assigned schools. According to the testimony of the Massachusetts Commissioner of Education, Boston's transfer policy effectively allowed white middle class children to abandon integrated schools in the city's core "to go to all-white schools in Boston on the periphery." McClellan asserted that if Boston were Little Rock, the Department of Justice "would be down there tomorrow" launching an investigation. The Arkansas senator suggested that the federal government's enforcement procedures gave preferential treatment to white students in Northern states and "discriminated" against their Southern peers. Boston's reputation as the "cradle of liberty," McClellan noted, should not protect it from federal oversight. In the wake of McClellan's comments, political commentators speculated that the senator hoped to spark nationwide resistance to systemic school desegregation by calling for standardized enforcement. As the *Washington Post* observed, "Pressure now in the North will produce resistance," and "if the Bostons of the country can ultimately ward off integration, so can the Little Rocks."[2]

During the 1970s, the terrain of the struggle to integrate American schools shifted. After finding that urban school districts in both the North and the South had manipulated school attendance zones to maintain racial segregation, federal courts demanded that school districts throughout the country take affirmative steps toward dismantling their dual school systems, even if this meant busing students. As an urban school district in the South, Little Rock was one of the first communities to be affected by this change. However, as the focus of the black freedom struggle expanded to include Northern communities and student transportation, national resistance to black activism grew. As conflict erupted around the nation, the memory of the 1957–59 school desegregation crisis in Little Rock functioned as a cultural lodestone against which new attacks on black students and school integration efforts were measured. Increasingly, distinctions were drawn between the events of 1957–59 and those of the 1970s, as reporters, cultural observers, and politicians rejected McClellan's call for standard enforcement procedures and insisted that what was at stake in student transportation cases was fundamentally different from the battles of the 1950s. In Little Rock, the city's black media and civil rights organizations attempted to cross this chasm, drawing historical parallels and arguing that the implementation of systemic desegregation strategies—both in the North and South—was a fulfillment of the goals for which they had struggled more than a decade earlier.

In the early 1970s, federal courts ordered the city of Little Rock to dismantle its dual system of education through student transportation and other remedies as a result of growing residential segregation in the city. Even after the courts struck down the pupil placement procedures that had allowed the Little Rock school district to minimize school desegregation, the city continued to maintain racially identifiable white and black schools. In his original proposal, Superintendent Blossom drew school attendance zones to minimize the impact of integration and contain it in the city's downtown core. The district gerrymandering that had been integral to the "Blossom

Plan" capitalized on urban redevelopment strategies that forcibly relocated black families to the city's east side, and exacerbated racial segregation in the city by encouraging white families eager to avoid integration to purchase homes on the city's west side. Indeed, since 1957, residential segregation in Little Rock had increased. Over the course of the 1960s, the population of the western sector of the city had grown by 26,000 and was approximately 96 percent white. The eastern section of Little Rock had lost approximately 12,000 white residents and was more than 90 percent black. Notably, these changes were not just driven by private real estate decisions but were shaped by school policy and redevelopment plans in the city; the Little Rock Housing Authority was the first public housing agency in the country to be sued by the Department of Housing and Urban Development for failure to comply with the 1964 Civil Rights Act.[3]

Under legal pressure in the late 1960s, the school board fell back on the zoning strategies embedded in the Blossom Plan, which relied on attendance zones drawn north to south rather than from east to west. Civil rights advocates initiated court suits to challenge the district's deliberate effort to separate black and white students on the basis of geographic residence.[4] However, the school district defended its policies as "constitutionally faultless." The district's attorneys suggested that any deliberate attempt to create "racial balance" in the schools would violate the Fourteenth Amendment and the spirit of the *Brown* decision because it would require the assignment of students according to race. The neighborhood school concept was "educationally sound" and the only "feasible means" of operating the school system "in view of community attitudes."[5] The school board's sole African American member, T. E. Patterson, objected to this line of argument. Patterson questioned why the school board had invested over $200,000 in attorney fees to defeat its own public commitment to work toward a unified school district. He urged his fellow members to be more forthright about their intentions and not to mask their desire to maintain segregated schools behind the rhetoric of racial neutrality. From Patterson's perspective, the school district's position was a new reiteration of the rhetoric of minimal compliance.[6]

In May 1970, the Eighth Circuit Court of Appeals rejected the school board's contention that they could take no further action to eliminate segregated institutions without violating the Fourteenth Amendment. The district had a constitutional obligation to produce an *effective* desegregation plan in light of all of the alternatives available; any plan submitted by the district should be designed "to promote desegregation rather than to reinforce segregation." The Little Rock school board's plan failed to meet this standard, perpetuating rather than eliminating entrenched student attendance patterns. The Eighth Circuit did not rule on the relative merits of the neighborhood school concept, nor did it prescribe alternative procedures like student transportation, but the court ordered the school district to fully implement a plan that met the requirements of the *Green* decision to eliminate segregation in the district "root and branch."[7]

The Supreme Court took up this question of neighborhood schools, racial balance, and busing in a group of cases from Charlotte-Mecklenburg County, North Carolina; Mobile, Alabama; and Clarke County, Georgia. In *Swann v. Charlotte-Mecklenburg Board of Education* (1971), the Supreme Court provided specific guidelines for the desegregation of large metropolitan areas that were residentially segregated. The Court asserted that "racially neutral" student assignment plans based on geographic attendance zones were inadequate if they failed to "counteract the effects of past school desegregation" and created or maintained "artificial racial separation." The Court noted that decisions made by school boards—such as the closure of facilities in integrated areas and the construction of new buildings in racially segregated areas—could compound residential segregation. In school districts like Little Rock that deliberately used such tactics and gerrymandered neighborhood zones to maintain dual school systems, the Supreme Court held that the lower courts could order appropriate remedies such as the clustering of identifiably white and black schools and the transportation of students to noncontiguous attendance zones.[8]

In 1971, the Eastern District Court of Arkansas issued a new school desegregation decree shaped by the principles and guidelines outlined in *Swann* and determined that bus transportation would be required to dismantle the dual school system in Little Rock. Instead of assigning students on the basis of geographic attendance areas, the new plan adopted a variety of techniques ranging from pairing and clustering to contiguous and noncontiguous zoning with the objective of completely eliminating racially identifiable schools.[9] During the 1970s, this plan produced meaningful and systematic integration in the Little Rock school system for the first time. However, its extensive use of desegregation remedies like busing was not without controversy.

As the transportation program went into effect in Arkansas's capital, the number of students bused to school jumped from 0.2 percent to 27.3 percent, one of the most acute increases in the country. The number of students attending public schools in Little Rock declined by more than 1,100 pupils—a decrease of nearly 5 percent. Statistics from the US Department of Health, Education, and Welfare indicated that the vast majority of students exiting the system were white; the proportion of minority pupils in the Little Rock school district climbed from 39.4 percent in 1970 to 43.8 percent in 1971.[10] During this transitional period, real estate magnate William Rector founded and built a new private school called Pulaski Academy in western Little Rock. Rector candidly admitted that he built the school as an outlet for families who wanted to avoid busing.[11] Many observers were particularly troubled that five of the seven members of the Little Rock school board decided to enroll their children in the county's emerging private schools when busing was first implemented in the junior and senior high schools.[12] Increasingly, "moderates" committed to the strategies of minimal compliance and opposed to systematic desegregation clamored for political intervention and placed pressure on local and national political leaders through coordinated letter-writing campaigns and public appeals in the mass media. Even as Little Rock implemented its busing plan, the national debate about student transportation increasingly occupied center stage in political discourse.

In this context, Little Rock school officials and civic leaders embraced a new memorial strategy designed to facilitate their ongoing effort to escape from federal court oversight and sweeping desegregation remedies like busing. As the city's schools achieved racial balance, school officials embraced the district's new status as a "model" community. They hoped that the demonstrable progress made in the city's schools would enable Little Rock to escape from the shadow of the 1957–59 school crisis as well as ongoing federal intervention in the operations of the school district. However, in their careful recitations of the city's history, district officials carefully constructed a narrative of passive progress—a story of transformation that deliberately obscured the mechanisms of change and the historical actors who had made it possible. In this iteration of Little Rock's history, it was not the actions of the Little Rock Nine or their peers who followed them into the city's "white" schools that instigated change; it was not federal enforcement of *Brown* through the deployment of the 101st Airborne; it was not lawsuits filed in federal courts that demanded an end to pupil placement, freedom-of-choice, or gerrymandered geographic zones that produced meaningful integration. It was not even busing itself.

Rather, it was the passage of time that had altered the "hearts and minds" of the city's population, or, alternatively, allowed Little Rock's naturally moderate and progressive character to reemerge.

In contrast, from the perspective of the local NAACP, the history of desegregation in the city was one of active agitation from civil rights organizations, timely intervention from federal courts, and the application of effective remedies like student transportation. Maintaining hard won gains required continued action, a willingness to identify and confront sources of opposition, a commitment to protect and perpetuate effective mechanisms of change, and a rededication to the principles of equal justice and educational opportunity. The decision of the Little Rock Nine to enroll at Little Rock Central High School in 1957 was one link in an unbroken chain of black resistance that extended deep into the past and animated ongoing struggles for social justice and educational opportunity in the present. In Little Rock, civil rights activists and plaintiffs in the *Clark* litigation viewed the school board's persistent defense of neighborhood schools as just one more tactic of delay in a long-term strategy of resistance.

In the memorial arena, litigants promoted their understanding of the relationship between past and present and rehearsed historical arguments and analogies in preparation for their deployment in federal courts of law. The narrative of passive progress undergirded the arguments of busing opponents in Little Rock and elsewhere. If the passage of time itself was a marker of racial progress, then aggressive federal intervention and systemic remedies like student transportation were not required. Busing opponents insisted vociferously that the newest generation of school desegregation remedies were not natural extensions of previous efforts to dismantle dual school systems. Instead, in their view, federal courts were attempting to create artificial racial balance in areas where residential segregation was not the product of official action; the city's settlement patterns were the result of the impartial operation of market forces. This account of residential development and school district planning was largely devoid of historical actors and was utilized to argue for "race neutral" strategies like residential zoning even after the implementation of busing orders and even while the district publicly celebrated its new status as a "model" community.

Nationally, the antibusing movement gained momentum when federal courts applied the school desegregation precedent that had been established in Southern communities to Northern districts that were also found guilty of manipulating student assignment plans and perpetuating segregation. In the midst of national controversy, the antibusing movement constructed a historical narrative that sought to legitimize their objections to student transportation by distancing them from earlier efforts to resist school desegregation—both geographically and temporally. Throughout the 1970s, public memory of the Little Rock school desegregation crisis of 1957–59 was actively deployed in service of contemporary political ends in Arkansas's capital as well as in the nation at large. Civil rights advocates highlighted historical parallels and drew connections between past and present, while antibusing organizations sought to disassociate themselves from the legacy of segregationist resistance by drawing distinctions between de jure and de facto discrimination. Comparisons and contrasts drawn between the school desegregation efforts of the 1950s—particularly the events in Little Rock—and the controversies of the 1970s functioned as means to illuminate the contours of arguments on both sides.

The antibusing movement garnered a powerful ally when President Richard Nixon took up the cause, not only as part of a "Southern strategy" calibrated to assuage the racial anxieties and concerns of Southern white voters, but also in a bid to appeal to their Northern counterparts who resented new legal challenges that sought to expose the official state action that underlay "de facto" segregation. In 1972, Nixon proposed a moratorium on court-ordered busing and legislation that would permit the use of student transportation only as tool of "last resort" under "strict limitations." Nixon's proposed Equal Educational Opportunities bill would also allow school boards to revisit existing court orders that went beyond the standards laid out in the legislation.[13] In the weeks and months that followed, Congress considered these proposals as well as amendments to the Constitution that would prohibit federal courts from utilizing busing or any other race-conscious remedies.[14]

Civil rights activists contended that the proposed antibusing amendments and bills under consideration in Congress would render the promise of *Brown* illusory. Without busing, minority students would be segregated into separate-but-unequal schools that lacked funding and resources. As the US Commission on Civil Rights noted, "To restrict busing in most communities is simply to restrict desegregation." The Commission asserted, "What you really say to these children when you say 'no busing' is 'stay in your place and attend your inferior schools.'"[15] Likewise, the NAACP insisted that antibusing legislation was "no different from the doctrines of interposition, nullification, and advocacy of defiance by manifesto" that were used to delay implementation of the 1954 *Brown* decision.[16]

In these public debates, Little Rock served as a symbolic site of the school desegregation struggle and acted as a rhetorical anchor for ongoing conversations about race and educational policy, particularly in the national media. For example, in 1974, Boston became the center of the school desegregation storm when federal courts determined that the city school board had deliberately created and maintained racially imbalanced schools by concentrating minority students in inferior facilities sized and located to serve residentially segregated neighborhoods. The court of appeals affirmed, "It is beyond dispute that the defendants [the school board] took every opportunity to maintain segregation where it existed and to foster segregation where it did not. To use the Supreme Court's language, the neighborhood school concept has not been maintained free of manipulation."[17] As part of his desegregation plan, Judge W. Arthur Garrity Jr. ordered African American students from Roxbury to be bused a short distance to nearby South Boston. When the school buses rolled into this nearly all-white enclave known as Southie, mobs greeted the black students with stones, signs, and threats. The taunts and angry faces of the gathered crowds generated comparisons between the events of 1957 and 1974, as scenes in South Boston evoked memories of Elizabeth Eckford's attempt to navigate through the mob outside of Central High School on the first day of classes. Boston quickly became known as the "Little Rock of the North." This comparison generated its own debate, with some arguing that the same issues and fundamental rights were at stake and others insisting that the circumstances surrounding the two cases were completely different.

In 1957, the mainstream media—particularly national news magazines and Northern newspapers—had presented the Little Rock school desegregation crisis as a battle between a cornerstone of American democracy—the rule of law—and the forces of massive resistance. For many reporters who covered the story, these two sides of the conflict were not equal adversaries. However, as civil rights advocates challenged established white privilege throughout the country, and exposed the official state action underlying "de facto" segregation, the generally sympathetic tone of coverage during the 1950s evaporated. In 1974, the voices involved in the Boston busing crisis

FIGURE 4. This photograph of Elizabeth Eckford attempting to enter Central High School on the first day of classes has become one of the most indelible images associated with the school desegregation crisis. As controversy surrounding busing escalated in Boston, the public memory of scenes like this one was repeatedly invoked by civil rights advocates who sought to draw historical parallels between the events of 1957 and 1974 and by antibusing advocates who insisted that the issues at stake were fundamentally different. (Will Counts Collection: Indiana University Archives)

were given equal weight and were presented as part of a legitimate debate over the use of busing and the authority of the federal courts to implement it. Under the mantle of balance and objectivity, speakers on both sides of the conflict were provided with space to express and articulate their grievances, but many reports did not acknowledge that the legal issues surrounding student transportation were already settled.[18]

As antibusing rhetoric gained traction in the court of public opinion, a "narrative breach" surfaced in media accounts and political rhetoric regarding civil rights. Earlier efforts to dismantle school desegregation in the South through token integration or freedom-of-choice plans were embraced and celebrated, even in Little Rock itself. However, efforts to achieve district-wide integration on a national scale were not recognized as natural extensions of these earlier campaigns. Although many activists stressed the continuity between the "struggles to gain political rights for southern blacks and the struggles to exercise them in productive ways," these connections were elided in public discourse.[19]

In the national media, few reporters made note of Little Rock's own long struggle with the issue of student transportation. Frozen in 1957, the press advanced a narrative that drew stark comparisons between efforts to dismantle de jure Southern school desegregation and the more complicated business of addressing what was popularly described as de facto discrimination throughout the country. For many who opposed busing, there was a "critical difference" between the school desegregation crisis in Little Rock and the controversy that gripped Boston. In the 1950s, they contended, Little Rock school children and their parents had pursued a desegregated school system with students assigned to schools regardless of their race. Despite a mountain of evidence to the contrary, antibusing advocates insisted that students in Boston and other Northern school districts had "long been assigned to schools solely on the basis of where they lived on a straight color-blind basis." Advancing this narrative of innocence, they argued that the courts were mistakenly deploying "race-conscious" remedies. From this perspective, busing not only tried to impose an "artificial" racial balance on "naturally" segregated communities, it also violated the "color-blind" principle established in *Brown* and defended in Little Rock.[20]

This defense of the status quo was rooted in a refusal to acknowledge the public policies that had shaped the nation's metropolitan communities: discriminatory federal mortgage guidelines that favored identifiably white neighborhoods and labeled integrated neighborhoods as "high risk," urban renewal programs that destroyed historically black communities in central cities and displaced residents to less favorable sectors, as well as the facilitation of suburban sprawl through federally funded highways and municipal zoning plans.[21] Middle-class antibusing advocates insisted that their suburban privileges were the rewards of their individual effort rather than these systemic forces. In this context, they framed residence in affluent white enclaves as the inevitable outcome of their hard work and their ability to make discerning choices in the housing market. Many antibusing advocates viewed their access to quality public schools as an extension of this individual meritocracy and middle-class entitlement. Court-ordered busing, and the transportation of their children to distant communities of color, threatened to undermine their upwardly-mobile status and was viewed as a violation of their consumer rights and an assault on their pursuit of the American Dream.[22]

The antibusing movement drew sharp distinctions between de facto and de jure discrimination.[23] In the media, this contrast was frequently framed as a stark binary contrast between the North and South. The Boston school board mobilized a defense of its policies rooted in its claims that the city was "not Little Rock" or "not Birmingham." This strategic formulation cast racism as a distinctly Southern problem, allowing Northern antibusing advocates to celebrate, affirm, and even co-opt the accomplishments of the Southern civil rights struggle while maintaining and perpetuating segregation at home.

Civil rights leaders in the late 1960s and early 1970s challenged this binary contrast in federal courts of law. In Northern cities like Boston, community leaders sought to amplify the connections between their demands for educational opportunity and those below the Mason-Dixon Line. As the historian Jeanne Theoharis has noted, Northern civil rights activists understood that the reification of the "southern movement as proof of the perfectibility of American democracy" threatened to overshadow and even undermine their own efforts to secure meaningful change. If racism was a distinctively Southern problem that had been addressed through the passage of civil rights legislation, then Northern campaigns for open housing, educational equity, economic opportunity, and proportional political power were not necessary. This binary contrast between North and South sought to displace racism geographically. In an effort to counter this narrative, Northern civil rights leaders drew attention to the similarities—rather than the differences—between the racial crisis gripping cities like Boston and earlier conflicts in cities like Little Rock. Exploring the intersections between the two regions provided community leaders in Boston with a "site through which they anchored the morality of their own struggle."[24]

In Little Rock, Southern civil rights advocates also illuminated the parallels between the events of 1957 and 1974. Sybil Stevenson, a Central High alumna who enrolled as one of a handful of black students when the city's schools reopened in 1959, publicly recognized the connections between her own experience and the African American pupils riding buses into Southie. In her view, the children in Boston were "change agents . . . links in a chain which has been forged throughout our struggle in this country; a chain of blacks committed to freedom and justice." This chain of change agents stretched back into the past through the length and breadth of American history up through the twentieth century to the Little Rock Nine and those who followed them, like Stevenson herself, and was being carried on by a new generation of young people. Like their predecessors, bused students were willing to "face perils as they participate in the effort to bring about racial balance in our public schools."[25]

Little Rock's black newspaper, the *Southern Mediator Journal*, also weighed in on the events unfolding in Boston and resistance to student transportation more broadly. The unfolding busing crisis in the "allegedly liberal North" revealed pervasive national discrimination and the segregation of black citizens in all sectors of American life. The "ballyhoo" in Boston and the national outcry against busing revealed "how whites think the country over." The paper's editorial board contended that the nation had still not learned its lesson from the Little Rock school desegregation crisis. "It was hoped," they wrote, that after events in Little Rock had established "the right of blacks to enter the public schools without segregation . . . people all over the United States would go about the business of making democracy work in all areas." The crisis in Boston, and persistent resistance to student transportation in Little Rock, revealed that this transformation had not occurred. Columnist and radio commentator Leo Collins expressed his disbelief that white residents in Arkansas's capital and elsewhere continued to try to evade the spirit of the *Brown* decision through "leftover Orval Faubus schemes." If white parents truly wanted to provide their children with the best education possible, Collins chided, they should "allow their children to attend school unmolested by their stereotyped thinking."[26]

National civil rights leaders also sought to reshape public opinion through the mass media. In an op-ed in the *Washington Post*, NAACP general counsel Nathaniel R. Jones cautioned reporters that it was a "fundamental error" to attempt "to draw legal distinctions between the Little Rock and Boston desegregation cases." Jones insisted that the issues were simple. In 1954, the Supreme Court had ruled that state-imposed segregation was unconstitutional. Public officials had created and maintained segregated schools in Little Rock *and* Boston. Their actions violated the equal protection clause of the Fourteenth Amendment and courts were required to develop remedial plans that removed all vestiges of segregation from the system. In both cities, resistance to efforts to eliminate segregation had resulted in violence. Indeed, the cases were so similar the Court of Appeals drew upon legal precedents established in Little Rock sixteen years earlier when it refused to overturn the Boston busing order because of community resistance and mob violence. "Rather than continuing fruitless journalistic probes for legal distinctions that don't exist," Jones urged reporters, "it is time for all people of decent instincts to come together to preserve the fragile but essential rule of law."[27]

In other venues, national civil rights leaders argued that the most important difference between Little Rock and Boston had nothing to do with a false distinction between de jure segregation in the South and de facto discrimination in the North, but the failure of the Nixon and Ford administrations to follow President Eisenhower's example and enforce federal law. Roger Wilkins, President Lyndon Johnson's former assistant attorney general, described the scene in Boston as "reminiscent of hundreds of others flashed on television screens at the opening of school in years gone by. There were angry whites chanting their opposition to a Federal Court order, throwing rocks at black school children and screaming defiance and hatred at a symbol of the Federal will to enforce the law." The African American civil rights leader acerbically asserted that the only difference between Little Rock and Boston was "geography and federal policy." School segregation persisted in the North, not because the constitutional rights at stake in the region were fundamentally different, but because the Nixon and Ford administrations encouraged resistance to Northern desegregation, publicly attacked remedies designed to ameliorate it, and refused to withhold federal funds from institutions that supported it. In this context, Wilkins concluded that the people of Boston were "worse off than the people of Little Rock" because they had been misled and failed by "demagogues playing anti-busing politics," not just at the state or local level but in the legislative and executive branches of the federal government.[28]

As controversy surrounding busing grew, Southern antibusing advocates sought the same insulation and political protection from court-ordered busing orders as their Northern counterparts. In this regard, they also worked to collapse regional distinctions between Southern de jure segregation and Northern de facto discrimination but to a different end. While civil rights leaders challenged this binary construction in order to legitimize Northern civil rights campaigns, Southern political leaders and antibusing advocates challenged the contrasts drawn between Southern communities like Little Rock and Northern communities like Boston as part of their strategy to evade ongoing federal intervention in their public schools. In the 1970s, Southern antibusing advocates argued that Southern communities and the federal courts had effectively eliminated de jure segregation, and that their metropolitan communities mirrored conditions in the North.[29]

Although Southern antibusing advocates could not displace the residue of state based de jure segregation geographically, they did attempt to distance themselves temporally. In Little Rock itself, the school district's protracted effort to avoid busing had been driven by widespread community opposition. Twice, during the late 1960s, the school board had considered alternative student assignment plans that moved beyond freedom-of-choice plans in an effort to avoid litigation, but the board had encountered stiff resistance from the city's affluent west end. Families in this predominantly white section of Little Rock had been insulated from most of the integration in the school district due to the construction of racially homogenous schools in the western part of the city. Notably, during the first decade of desegregation, voters in this sector of Little Rock had developed alliances with black voters to support moderate candidates for the school board who advocated minimal compliance, rather than segregationist school board candidates who promoted more extreme forms of resistance. Yet this electoral coalition collapsed when the school district considered and the federal courts ultimately ordered student assignment plans that affected them directly. West End residents rallied against comprehensive desegregation plans, worked to defeat board members who supported them, and rejected bond issues that would facilitate their implementation.[30]

In their effort to resist the systematic transformation of the city's school system, West End residents who joined antibusing organizations like Education First were careful to distance themselves from the images of massive resistance that had colored the city's past in 1957–59. As the historian Ben F. Johnson III has noted, members of these organizations "employed the language of neighborhood unity and individual freedom rather than the citizens' council rhetoric of heritage and racial integrity."[31] As the litigation in the case evolved, antibusing advocates even disassociated themselves from the pupil placement procedures and freedom-of-choice plans that had governed the school district's assignment plans for a decade. In its rejection of court-ordered busing, the *Arkansas Democrat* acknowledged that the use of freedom-of-choice plans, like the one that had been in place in Little Rock, were little more than an effective form of "subterfuge" designed to keep schools segregated, but the paper insisted that geographic zoning was inherently fair and that establishing racial balance in the city's schools was not mandated by the Constitution. A student shouldn't be forced "to go to a different school—one that he wouldn't normally attend—because some judge has prescribed [it]." The *Democrat* rejected the logic of the federal courts, and insisted that mathematical ratios measuring the number of black and white students attending the city's schools should not be used to measure the efficacy of the district's desegregation policies. To do so would make "school kids the creatures of the state" and threaten the "theory of individual freedom we prize so highly in our country." This rejection of the Supreme Court's interpretation of constitutional law contained echoes of the past. But by the early 1970s, the paper's editorial board justified its stance by deploying the rhetoric of the civil rights movement itself. "Color shouldn't make any difference" in student assignment, the *Democrat* asserted; "either all of us are equal before the law or we aren't."[32]

Ben F. Johnson III has suggested that this rhetoric reflected a general lack of knowledge about the public policies that undergirded residential segregation in the city. The constructed landscape and the virtually all-white character of the West End had become naturalized by the late 1960s, Johnson maintains, and residents of the area were "innocent of how they benefitted from concerted policies" designed to foster residential segregation.[33] However, many well-connected civic leaders who lived in the area were well aware of and in some cases had deliberately helped to orchestrate the policies that increased racial isolation in the 1960s. Certainly, many homeowners consciously capitalized on these developments with the aid of real estate agents and developers. The argument that residential segregation arose from "market forces and personal choice" was carefully crafted and strategically deployed in *defense* of these arrangements and was more than an expression of ignorance. Notably, many white antibusing advocates in Little Rock maintained this calculated posture of historical innocence even after the de jure roots of residential discrimination in the city were exposed in federal courts of law. This position allowed antibusing advocates in Little Rock to displace racial discrimination as a thing of the past while preserving their privilege in the present.

President Nixon's public statements in support of his proposed busing moratorium appealed to antibusing voters on precisely these grounds. Nixon appealed to white voters who hoped to maintain or benefit from residential segregation and racially isolated schools by drawing a sharp distinction between segregation fostered by educational policy and segregation in housing markets. Regardless of region, the president suggested that residential segregation was a de facto phenomenon, and school districts could not be compelled to redress it through legal action. In this sense, the president also challenged the North/South binary that had dominated public discourse, but his intervention was designed to insulate public school districts in both regions from further court orders. In doing so, Nixon explicitly rejected the determination of the federal courts that official state action underlay residential segregation in communities where student transportation was required. Nixon insisted school desegregation was "substantially completed" and any further measures must be "achieved with a greater sensitivity to educational needs" without "disrupting communities and imposing hardship on children."[34]

In Little Rock, the progress that had been made under the city's new comprehensive desegregation plan would unravel if the president's proposals were implemented and busing was eliminated as a remedy. Arkansas's capital was listed by the Justice Department as one of forty-five school districts with pending court orders that would be directly and immediately affected if Nixon's proposals were to become law.[35] Superintendent of Schools Floyd W. Parsons asserted that the Little Rock school district had been "required to go beyond the Supreme Court's requirements" and expressed confidence that the proposed busing moratorium could have the effect of halting busing completely at the elementary level and scaling back the extent of the city's desegregation efforts at the junior and senior high school levels.[36] African American attorney John W. Walker scoffed at Parson's assertions, however. He noted that Nixon's proposals to provide "compensatory" funding to racially isolated schools only underscored the fact that segregated schools throughout the South were and would continue to be unequal. The president's proposals also exceeded the scope of his authority. "Obviously, the President cannot run the judiciary," Walker asserted.[37] However, while Nixon's direct influence over the federal courts was restrained by the separation of powers, he would have the opportunity to profoundly reshape Supreme Court jurisprudence. During his tenure, Nixon would appoint four new justices to the bench and recast the ideological outlook of the Court. In this respect, political resistance threatened to undermine the legal gains only recently secured by civil rights organizations.

At this critical juncture, the civil rights community moved to defend the gains made in federal courts of law in the memorial arena. In doing so, they advanced an oppositional history designed to counteract efforts to disconnect the legacy of the 1957–59 Little Rock school desegregation crisis from struggles to secure educational equity a generation later. By advancing an alternative public history of the process of school desegregation in Arkansas's capital, local and national activists were participating in a broader effort to challenge the interpretation of the African American experience and its representation in public space. In the 1970s, this deep cultural ferment was reflected in the emergence of black studies programs in institutions of higher education, the development of the black museum movement, the celebration of West African cultural traditions, and public demands for an inclusive national bicentennial.[38] In her study of commemorative practices during the mid-1970s, Tammy S. Gordon observed that activists on the left tapped into the knowledge generated by the new social history and became "attuned to the potential of historical knowledge to motivate people to enact or accept the social, economic, or political changes they were advocating."[39] In this regard, they tapped into a long-standing tradition in African American communities that Manning Marable has described as an effort to connect "scholarship with collective struggle" and "social analysis with social transformation."[40]

In Little Rock, local African American leaders responded to the NAACP's national call to action against Nixon's proposed antibusing legislation through a memorial ceremony held on the steps of Central High School. The NAACP rejected the president's distinction between de jure and de facto segregation and framed the administration's actions as an attack on the 1954 *Brown* decision. The national civil rights organization urged its allies not to "stand still while the protections we have won at such cost are swept away by our enemies." Members were urged to write letters to their congressmen, senators, local newspapers, and the president himself reminding them that the "*real* issue is ending segregated education and that busing is only one way—but often a necessary way—to end segregation."[41] The national organization also urged local branches to schedule rallies and mass meetings in opposition to the president's proposals.[42]

Within days of this appeal, 200 delegates from the NAACP Region Six leadership conference converged in Little Rock. In his rousing address to those gathered, NAACP board member Dr. George D. Flemmings warned his colleagues that the Nixon administration and its allies were not only undermining the enforcement mechanisms written into the 1964 Civil

FIGURE 5. In 1972, representatives of the NAACP rallied on the steps of Central High School to publicly denounce President Nixon's antibusing policies and called on the broader community of Little Rock to take action to preserve the city's student transportation plan. (*Arkansas Democrat*)

Rights Act, but were now devoting "a lot of time and energy . . . into the idea of breaking down the gains we've made in recent decisions of the Supreme Court."[43] Historic parallels between past and present occupied center stage as the assembly condemned President Nixon's antibusing position in a public resolution read in front of Central High School. Likening the president to Governor Orval Faubus, the delegates accused Nixon of acting "for selfish political advantage" and using his office to "encourage a national mood of reaction and oppression by emotional appeals and obvious deceit." Despite the fact that Nixon had staked his political reputation on a commitment to preserve "law and order," the delegates observed that Nixon sought to undermine the authority of the federal courts just as Faubus had done when he called out the National Guard to prevent the integration of Central High

School. As NAACP representatives stood in front of the school's iconic facade and joined hands singing "We Shall Overcome," Rev. C. Anderson Davis, director of the NAACP Houston chapter, referred to Central as an important "symbol of the Negro's struggle for integration in the schools." This symbolism was multivalent. Central High was both a historic and contemporary symbol of the black freedom struggle because its integrated student body had only recently been secured through student transportation. This reconfiguration of Central's symbolic status directly challenged efforts to freeze the school district's image in 1957 in an attempt to draw geographic distinctions between Southern and Northern desegregation efforts, as well as efforts to distance the antibusing movement temporally from the longstanding effort to resist meaningful school desegregation.

Although she was no longer NAACP Arkansas State Conference president, Daisy Bates was still an active leader in the organization and also spoke to the assembled delegates. In her address, Bates echoed Dr. Flemmings's warning that "slippage in civil rights is apparent on every hand," but she emphasized that the battle in Little Rock and elsewhere was not over. "Freedom is something we must fight for every day and every hour," she asserted. Bates invoked the public memory of Elizabeth Eckford's solitary courage as she walked in front of Central High School with a "mob at her heels" and urged the crowd to "rededicate" themselves to the "fight for freedom." In response to this public appeal, the delegates pledged to challenge the president in "the Congress and the courts" and to "appeal for justice before the nation and the world" in order to prevent resegregation in this symbolic city of the struggle.[44]

The US Commission on Civil Rights also mobilized the image of Little Rock in its efforts to counteract antibusing sentiment. In its public information campaigns, the Commission attempted to redirect the comparisons that were already being drawn between Arkansas's capital and the newest foci of the desegregation struggle. In mass media accounts which drew sharp distinctions between controversies surrounding Southern segregation in the past and Northern battles in the present, reporters failed to recognize that school desegregation litigation in Little Rock had evolved over the course of two decades. In contrast, the US Commission on Civil Rights highlighted Little Rock not only because of its iconic status as a symbol of massive resistance, but also because the dual system of schools that had made the city famous was being dismantled through a court-ordered district-wide busing program. The Commission suggested that if the city of Little Rock—"the example segregationists used to argue that black and white students would never go to school together in peace"—could transcend its divisions and successfully desegregate through busing, the same could be accomplished almost anywhere. The district was applauded for offering students the opportunity to learn "how to live and work with people of different skin colors and cultural backgrounds."[45]

The US Commission on Civil Rights believed that public opinion had hardened against busing because many politicians and antibusing advocates opposing desegregation had deliberately clouded the issues and the media had not clarified them. The Commission worked assiduously to dispel the "groundless fears" that had been substituted for fact in the busing debate, providing studies and statistics to demonstrate that the safety of school children was not jeopardized by busing and that the academic achievement of white and black students remained stable or improved under integrated conditions. The Commission also underscored that mandatory busing was implemented as a tool of last resort in school systems where racial isolation had been deliberately fostered and perpetuated, not maintained by "chance or free choice."[46]

In this context, Little Rock's experience with busing was advanced as a model of successful desegregation, not because of the token integration associated with the Little Rock Nine in 1957 but because of a student transportation program that had been implemented with little violence or administrative difficulty.[47] Positive images of busing in Little Rock were used to counter the negative images streaming out of cities like Boston and Pontiac, Michigan. At the urging of John Walker, the attorney for the black plaintiffs in the Little Rock school desegregation litigation, the NAACP Legal Defense Fund (LDF) also highlighted the successful implementation of busing in Little Rock to demonstrate "that integration can be made to work." The pamphlet, *Little Rock, 17 Years After*, highlighted testimonials from students, teachers, and administrators to present a positive image of student transportation and its effects. Due to the school district's own experience with violent resistance, the LDF suggested that Little Rock citizens were uniquely positioned to "speak truth to hate" and counteract antibusing rhetoric circulating throughout the country. Yet the LDF did not attribute progress in the city to changes in the "hearts and minds" of Little Rock's residents, but rather to persistent pressure applied by civil rights organizations.

If busing remained politically unpopular in the court of public opinion, the kind of progress Little Rock's student transportation program had fostered might only be achieved elsewhere or retained in Arkansas's capital through extensive and costly court litigation. The LDF highlighted Little Rock's "success" story to solicit donations in an effort to continue its work.[48]

Ironically, as Little Rock approached the twentieth anniversary of the 1957 crisis, school administrators, students, and local residents also embraced their new role as a model school district. However, while it was precisely the city's well-known resistance to school desegregation that made it such a valuable symbol for the US Commission on Civil Rights and the NAACP Legal Defense Fund, many in Little Rock preferred to keep the spotlight squarely on the present rather than the past. As one retrospective newspaper account put it, "The turmoil of that September is easily remembered and that's the way everyone wants it to remain—just memories."[49] While civil rights organizations highlighted the central role of pioneers like the Little Rock Nine and countless others who participated in the school desegregation litigation, city boosters sought to emphasize Little Rock's accomplishment and downplay the struggle required to attain it. Vague references to the events of 1957 merely served as a foil to highlight the lack of racial tension in the city's schools twenty years later. Moreover, the mechanics of the process of desegregation—including the central importance of busing—were murky in official public accounts, despite the efforts of civil rights organizations to place them front and center.

Two decades after the school desegregation crisis in Little Rock, the mainstream press focused on the signs of progress at the city's most infamous institution—Central High School. By the mid-1970s, Central High's student body was half white and half black, and the principal, Morris Holmes, was African American. Although most media accounts made note of the even ratio of black and white students, reporters also made note of a spirit of racial "harmony" and "cooperation," suggesting that integration amounted to more than a mathematical formula at Central High. At the beginning of the 1976 school year, the *New York Times* reported that "racial violence had practically disappeared" and "tension seemed nonexistent" at Central. Superintendent of Schools Paul R. Fair stated proudly, "I think the problems we've experienced in the past have been in large measure eliminated. We have an apparent attitude of cooperation here, not only among students but among the faculty." Over ten years, the school had been able to narrow the achievement gap between black and white students, with black students scoring "considerably higher" and white students scoring "slightly better" on tests. Student government, athletic teams, and other organizations were completely integrated after years of delay, and both black and white students expressed pride in the school's accomplishments.[50] Superintendent Fair conceded that every school district had to confront its own unique challenges, but urged urban school districts to devote considerable time and resources toward resolving racial issues. "I didn't believe at first that this could be done," he said. "Now I believe anything can be done. It's obvious to me now that desegregation of schools is best. In order to build a solid, cohesive community, you have to have it." Fair asserted that this was true in all areas of the country. "The Constitution wasn't written to apply only to some sections and not to others," he said.[51] Although Fair's comments obliquely addressed the national controversy surrounding busing, few retrospective media accounts explicitly addressed persistent tension in Little Rock itself related to student transportation or even acknowledged that the celebrated racial balance at Central High was the product of a court-ordered busing plan.

Indeed, Little Rock's celebration of progress came at the expense of cultivating an active historical understanding of the process of school desegregation in the district. By the twentieth anniversary of the 1957 school desegregation crisis, none of the students attending Central High had even been born when the racial turmoil in Little Rock captured the world's attention. Several told journalists that they had difficulty understanding the tension in Boston and elsewhere. Greg Means, a white senior, explained, "Really, we talk about what happened in Louisville and Boston and we laugh about it . . . We can't comprehend it. We don't see people here throwing rocks at school buses. We don't see parents yelling at the police in front of school. It's all so hard to comprehend." Pausing reflectively, he added, "Of course, none of us here can really comprehend 1957 either." Other students admitted how little they knew about the school desegregation crisis. The events of 1957 were covered only superficially in history courses and many students were "surprised to learn that their school helped blaze a new frontier for the civil rights movement," according to the *Los Angeles Times*. At least one teacher reacted with hostility to a reporter's questions about the crisis, accusing him of "trying to relive the Civil War all over again." A school administrator admitted that the controversy in 1957 and the closure of all three of the city's high schools in 1958–59 was "purposefully played down" because "a lot of people don't want to open up old wounds."[52]

Even the commemorative ceremony organized by the school district to publicly mark the twentieth anniversary of 1957 crisis evaded a close accounting of the historical events that had shaped the trajectory of school desegregation in the district. Although three of the Little Rock Nine were present and received standing ovations from Central High's student body, the program was described by the *Arkansas Gazette* as "not so much on occasion for recalling the 1957 school desegregation crisis . . . as it was a time for noting the progress that had been made since then." The ceremony was on occasion for "tuning up the choir and tuning up the band in salute to those who helped build what one speaker called a 'new Central High School.'" With some relief, the paper noted, "Heroes received rousing tributes, while the villains, mercifully, were not mentioned." When Ralph Brodie, the student body president in 1957–58, rose to speak, he asserted that only a "small group of Little Rock residents were responsible for the city's bigoted, violent, and prejudiced image," according to the *Gazette*. "For most of us," he insisted, "that image remains entirely undeserved." Although Brodie saluted the courage of his black classmates who had "done much to assure the rights of others," he also paid tribute to the "moderate" and "quiet" voices who urged others to comply with the law."[53] In this iteration of the history of the crisis, the voices of "moderation" and tokenism were given just as much credit for the district's success as the civil rights activists and black plaintiffs who had pushed for substantive desegregation. Even the title of the program, "Twenty Years of Integration: A Model for the Nation," implied that the racial balance only recently achieved in the city's schools was a long-standing achievement.

This narrative of passive progress was remarkably devoid of historical context, conflict, or substantive reflection. Longstanding claims that the school desegregation crisis had been precipitated by outsiders stood unchallenged; the ideological differences which separated segregationists committed to massive resistance, moderates who charted a course of minimal compliance, and civil rights organizations who demanded systemic desegregation were unexplored; the winding road of court litigation and the evolving landscape of school desegregation in the city was uncharted; and the persistence of resistance to equitable integration in the district was unexplored. In order to advance claims that Little Rock had always been a "progressive" Southern city and that the city's "model" status could be attributed to the efforts of white moderates to persuade their peers to comply with the law, the history of school desegregation in the city was vacated. Those who sought to preserve white privilege in Little Rock through neighborhood schools and resistance to court-ordered busing maintained that the city could maintain "harmony" without extensive court intervention because of the racial moderation of the community. These actors adopted a posture that paid lip-service to the principle of integration, while obscuring the state action, housing policy, and school zoning plans that had fostered residential segregation, and rejecting the mechanisms required to remedy their effects. They finessed the contradictions between the city's image of itself as "progressive" and the persistence of racial isolation in city neighborhoods by defending them on the grounds of "freedom of association" and the economic stratification of the real estate market. They embraced Little Rock's status as a "model" community by situating resistance to meaningful school desegregation in the past, and attributing it to historical actors they defined as "outside" of the community, in an effort to legitimize their own claims of historical innocence in the present.

The city's selective historical memory produced a convoluted public discourse. Political leaders and school board members publicly embraced the principle of integration while declining to endorse the busing program required to achieve it. For example, in 1977, on the occasion of the twentieth anniversary of the school desegregation crisis, the Little Rock school board pledged to uphold its obligations under federal court orders. In a public resolution, the board proclaimed, "The achievement of the highest quality education in the Little Rock Public Schools cannot be subjugated to any other policy in this district." In previous years, this statement would have served as the preamble to the announcement of yet another pupil placement procedure or transfer program designed to delay desegregation. But in 1977, the board announced, "It is the conviction of this Board that this goal cannot only be achieved with integration but improved by it. A vital part of the education of any student is learning to live with others. Integration of our schools is essential if our children, both black and white, are to live in harmony in an integrated city." The alternative course, which the board referred to as "separatism," would produce nothing but "crippling consequences for generations to come." Yet while school board members expressed their support for the principle of integration, they were decidedly less enthusiastic about the mechanics of the court-ordered desegregation plan that had fostered racial balance in the district's schools. The school board's 1977 pledge contained only a tepid commitment to the busing program; the document described student transportation as an "expensive and difficult" program to administer, though the board promised to continue to implement it until the district was "able to institute a better program."[54]

Indeed, in this respect, the school board's position was carefully calibrated to resonate with broader public opinion in the school district. A 1976 survey of black and white residents in Little Rock revealed ambivalence about school desegregation in the district and persistent white resistance to "forced" busing. While the US Commission on Civil Rights highlighted the implementation of the busing program in Little Rock as proof that student transportation was a necessary tool for achieving school desegregation, it recognized the persistence of racial tension in the district in its report *School Desegregation in Little Rock, Arkansas*. Black parents, students, and teachers interviewed generally agreed that African American pupils had access to better schools and instructional materials under the desegregation plan. Many black teachers expressed their belief that equal educational opportunity could only be attained through integration and agreed that the busing plan had improved educational equality. For their part, black students felt that "opportunity for a better for education for all students" was attainable in Little Rock. Due to their access to educational resources, higher percentages of their peers were graduating from high school and finding employment. When African American interviewees expressed dissatisfaction with the busing plan, their complaints were primarily directed at the unequal burden they felt the desegregation plan placed on black families, teachers, and historically black educational institutions.

White parents and teachers were more likely than their African American counterparts to challenge the premise that the desegregation plan improved educational equality in the district. Moreover, they implied that if the plan did so, it achieved this end at the expense of white students. Although some parents believed that the desegregation plan had improved the school system through a general restructuring, the interviewers encountered "parental hostility about completely desegregating the school system." Many resented that their children were "compelled" to attend interracial schools. Likewise, white teachers were "generally pessimistic" about school desegregation. While some white teachers indicated that black students benefitted from the integration of schools, they contended that desegregation hindered white students academically. White students themselves suggested that the plan gave black students access to better educational facilities and provided white students with the chance to meet people from other backgrounds, but they did not believe the plan offered them any educational benefits. For their part, school administrators did not believe the greatest problem facing the school system was the unequal burden the desegregation plan placed on the black community, but rather "the apathy of black students and parents, violence in and around schools, and financial problems." The elements of the busing plan spoken of favorably by white parents were those that *reduced* the busing of white students and allowed white pupils to continue to attend Hall and Parkview High Schools in the city's West End. Parents also praised the feeder system that allowed students to continue through elementary, middle, and high school with a consistent group of friends.[55] The survey revealed the need for court-ordered busing in order to secure effective desegregation, since it seemed unlikely that the community of Little Rock would endeavor to dismantle the white privilege embedded in neighborhood schools voluntarily.

Indeed, even as the school board affirmed its commitment to the principle of integration, it acknowledged that this undercurrent of resistance threatened to undermine the stability of the city's public schools. The school board noted that white flight had disrupted the economic and social fabric of "other cities" and cautioned parents that Little Rock, too, would "be destroyed" if parents and community leaders did not continue to support the public schools "with their dollars, their time, their good will, but most importantly, with their children in our schools."[56] Concerns about white flight to Little Rock's western suburbs lurked behind the school board's promise to implement a "better program" than busing as soon as it was able. In interviews with staffers from the US Commission on Civil Rights, school administrators cited "white flight, parental opposition, and community attitudes" as the largest challenges still facing the school district.[57] In the 1980s, these concerns would drive school administrators to consider a consolidation suit to merge Little Rock's city schools with the surrounding Pulaski County Special School District, and would ultimately result in a return to more limited desegregation measures designed to appease white patrons in the school district and counteract the "blackening" of the city's schools.[58]

In the 1970s, the national controversy surrounding busing overflowed into the memorial sphere. Civil rights and antibusing advocates grappled over the definitions of de jure and de facto segregation, and engaged in contested debates related to the spatial geography of segregationist resistance and its expression over time. In Little Rock and the nation at large, antibusing advocates crafted a memorial narrative designed to cast the civil rights movement as a relic of the past rather than an active force in the present. This strategy was carefully calculated not only to obscure the continuity between earlier demands for access to equal education and their reiteration in the 1970s, but also to elide the connections between minimal compliance and the new rhetoric of "colorblind" student assignment. This narrative disjuncture allowed those who resisted systemic desegregation to claim the legacy of the *Brown* decision for themselves and to argue that neighborhood schools that assigned students on the basis of the geographic residence were "constitutionally faultless" because they avoided invidious racial distinctions.

In contrast, local and national civil rights activists deployed a careful recitation of history and evoked powerful symbolic memory in an attempt to defuse the willful amnesia of their antibusing counterparts. If a community like Little Rock was in a unique position to "speak truth to hate"—if it had undergone a transformation from being a symbol of massive resistance to "one of the most successfully desegregated school systems in the nation"—it was only because of continuous and sustained litigation, community activism, and the use of busing. This painstaking account of the evolution of the school desegregation landscape was designed to inspire a recommitment to the principle of integration, but also to expose the official school and housing policies that undergirded residential segregation and made student transportation necessary.

At its root, the narrative of passive progress was founded on the argument that the passage of time itself was sufficient to erode the legacy of centuries of state-sponsored discrimination. For a generation, school districts had delayed meaningful and systematic desegregation in the name of proceeding with "deliberate speed" rather than haste. The apostles of minimal compliance had always insisted that more time and the gradual application of the law in accordance with local mores would resolve the nation's deep-seated racial problems. By the 1970s, those who resisted the systemic desegregation required by the *Green* and *Swann* decisions inverted this argument. If time itself was all that was needed to foster change, and time had passed, then this itself was sufficient to demonstrate that change had occurred and school desegregation had been "substantially completed." When this argument was first advanced in federal courts of law, it was not received hospitably. However, the incubation of this narrative in the public sphere impacted the political process and ultimately reshaped the cast of school desegregation litigation through President Nixon's appointments to the Supreme Court. As a result, in the final quarter of the twentieth century, civil rights litigants would struggle to convince the justices on the bench that persistent inequities in American society were "vestiges" of discrimination.

— CHAPTER THREE —
Recasting Moderation and Resistance

Over the last third of his life, in the midst of financial insecurity, a troubled family life, and several unsuccessful attempts to regain office, Orval Faubus dedicated himself to reshaping his historical reputation. He granted hundreds of interviews to journalists, historians, sociologists, political scientists, and other interested citizens, and spent innumerable hours writing and gathering material for his political memoirs *Down from the Hills* (published in two volumes, in 1980 and 1985). Although he brought his considerable charm and skills as a politician to this project, by the late 1970s Arkansas's longest-serving governor had become a political pariah. After his retirement in 1966, Faubus never regained the influence and prestige he had once accepted as his due.[1] Without the assistance or patronage of those he once called his friends, Faubus was unable to find a publisher interested in distributing his memoir. The governor's rhetoric in *Down from the Hills* was wrought from the political arguments, propaganda, and states' rights appeals of the past; the text offered no hope of individual transformation, local change, or national progress.[2] As a result, the governor's story was out of step with the triumphal narrative of progress that dominated public accounts of the civil rights movement by the early 1980s. These factors, combined with Faubus's political fall from grace and his status as a figure of public opprobrium, may have discouraged potential publishers from moving forward with the project.

Despite this lack of interest, Faubus was determined to move forward with self-publication. "It would be tragic for me and for the history of the period in which I served as governor, if the principal source of material for historians and future studies should be mainly newspaper files such as the *Arkansas Gazette*," he reflected.[3] However, the governor's efforts to recast his legacy were unsuccessful. His first-person account was largely dismissed as a poorly written and self-serving narrative. Although he still had some well-placed friends who praised the text in favorable reviews,[4] most readers contended that the book offered little that had not been heard before. The notoriously anti-Faubus *Arkansas Gazette* rejected the "implied theme" that the narrative was "an objective history" of the governor's time in office. "Above all, it is dedicated to the sympathetic treatment of the author," reviewer Leland Duvall asserted. "When Faubus was governor, he issued statements that served his purpose; on other occasions, he held his peace. This practice, generally accepted among politicians . . . can be a bit of a disappointment to those who shell out $25 in the hope they will learn something new about the turbulent period." The former governor contemptuously dismissed such commentary, noting that although Duvall was a credible journalist, "he would have been fired if he had written anything good about me."[5] However, a review in the *Arkansas Historical Quarterly* also charged the governor with "skew[ing] the facts." While Faubus's political skills were legendary, his reputation for dissembling ultimately served him poorly with historians.[6]

Despite his "untiring revisionism" and "endless pleading and explaining to justify the past to the future," Faubus never quite escaped his reputation as an opportunist who exploited racial tension when it served his electoral fortunes. The arguments that had once been so persuasive with voters no longer resonated. Without a publisher, the man who was once the most powerful political figure in the state of Arkansas had his book printed privately and found himself spending the final years of his life selling copies out of the trunk of his car at courthouse lobbies, Civil War reenactments, county fairs, and political events and speaking "charmingly and lengthily and with much cordiality to the odd reporter or historian or odd constituent" who sought him out.[7]

In contrast, Little Rock's white moderates found a ready market for their retrospective accounts of the school desegregation crisis in the 1980s.

Publishers and television executives embraced their accounts of "good people" doing the best they could under terrible circumstances and presumed that civil rights stories written from the perspective of moderate white protagonists would have widespread appeal. In this context, historical actors associated with massive resistance like Orval Faubus struggled to find an audience—but so too did African American civil rights activists. While the memoir of Central High School's Vice Principal of Girls, Elizabeth Huckaby, was adapted for broadcast on national television, Daisy Bates reported that her memoir received a hostile reception from television producers because it was the "wrong color."[8]

The elevation of white moderates and their presentation as heroic figures in the mid-century civil rights struggle was dependent on a variety of factors beyond the profit-driven imperatives of the culture industry. Most notably, the narrative of passive progress advanced in the previous decade had divorced the actions of African American civil rights activists from the fruits of their labor. With their contributions obscured, white moderates easily stepped into the frame as the primary drivers of change. This transformation allowed the programs that white moderates promoted in the 1950s and 1960s to be advanced by school administrators as model desegregation policies two decades later, camouflaging the fact that many of these policies had been designed to limit and not to encourage the dissolution of dual school systems.

White moderates marketing their accounts in the early 1980s benefited from their liminal status during the mid-century civil rights struggle. Politically pragmatic, moderates had frequently promoted tokenism and gradualism as the most effective way to control and limit the pace of school desegregation. Indeed, their selective screening procedures, pupil placement laws, freedom-of-choice plans, and gerrymandered attendance zones achieved precisely this objective in communities across the country. The legal foundation for their approach rested on the admittance of a handful of black students to "white" schools where they were frequently relegated to a second-class status, forbidden from participating in organized sports, student organizations, and seasonal concerts or from attending school dances and extracurricular activities. Even this, however, was too much for ardent segregationists committed to the course of massive resistance. These actors accused white moderates of being "integrationists" who wittingly or unwittingly were opening the floodgates of desegregation. In the late 1950s and early 1960s, well-connected and politically active moderates vigorously denied this charge in order to preserve their influence in public life. Their approach, they argued, would survive court challenge and sustain the Southern way of life, while overt obstructionism would only produce massive federal court intervention and enforcement. Twenty years later, however, many white moderates sought to distance themselves from this position. With a wink to the past, they suggested that their critics had been right all along—they *had* been closet integrationists—committed to advancing the cause of civil rights with subtlety in a hostile environment. Moreover, they too had been victimized and targeted by extremist segregationist organizations who sought to undermine their influence and credibility in the community-at-large. This maneuver allowed white moderates to recast their role, and to emerge in popular civil rights histories as allies rather than as obstructionists or silent bystanders.

This celebration of the experiences and perspectives of white moderates occurred just as demographic shifts threatened the racial balance of Little Rock's school system. Well-connected white moderates had evaded the impact of token integration plans through their residence in Little Rock's "silk-stocking" district on the western side of the city, which was nearly all white. As busing transportation produced systemic change, some segments of this population continued to drift westward and abandoned public education in the district—taking up residence in the surrounding suburbs or sending their children to rapidly expanding private schools. In the early 1980s, Little Rock school officials became increasingly concerned about the "blackening" of the city's schools in the wake of systemic desegregation. Following the failure of a plan to consolidate city and suburban schools in the county, district officials fell back on the "moderate" principles that had guided their efforts to limit the impact of integration and appease white parents for decades. However, this time, these measures were not advanced as a means to inhibit school integration but as tools to salvage desegregation and save the district from continued white flight.

The effort of white Southern moderates to transform their legacy was particularly evident in the memoirs of Little Rock congressman Brooks Hays and the evolution of his self-presentation between the late 1950s and early 1980s. In the mid-twentieth century, Hays defined his moderation within the framework of a "states' rights liberalism" that largely preserved

FIGURE 6. This 1958 political advertisement depicted white "moderate" school board candidates as unwitting integrationists. Although they were publicly committed to the principle of segregation, moderates argued that massive resistance would lead to the destruction of the public education system and favored a policy of passive resistance that utilized tokenism and gradualism to evade the full impact of the *Brown v. Board of Education* decision. This image circulated by the Capital Citizens' Council suggested that moderate candidates who promoted this position were not segregationists, as they claimed, but instead were a "slate of integrationists" misled by civil rights activists like Daisy Bates. (*Arkansas Democrat*)

white Southern prerogatives by retaining local control over the pace of change in American race relations.⁹ Hays advocated various forms of local control, tokenism, and gradualism in a bid to avoid direct federal intervention and enforcement of school desegregation. Yet a generation later, Hays claimed that the moderate positions he staked out at the peak of his political career were a smokescreen for more liberal and progressive inclinations. The congressman published three memoirs over the course of his career, with *Politics Is My Parish* (1981) released nearly twenty-five years after the Little Rock school desegregation crisis. This text recast some of the positions Hays articulated in his first retrospective account, *A Southern Moderate Speaks* (1959), published in the immediate aftermath of the 1957–58 school year.

In the 1950s, Hays argued that the question of civil rights was primarily an ethical and moral problem best addressed by local civic and religious organizations, which had the influence to shape public sentiment and create lasting change. The Arkansas congressman contended that any law that violently tore apart the fabric of Southern life not only violated the nation's "dual form of government with some powers reserved to the states," but was also destined to produce nothing but frustration and resistance without the support of the American people. Hays asserted that gradual programs of change directed at the local level would be more accepted and would ultimately be more effective. If this kind of approach came at the expense of America's black citizens, that was a secondary consideration.¹⁰

As an expression of dissent, Hays signed the 1956 "Southern Manifesto" decrying the Supreme Court's *Brown v. Board of Education,* a decision he later said he regretted. In the months that followed, he expressed hope that the South could come into compliance with the *Brown* decision through a policy of "permissive integration" that placed responsibility for school desegregation with local communities and school boards. For the congressman, the school desegregation plan put forward by Little Rock superintendent Virgil Blossom and approved by the school board represented the best hope for a moderate solution to the racial crisis precipitated by *Brown.* Like the superintendent himself, Hays viewed himself as a man of the middle, trying to steer a pragmatic course through extremists on all sides—not only between civil rights advocates and ardent segregationists, but, at the national level, between Northern liberals and Southern conservatives. Hays hoped that Blossom's plan of "slow, gradual, voluntary integration" would serve "as a model for many cities in the South." If the plan had been implemented without controversy, it might have validated his political philosophy.[11] Instead, Little Rock's struggle came to symbolize a titanic confrontation between Southern massive resistance to and federal enforcement of the *Brown* decision.

Hays had been working to avert such a conflict throughout his political career, but in 1957, the "clash between state and federal authority" unfolded in his own district. Eager to fashion a compromise, Hays brokered a meeting between President Eisenhower and Governor Faubus in the hope that the president would grant a reprieve in order to resolve conflicts between state and federal law.[12] Hays's long held belief that "extremists" were pushing the nation toward crisis seemed to have been realized in Little Rock. He expressed impatience with partisans from "other states" who were determined to stir up resistance to desegregation in the city, and maintained hope that Arkansas's capital "could yet become a symbol for harmonious race relations" if its citizens worked to resolve the conflict through the orderly processes of law.[13] In speeches before civic groups and in conversations with community leaders, Hays tried to cultivate a spirit of conciliation, moderation, and respect for law and order.

Hays's position during the school desegregation crisis and his support of the Blossom Plan made him vulnerable to political challenge. During his 1958 reelection campaign, the congressman faced charges that he was a "race-mixer" and a "fence-straddler" betraying the Southern way of life. Defeated by segregationist school board member Dr. Dale Alford in an eight-day write-in campaign, Hays discovered that his moderation was a liability at the local level. Alford accused Hays of playing both sides of political issues and argued that the moderate course charted by Hays "only ends in integration for us here at home."[14] However, if Hays's moderation was a liability in the local political arena, it was an asset in the national sphere. Ironically, Hays's defeat generated more respect for the political risks that he and other Southern moderates courted.[15] Nationally, the former congressman was canonized by the press as a political martyr for standing up for his "principles," though little mention was made of what those principles were and little effort was expended to elucidate what Hays stood for as a states' rights liberal.

Hays's celebrity contributed directly to the publication of his first book, *A Southern Moderate Speaks,* in 1959. The congressman claimed that his stance on American race relations had been "distorted" in the press and his public statements taken out of context. Consequently, Northerners had not appreciated or recognized his refusal to adopt a hardline position, while constituents in his own district had judged him harshly without grasping the nuances of his defense of local control, gradual change, and the flexible application of federal law. *A Southern Moderate Speaks* chronicled Hays's actions throughout his political career and during the school desegregation crisis in light of his political philosophy, but it also served as a launching pad for his future endeavors. In the wake of his defeat, Hays's reputation as a "hero-martyr of moderation" served him well for the remainder of his career. As he reflected, "I had unintentionally become a momentary symbol of something that would bring pride and satisfaction to a far greater degree than continuation in office could have produced." Although he had been defeated, he observed, "my moral position was impregnable."[16] Hays never held elected office again but was able to leverage his reputation to secure political appointments in the Eisenhower, Kennedy, and Johnson administrations.

Hays's reputation as a moral statesman, and the hazy public understanding of his policy positions, would have important implications for his legacy. Although he acknowledged the courage of the Little Rock Nine in the 1950s, he was not their advocate. Hays hoped that token desegregation and minimal compliance would appease the federal courts and satisfy civil rights organizations so that the region could avoid "immediate" and "massive" integration. Hays did not believe that the *Brown* decision required systemic desegregation and felt it could be satisfied as long as African American children were provided with educational facilities in their own school district, pupils were able attend specialized courses not available in their own schools, and a handful of "exceptional students" were admitted to white institutions and provided with the opportunity to benefit from their "higher" educational standards. The congressman suggested that these limited concessions would satisfy African American citizens and create a "psychological release" that might relax pressure for more substantive change.[17]

However, over the years, Hays downplayed these aspects of his record and suggested that he had truly been a Southern white liberal, promoting token integration as only the first step in a good-faith effort to dismantle racial discrimination and systems of segregation in the region. In his final memoir, Hays suggested that he adopted a moderate stance in order to "induce" his Southern colleagues to move toward fulfilling the "aspirations of our black minority for complete equality."[18] This motivating force, or even sympathy for this outcome, was not evident in his earlier book *A Southern Moderate Speaks*. Nevertheless, in his twilight years, Hays was able to take advantage of the accusations leveled at him by his political opponents two decades earlier—that as a moderate he had been an integrationist who took a "moral" position on civil rights during the school desegregation crisis. While filming a public television documentary focused on his statesmanship titled *Brooks Hays: Return to Little Rock* (1980), the congressman explained the "moderate" position he staked out during the crisis to a small group of students at Central High School. Hays expressed pride in his refusal to abandon his political principles and his public support for a "morally correct law which ruled out segregation."[19] This statement reversed Hays's position in 1957 that a matter of conscience—like civil rights—could not be legislated.

The production and distribution of *Brooks Hays: Return to Little Rock* generated controversy in the state, but not as result of Hays's misrepresentation of his policy positions. Indeed, Hays's reputation as a moral moderate went largely unchallenged. Filmmaker David Solomon envisioned a celebratory portrait of Hays that featured the former lawmaker as part of a series that focused on politicians who took principled stands in the midst of "moral ambiguities." The film featured Hays, the sources of influence and inspiration that informed his actions in 1957, and highlighted the congressman as a positive example of the best traditions in American statesmanship. In his proposal for the project, Solomon indicated that he did not envision a film dedicated to "trying to dissect a tragedy," but rather planned to create a biopic that created a "positive portrait of a man." This approach, the filmmaker believed, would be instructive and inspiring.[20]

Despite this focus, the proposed film provoked debate throughout Hay's native state when programmers at the Arkansas Educational Television Network (AETN) threatened not to air the program if it portrayed a "biased" portrait of the Little Rock school desegregation crisis. These powerful cultural gatekeepers questioned the balance and objectivity of a film that might elevate Hays's own reputation at the expense of the citizenry of Little Rock. This position provoked a storm of controversy about the role of public television, mediated representations of the 1957–59 desegregation crisis, and the appropriate balance of tragedy and transformation in historical accounts of those events. Public debate surrounding the production focused primarily on whether the film portrayed Hays as a lone and isolated moderate figure or served to highlight the plight of a large and unrecognized moderate majority in the city of Little Rock.

Public debate about the merits of Solomon's film surfaced after the filmmaker sent a prospectus for *Brooks Hays: Return to Little Rock* and other materials related to the project to station programmers at AETN. Solomon had secured funding from the Arkansas Endowment of Humanities to produce the project, and he imagined distributing it to public schools and libraries after it aired on local public television outlets.[21] The filmmaker planned to intercut archival NBC footage filmed outside of Central High School in 1957 with scenes of the city, the school, and its students in the late 1970s. In addition to interviewing Hays about his role in the crisis, Solomon had been in communication with other prominent figures in American politics who had agreed to participate in the project and give the film the "armor of authority."[22] However, when AETN program director Fred Schmutz was informed that Solomon planned to use archival footage from NBC, he took "exception to this particular part of the film," and indicated that he would review the film closely and would not air it on the network if there was "anything embarrassing to Arkansas" in the final product.

Schmutz had worked for Little Rock's NBC affiliate KARK-TV in 1957. After shooting footage outside Central High School, NBC News had edited and transmitted programming to the network in New York from the local outlet. Schmutz explained his objections to *Brooks Hays: Return to Little Rock* in relation to this practice:

> The local outlet had no control over the content of the NBC film segments. I personally was on the scene at the time the film was shot, I was with the members of the NBC crew as they edited the film and prepared it for transmission. On many occasions, I questioned the particular incident which was featured, and suggested other incidents which presented a more sane and intelligent approach to the problem. At no time were my suggestions accepted, and on one early morning hour, between hourly feeds to the NBC "Today" program, the newsman, Mr. Frank McGee, informed me that those incidents which I had suggested "would not sell." In other words, they were interested only in that which was sensational. As a result, I feel that the coverage originated by NBC was definitely biased.[23]

In a letter to Solomon and the Arkansas Endowment of Humanities, Schmutz informed them that if the "sensationalism" of the NBC reports was incorporated into the film, through footage "showing violence without showing the other side," AETN would not broadcast it.[24] As Renee C. Romano has noted, during the civil rights era itself, many white Southerners assumed "the mantle of aggrieved victims," rejecting claims that they bore responsibility for racial violence and "blaming protestors for instigating violence or outsiders for exposing it, rather than considering the ways in which they may have contributed to a political environment that cultivated it."[25] This same spirit animated the actions of AETN representatives like Schmutz as they considered film treatments for *Brooks Hays: Return to Little Rock*. Indeed, the program director felt that the city of Little Rock had been unfairly vilified in the popular press and demanded that Solomon's film correct this injustice with attention to the moderate forces of minimal compliance.

Lee Reaves, a Faubus appointee and the director of the Arkansas Educational Television Commission, subsequently told commission members and reporters that he and Schmutz would review the documentary and would not air it if they found it "biased" or "unfair."[26] If AETN refused to broadcast the film, it was unlikely that Solomon would be able to find another broadcast outlet in the state. In the early 1980s, most commercial networks declined documentaries that were produced by independent filmmakers, leaving public television as the sole outlet for their work. Within a decentralized system where local public television affiliates screened and recommended programs for national distribution, it was also unlikely that Solomon would be able to air the film outside of Arkansas. Relatively powerless in the centralized structure of a commercial network, where the "local outlet had no control over the content of NBC film segments," Schmutz had considerably more power to control content as a programmer of a local public television affiliate. Within a broadcasting system that celebrated localism, he argued that national perspectives on the crisis should not be privileged over local experiences.[27]

In the 1967 Public Broadcasting Act, the public television system was charged with the responsibility to develop and air programs "with strict adherence to objectivity and balance in all programs or series of programs of controversial nature." This standard goes beyond the requirements for "fairness and accuracy" imposed by the US Federal Communications Commission on all broadcasters.[28] In his review of controversial documentaries aired on public television, B. J. Bullert observed that once private deliberations between stations and producers entered the public sphere, charges of "unfairness" and "lack of balance" were frequently used to undermine a filmmaker's credibility and the quality of the proposed project. Thus, charges that a film "lacked balance" or was "biased," as those terms were defined by station programmers, carried significant weight. Gatekeepers like Schmutz and Reaves could wield these standards to determine "which views of reality will contend on the airwaves, when they will be broadcast, and in what context."[29]

In response to these public warnings from AETN, Hays defended the project, assuring the community that his stance during the desegregation crisis would be represented as a reflection of a deep and unrecognized reservoir of moderate public opinion in the city. The film would depict the moderate stance of a states' rights liberal and a statesman working to support the rule of law. Consequently, Hays promised, "the total view will be favorable and our image as a law-abiding people will be preserved." He assured reporters that the documentary would be "faithful to history." In this public appeal, Hays suggested that the film would not reproduce a one-dimensional image of the crisis. Rather, it would counteract it by emphasizing the moderate forces at work within the city. At the annual banquet of the Arkansas Endowment for the Humanities, Hays urged his audience not to "entertain fears that Little Rock and Arkansas will be presented in any except a favorable light" and assured those present that focus would also be placed on the community's progress with school desegregation in the intervening years.[30] This argument appealed to those who wished to reclaim the city's reputation for progressive race relations.

AETN's warning to the film's producers became a front-page news story and the subject of editorials and letters to the editor in both the *Arkansas Gazette* and *Arkansas Democrat*. Several regional newspapers suggested that Schmutz's concern that the film would focus on sensationalism—but not the "other side" of moderate approaches to the issue of school desegregation—made little sense. The entire purpose of showing the mob scenes outside Central High School was to illustrate what Hays and, by extension, the state of Arkansas had transcended. It would be difficult for viewers to understand why Hays's moderate position was so controversial in 1957 without capturing the "Great Faubusfear he rose above." Likewise, it would be difficult to measure the state's "progress" without showing the "depths" to which it had descended.³¹ "A film on 'Little Rock,'" the *Arkansas Gazette* asserted, "cannot rewrite or scrub up that melancholy chapter in our national history, nor make it appear that popular opinion in Arkansas was not grievously in error at the time." Sensationalism, the paper noted, "is a highly subjective term," but "one must concede that the performance of the rowdy crowd at Central High was pretty sensational material, as was the first test of whether racism was to prevail over the rule of law in this country." The crowd outside Central "was engaged in something other than peaceful demonstration on a September morn," the *Gazette* observed. Yet incorporating infamous images of "rowdy" behavior outside of Central High School served a greater purpose in Solomon's film. These scenes were not intended to cast shame on the city of Little Rock as a whole. In the film, Hays was not a lone and isolated figure but rather represented a broad swath of public opinion in the city. The congressman "was and is the very symbol of 'the other side,' as a leading advocate of settling the Little Rock crisis peacefully within the rule of law," the *Gazette* averred.³²

As a state-financed public television network, AETN's threat not to air the film provoked commentary about the purpose of public television and the power of cultural gatekeepers like Schmutz and Reaves, who effectively functioned as a "two-man censorship board."³³ Arkansas governor Bill Clinton responded to the growing controversy by assigning a member of his staff to investigate AETN's policies and its statements about the *Brooks Hays* film. The governor acknowledged that AETN had an obligation to review programs to determine if they were acceptable for broadcast, but asserted that the commission overseeing program decisions should adopt clear and transparent guidelines. From the governor's perspective, Arkansans needed to learn about their recent history. "The idea that we should not know about it or learn about it or see it is ridiculous," he said. Clinton later described Hays's career as a "shining example of the highest standard of public service" and asserted that his contribution to the state of Arkansas was "virtually unparalleled." The eight commissioners on the network's board served by gubernatorial appointment and Clinton told reporters that the controversy had given him a "keen awareness" of his responsibility to appoint members that were "not interested in undue censorship." With two of the commissioners' terms expiring, the *Arkansas Gazette* applauded Clinton's well-timed statements and hoped that the governor's remarks would damper further threats not to air the program.³⁴

FIGURE 7. The Arkansas Educational Television Network's threat not to air the film *Brooks Hays: Return to Little Rock* if it proved to be "embarrassing" to the state of Arkansas provoked widespread accusations of censorship and generated heated debate about public representations of the Little Rock school desegregation crisis. In this cartoon, George Fisher lampooned AETN's position and the claim that events in Little Rock had been "distorted" by the national press by imagining what an unapologetically positive portrayal of the crisis might look like. (*Arkansas Gazette*)

Indeed, after months of public debate, the film was shown on AETN and WFMY in North Carolina. At the film's premier on his eighty-second birthday, Hays received congratulatory letters and telegrams from Governor Clinton as well as President Jimmy Carter, Senators Dale Bumpers and David Pryor, Congressman Ed Bethune, and others.[35] Despite these accolades, reviews of the production were mixed. While some asserted that the film fulfilled its promise, producing an "account of Hay's courage, devotion and inspiration,"[36] others asserted that it fell far short of the mark. In the final cut, the film placed the spotlight almost entirely on Hays's broader political philosophy rather than on the events that propelled him to national attention as a political figure. In scenes where Hays reflected on his role in the school desegregation crisis, he not only proclaimed his support for the *Brown* decision as a "morally correct law" but also assured Central High students more than two decades later that the silent majority of Little Rock's citizens agreed with him in 1957 despite their lack of support for him at the polls.[37] If, as many observers had suggested, some contrast between Hays's position and the forces of massive resistance was necessary to illuminate the congressman's moderate stance, the absence of this context in the final production raised questions about whether David Solomon had deliberately shifted attention away from "embarrassing" scenes related to the school desegregation crisis in an effort to appease AETN programmers. Journalist Elizabeth Shores had followed the development of the project since its inception and asserted that the film was fatally flawed because it downplayed historical context, sidestepped Hays's own "ambivalence" about Southern race relations, and failed to address the politician's internal conflict about whether and how to support a Supreme Court decision that violated traditional social practices and his own political philosophy as a states' rights liberal. In this respect, the picture of moral crisis Hays confronted in 1957 was unclear and incomplete.[38] In his film, Solomon adroitly sidestepped a direct recounting of the congressman's political position in relation to school desegregation in 1957. Instead, *Brooks Hays: Return to Little Rock* idealized Hays's call for "law and order" and celebrated the ultimate triumph of his ideals in the capital city of his native state. "I love my city," Hays asserted, "and I was proud of the rapidity with which it healed wounds and moved into compliance with the law."[39]

Although residual resentment of national news coverage in 1957 provoked threats of censorship and stimulated controversy across the state,

Brooks Hays: Return to Little Rock was not suppressed. Politicians, newspapers, and well-placed friends of the congressman did not hesitate to come to the defense of a man whose reputation as a "hero-martyr of moderation" was "impregnable." Solomon was able to broadcast his film on AETN and burnish Hays's reputation as a man of moral courage while adroitly sidestepping a direct recounting of Hays's political position in relation to school desegregation in 1957. Although the film's defenders and critics acknowledged that a film focused on Hays's role in the school desegregation crisis had the potential to unearth "embarrassing" incidents, it was state of Arkansas and not Hays himself that they imagined might be negatively impacted. In order to offset these concerns, Hays promised that efforts to highlight his position would only serve to illuminate the influence of unacknowledged moderate forces in the city. Any return to Little Rock, he suggested, could only underscore the extent of Little Rock's progress in the field of race relations. Discussing the crisis in this context had the potential to turn a tragedy into a source of inspiration. This carefully contained narrative was designed to recast Little Rock's history, to recall attention to its progressive reputation and tradition of racial moderation, and to reshape public perception of moderate policies in favor of minimal compliance.

Despite the appeal of this approach, the elevation of the stories of white moderates during the school desegregation crisis continued to provoke controversy in the city. Just a year after *Brooks Hays: Return to Little Rock* aired on AETN, public controversy surrounding Vice Principal Elizabeth Huckaby's memoir and its adaptation as a televised docudrama erupted in relation to the school administrator's depiction of the broader community and white students inside Central High School. In Huckaby's memoir *Crisis at Central High* (1980), the administrator described a school under siege. While she and her colleagues struggled to make the best of a difficult situation, she suggested that others had abdicated their responsibilities. Successful school desegregation was nearly impossible in the face of ongoing obstruction and harassment from the state government, the indifference of businessmen and civic leaders, the active opposition of segregationists, and "half-hearted" support from the Eisenhower administration in the form of inadequate numbers of troops. According to Huckaby, Central High faced a "crisis" during the 1957–58 school year because the school administration carried the "complete burden" of trying to make school desegregation work with little or no help and plenty of interference from outsiders.[40]

Throughout her book, the vice principal portrayed herself as a moderate pragmatist pummeled by hostile segregationist forces and abandoned by the broader community.

Huckaby's account rested on her description of Central High School as an isolated island in a sea of overt hostility and general apathy. This characterization provoked significant debate in Little Rock about the culpability of vocal segregationists and silent bystanders in 1957–59. As Central High School's vice principal of girls, Elizabeth Huckaby was responsible for investigating conflicts, counseling students, and enforcing discipline among the female student body. She believed her account of the crisis year from within the halls of Central High School offered a unique contribution to the historical record. *Crisis at Central High* provided readers with an insider's view and focused on the day-to-day experience of students, teachers, and administrators inside the building, not the political conflict that occupied other writers.[41] However, after Huckaby's book was published and adapted for television, she faced charges that her memoir offered the public a distorted version of events that vilified the community-at-large and white students in the school in order to glorify the administration's efforts to maintain calm and order. Several critics, particularly representatives of Central's student body, argued that Huckaby's narrative and the television adaptation of it lionized the administration at their expense and unfairly characterized their actions. In defining her own pragmatic position against the stance adopted by the majority of Little Rock's citizens, and using the dark days of segregation to underscore the city's progress in more recent years, these reviewers asserted that Huckaby obscured the generally progressive and "moderate" tone of the city's race relations twenty-five years earlier. Public criticism of Huckaby's text revolved around the claim that most residents of Little Rock were racial moderates who did not deserve to be castigated for their lack of action during the school desegregation crisis or their failure to stand up to the strident rhetoric of ardent segregationists.

Throughout the 1957–58 school year, Huckaby maintained a position of silent neutrality in relation to the merits of school desegregation. Although she later asserted that she was "eager" to help implement the *Brown* decision, her first loyalty lay with Central High School. As she explained, "As public school teachers and administrators we felt that education was our major responsibility and integration a secondary problem in the social revolution of our times."[42] During the crisis, Huckaby counseled students to maintain high standards of public behavior and decorum that would reflect well on them and their school. She urged students to focus on their studies and not to concern themselves with the public controversy surrounding school desegregation. Indeed, the vice principal dedicated her memoir to the "hundreds of boys and girls" who heeded her advice and "were too busy just getting their lessons and helping at home and working . . . to pay much attention to their elders' stir and confusion over the color of their classmates' skin."[43]

However, some students refused to acquiesce to the integration of Central High School. *Crisis at Central High* presented a detailed account of the harassment of the Little Rock Nine, the punishment and dismissal of segregationist perpetrators, as well as the anxiety of the faculty and staff as they searched the building after bomb threats and were harassed by community members and the state police. In Huckaby's account, the organized campaign of harassment against the Little Rock Nine escalated rather than abated over the course of the year as the 101st Airborne and the federalized National Guard were slowly pulled out of Central High School. Nevertheless, the vice principal was careful to note that the litany of disciplinary problems and incidents described in her text were planned and executed by a small handful of segregationist troublemakers who were either unduly influenced by adults or used the crisis as a pretext to behave badly.[44]

In her memoir, Huckaby vigorously defended administrative decisions and disciplinary policies developed to deal with these "hard cases" in light of the hostile climate created by segregationist resistance. The vice principal insisted that the administration's actions were driven by the pragmatic and practical needs of running an operational school while protecting the nine African American students from physical injury. For example, early in the school year, Central established a policy of only punishing incidents of harassment witnessed by an adult. In practice, this meant that unless a teacher or a guard could provide eyewitness testimony, nothing was done even when evidence that an incident had taken place was presented, a black student could identify their assailant, or administrators believed that a repeat offender was responsible. Huckaby defended this policy on two grounds. In the absence of a policy of "teacher verification," she maintained, segregationist students could have manufactured reports that would have resulted in the dismissal and expulsion of the black pupils. Moreover, she argued that school administrators had to be prepared to defend the punishment of a white student without any doubt about what had transpired.

Segregationist students and their parents often challenged disciplinary actions, and segregationist organizations in the city decried them. The vice principal acknowledged that the school's policy may not have been effective, fair, or just, and conceded that it left the Little Rock Nine "vulnerable to indignities," but she justified the decision on the grounds that it permitted the school to continue functioning on a daily basis.[45] Indeed, for Huckaby, the daily operation of Central High School throughout the 1957–58 school year was the primary marker of the administration's success and their ability to transcend segregationist hostility.

Encouraged to keep a record of her experience by an editor and old friend at the *Journal of Arkansas Education* as the school desegregation crisis unfolded, Huckaby drafted her account during the summer of 1958 and completed it during Little Rock's "lost year" when the city's high schools were closed in defiance of federal court orders to integrate. She later recalled that "freedom from paper grading and discipline of students" gave her time to write her memoir, and she submitted it to a literary agent in May 1959.[46] However, Huckaby quickly reconsidered her decision to seek a publisher in the immediate aftermath of the crisis. While the schools were closed, the vice principal was one of forty-four teachers fired by segregationist members of the Little Rock school board on the grounds that they were "integrationists" or "collaborators" who sought to dismantle Little Rock's system of segregated schools. Huckaby and most of the other teachers were reinstated. Nevertheless, this experience may have made her reluctant to publish an account that compared the situation in Little Rock to Nazi Germany and contained her relatively unvarnished opinions of students, their parents, fellow administrators, the US Army, the National Guard, the NAACP, the White Citizens' Council, and the community of Little Rock. After her brief flirtation with a literary agent, Huckaby put her manuscript away for the duration of her career at Central High School. "Feelings were too high in Little Rock," she wrote, "the town too disrupted for me to consider trying to publish my account. I wanted to keep my job at Central, as I did till I retired in 1969."[47]

In retirement, Huckaby found time to rework her manuscript and reflect on the significance of her experience, but her memoir's narrow focus and its distance from current events made it difficult to find a publisher. Her retrospective account was considered too dated to be "current" and too recent to be considered "history." The vice principal received a slew of rejections, but an editor at Random House expressed interest in the project if it could be brought "up to date." She urged Huckaby to consider co-writing a book with an administrator from South Boston in an effort to draw parallels between the two events. Huckaby rejected this proposition, echoing the arguments of moderates across the nation and asserting that the "situations were too dissimilar." Huckaby insisted that Little Rock and Boston were shaped by different "cultural and ethnic backgrounds," the legal issues involved had changed, and government involvement in school desegregation had evolved. The editor asked Huckaby if she would consider doing a study on how the crisis had influenced black and white students who attended Central in 1957–58 over the course of their lives. Again, Huckaby demurred, asserting that she had "no instinct nor skills for investigative reporting" and "no psychological or sociological skills" that would enable her to interpret the results of such a study. Her account was narrowly focused on her perspective of historical events in Little Rock—it would stand or fall alone.[48]

There was, however, interest in publicizing the administrator's account in another medium—television. The editor at Random House who had tried to revamp Huckaby's project mentioned the vice principal's story to the head of the film division at NBC. Although NBC ultimately declined the project, the option on her manuscript was picked up by Time-Life Films for adaptation as a television docudrama shortly thereafter. When the film was first proposed, Huckaby was unenthusiastic. She later recalled, "A movie was not what I really wanted. I wanted a book—something *real*." However, she agreed to sell the rights to her manuscript with the understanding that a book might be more salable if her story was broadcast on television. The strategy worked. After the script was written in the fall of 1979 and the film was in production, Huckaby finally found a publisher for her memoir—Louisiana State University Press. The press moved quickly, and Huckaby's "true narrative" hit the bookstands in October 1980, nearly five months before the film aired on CBS in February the following year.[49]

When Time-Life Films acquired the rights to Huckaby's book, they hired writers Richard Levinson and William Link to write the teleplay and cast actress Joanne Woodward to depict Huckaby. Together, Levinson and Link had created the popular television series *Columbo* and had written a number of "long form" television movies that explored controversial social issues. The writers believed that it was possible to maintain ratings and address controversial topics if it was done "without polemicizing, without self-congratulatory grandstanding, and without putting the audience to sleep." When adapting material for a screenplay, Link and Levinson strove to preserve the essence of what had appealed to them in the original text.[50] They were attracted to the idea of writing the script from the perspective of a vice principal inside Central High School. In press interviews, Levinson said, "What fascinated us was dealing with a major historical event without dealing with Eisenhower and Faubus.... You hire actors to play Eisenhower and Faubus and you wind up with a waxworks tableau." He recalled, "What appealed to us was the workings of a school under an extraordinary crisis."[51]

In the 1980s, "relatability" was a guiding principle in movies created for television. Networks strove to create storylines that their primary target audience, women ages eighteen to forty-nine, could relate to. Many television films from this era featured white, middle-class, female, suburban protagonists. Making a movie about the crisis at Central High from the perspective of Elizabeth Huckaby was in keeping with this broader trend.[52] Indeed, many civil rights films produced in the 1980s and 1990s featured the actions of moderate whites rather than the grassroots activism of African American communities. Cultural studies scholars Allison Graham, Edward P. Morgan, and Renee C. Romano have suggested that these cinematic representations of the civil rights movement were underwritten by the culture industries precisely because they appealed to white audiences—who wished to believe that equality had been achieved with generous contributions from the moderate or racially progressive white protagonists featured in the films. These narratives resonated with the audiences targeted by television and film producers not only because they underwrote a political agenda that helped to preserve their prerogatives, but also because they reinforced the popular view of the nation as a beacon of democracy, freedom, and equality.[53]

As *Crisis at Central High* moved into production, Huckaby fretted over changes made to her manuscript and expressed concern that the filmmakers' need to center the conflict around a "star" would make her actions seem "noble" and "dramatic" in relation to other figures in the story. As a former English teacher, she accepted the necessity of adapting her words to the screen and understood the need to restructure and consolidate characters, to create incidents and scenes that were representative of broader historical processes, and to fabricate dialogue that was not included in her written text.[54] Nevertheless, she expressed anxiety about her own portrayal in the docudrama. The vice principal contended that the television writers "exaggerated" her influence over administrative decisions in the school and cast other historical actors to the sidelines. She expressed relief that her written memoir had been accepted for publication and would be available for "serious students of history to read . . . before seeing the docudrama, which because of the limits of dramatization cannot be accurate history."[55] Despite Huckaby's concerns, many of the primary themes of her text were maintained in the film. Like the author, Levinson and Link portrayed a school administration struggling to keep the school open in a hostile environment with little community support.

Nevertheless, in several scenes, Huckaby's actions were reframed to make her actions seem nobler and to reposition her as a clear advocate for the Little Rock Nine. In her memoir, Huckaby insists that the pragmatic and practical needs of the school required administrators to make compromises and to take positions they felt were not "morally right" but were necessary if they were to survive the year. However, in the film, the writers presented Huckaby as an idealistic figure by developing dialogue between the vice principal and Principal Jess Matthews, in which she vigorously protested the expulsion of Little Rock Nine student Minnijean Brown as pure "expediency."[56] This fictionalized conversation did not reflect the vice principal's views as expressed in her text, however. In her memoir, she argued that it was impossible to govern the school with Brown present. She acknowledged that the segregationist students targeted Brown more than others, but suggested that Minnijean had "selected" herself for harassment through her impulsive behavior. In the memoir, Huckaby implied that Brown lacked the integrity, maturity, diplomacy, and restraint that enabled the other eight students to survive the year. In a narrative that concealed the names of segregationist perpetrators with pseudonyms, the degree to which Huckaby dissected Brown's academic achievements, personality traits, and student record in her effort to defend the administration's decision is remarkable, but this perspective was completely inverted in the film.[57]

While Huckaby may have had some concerns about her elevation as a "hero-martyr of moderation," others in Little Rock certainly expressed their own reservations. The television writers consolidated many characters and adopted Huckaby's practice of using pseudonyms to conceal the names of segregationist students in early drafts of the script, but they did not modify the names of prominent figures like Daisy Bates, the Little Rock Nine, or the three principals at Central High. However, Time-Life Films was unable to persuade some of these figures to sign waivers permitting the use of their names in the docudrama, including Bates and Eckford. "I received a letter that they wanted a complete release from me so that they could do anything they wanted with Daisy Bates," the civil rights leader explained to reporters. "They wouldn't let me see the manuscript. How did I know what they were saying about me?" Little Rock's black newspaper, the *Southern Mediator Press*, commented on the small proportion of African Americans included in the cast and noted that the film privileged the experience of white moderate figures like Huckaby rather than illuminating the role of the black community. As George Lipsitz noted in his book *Time Passages: Collective Memory and Popular Culture*, individuals frequently utilize residual counter-memories based on lived experience to challenge and interrogate narratives advanced in dominant popular culture. From the perspective of the *Southern Mediator Press*, the principal players in the school desegregation crisis were not Vice Principal Huckaby, Principal Matthews, or Superintendent Blossom. Rather, they were the members of the Little Rock Nine, their brave parents, and their mentors from the NAACP, Daisy Bates and Thurgood Marshall. While the stories of these figures may not have been considered "relatable" as television producers defined the term, Little Rock's black newspaper, the *Southern Mediator*, boldly proclaimed, "The Little Rock Story is Being Told Without the Help of Major Participants" in a front-page headline.[58]

Meanwhile, white residents of Little Rock failed to demonstrate the enthusiasm for the project that film producers expected. *Crisis at Central High* was shot on location; thousands of extras were required to shoot scenes on the exterior of the school and to represent Central's nearly 2,000 white students in the hallways. Initially, the production team thought they would have no trouble attracting participants without pay. However, on the first day of filming, only 500 people appeared on set for an outdoor graduation scene requiring 5,000. Film producers also struggled with the disproportionate presence of African American volunteers on set, particularly since the forces of massive resistance and minimal compliance had ensured that the presence of black residents on the grounds of Central High School was sharply limited in 1957–58.[59]

In the midst of these signals that local support for the project was weak, Time-Life Films assured residents that the film would depict the city of Little Rock favorably. As the date of broadcast approached, television writers Link and Levinson actively promoted the project, picking up on Huckaby's emphasis on Little Rock's progress and describing the televised version of *Crisis at Central High* as "an American success story." The written version of *Crisis at Central High* leapt abruptly from the spring of 1958 to 1980 in a celebration of the city's racial "progress." Like many others in Little Rock, Huckaby suggested that the city had overcome its problems with school desegregation. The vice principal asserted that Central High's diverse student body in 1980 was a "living memorial," not to the persistence of Little Rock's civil rights community, but to the predominantly white students, teachers, and administrators "whose fortitude helped it endure" through one of its greatest challenges.[60] Huckaby maintained that Central ran "much more smoothly" than "some of the newer desegregated schools" because of its "long experience" with integration. Although the vice principal acknowledged that the integration of Central High School was "maintained by a fleet of eighty buses that crisscross the town," she did not address the long history of civil rights litigation that imposed systematic desegregation on the city or persistent resistance to it, nor did she acknowledge the strategies of tokenism and gradualism that undermined meaningful integration at the high school throughout the 1960s.[61] In this regard, Huckaby drew heavily on the narrative of passive progress that had been constructed by Little Rock civic leaders in the previous decade. Indeed, the elevation of white moderates to the center stage of Little Rock's civil rights story required this temporal elision.

Producer Fryeda Rothstein assured the local press that the film would not rebrand Little Rock as a "city filled with hate." Using rhetoric that was strikingly similar to efforts to defend the *Brooks Hays* film a year earlier, Rothstein contended that the production should be viewed as an opportunity to "change Arkansas' image." She suggested, "It's a very pro-American story that says cooler heads did prevail . . . We're not doing this to excoriate, to sensationalize." She hoped the film would demonstrate "how far we've come." In press interviews, Levinson was also careful to distance the film from contemporary arguments about education and race. He was quick to point out that his film was about integration, "not about bussing." He stated, "There is . . . a legitimate debate about bussing. But about integration there simply should be no debate. It's the law of the land."[62] In this defense of the film, Levinson borrowed heavily from antibusing rhetoric, failing to acknowledge that busing was a court-ordered remedy designed to dismantle segregation even as he paid lip-service to promoting racial integration.

Despite the shortcomings of this narrative, Little Rock's "success" story was well received by the national media. The television press applauded the performances, and Joanne Woodward's portrayal of Huckaby earned her an Emmy nomination. The national media embraced the film and asserted that it offered an "important lesson" about a "traumatic period" in US history—namely, that despite the difficulties and the controversies involving race and the schools, the "good guys"—black and white—had been victorious.[63] In these reviews, Little Rock's determination to overcome segregationist hostility could be traced back to figures like Huckaby during the 1957–59 crisis itself. Following the film's broadcast, the faculty and staff at Central High commended Huckaby for her "role in preserving the image of Central High." The author also received kind letters of support from family, friends, former teachers, and some students. Huckaby was delighted with this response.[64]

The book and film were not universally praised in Little Rock, however. Despite the fact that Huckaby had dedicated her book to Central High students who had avoided controversy throughout the school year, she was criticized by alumni for placing too much emphasis on the activities of segregationist students. Ralph Brodie, president of the student body in 1958, released a public statement asserting that Huckaby's account was "distorted." Brodie argued that because of Huckaby's narrow focus,

> her manuscript does not develop a historical background with which to judge the events or other people of that year; nor does it present with much force the attitudes or actions of the responsible white students at Central High, over 90 percent of the student body who, along with the faculty, obeyed the law and held the school together that year. Rather the docudrama emphasizes the troublemakers who were a very small minority of the nearly 2,000 students at Central. Even though the news media made no distinction, the problems experienced inside Central that year were relatively minor compared to the problems outside Central and those invented by the media itself. In fact, those problems now seem insignificant compared to the problems other schools have experienced when faced with integration. There is a reason for that—there were many responsible people inside Central who, regardless of their personal feelings about integration, believed in both the rule of law and their obligations as citizens to obey and uphold the law. This part of Central's story is not as dramatic as the political confrontation nor as significant as the social change made that year, yet in the face of history I believe that it is equally important.[65]

Brodie emphasized that the vast majority of students had accepted *Brown v. Board* as the law of the land, along with the decision of the courts in the local case *Aaron v. Cooper* that Little Rock Central High would have to be desegregated.[66] He bridled at the suggestion that the majority of students were indifferent about the integration process—"to say we were 'indifferent' implies that we didn't do something we should have done, or that we did something we shouldn't have done. And I don't think that's true." He also rejected the contention that even students who did nothing were "culpable" because they had not stopped the harassment. In a small survey of members of the Class of 1958, the *Arkansas Gazette* reported that Brodie's classmates supported his remarks.[67]

In her correspondence, Huckaby responded to several students who had expressed their dissatisfaction with the docudrama directly. As a former English teacher, she pointed out that the televised version of her account was necessarily "built around conflict" and suggested that the film exaggerated the activities of the segregationist students because of the requirements of "good drama." She urged her critics to read her written account, asserting that it provided a more balanced picture.[68] Brodie, however, offered a critique of the vice principal's book and not simply the televised docudrama. Indeed, the film was actually more sympathetic than the book in its portrayal of Central's "silent majority" of white students. While the majority of white students "going about their business" were largely absent from the pages of Huckaby's narrative, they had to be represented in the film by the extras filling hallways, classrooms, stadiums, and stairs. Even the film's portrayal of the segregationist students was relatively mild since the filmmakers selected representative incidents of racial harassment to stand in for the litany of daily occurrences that made up a good portion of Huckaby's book.[69]

Nevertheless, several scenes in the film provoked the resentment of Central's alumni. Early in the film, the director attempted to restage Elizabeth Eckford's iconic walk through the mob gathered outside the high school after members of the Arkansas National Guard refused her admittance. However, most of the volunteers who agreed to appear as extras in the scene were young adolescents without other commitments.[70] In 1957, nearly all observers reported large numbers of adults—men and women—gathered outside the school as the Little Rock Nine attempted to attend classes. In the final cut of the docudrama, nearly all the participants in the mob scene appear to be students. After the film's broadcast, some alumni would

FIGURE 8. The nationally televised docudrama *Crisis at Central High* strove to evoke the iconic images of the 1957 school desegregation crisis. Some critics worried that audiences would not be able to discern fact from fiction, particularly because the film was broadcast through the same medium as the original television news coverage of the events themselves. In this scene, film producers sought to recreate the escort of the Little Rock Nine into Central High School. (University of Arkansas Libraries, Little Rock)

point to this scene and others like it to bolster their claim that the televised docudrama exaggerated vocal segregationist sentiment within the school.[71] Although *Crisis at Central High* was not shot in a journalistic style and did not gesture toward the conventions of a documentary or attempt to capture the aura of historical veracity through the use of black-and-white film, the fact that it was broadcast on the same medium that had spread the iconic images of the crisis in 1957 threatened to collapse the boundaries between fact and fiction.[72] Moreover, the third-person perspective of the camera lent Huckaby's subjective description of events a concrete sense of reality. In a context in which even the legitimacy of archived footage from NBC news broadcasts was questioned as a representation of "truth," it was hardly surprising that a format which reenacted the iconic images of 1957 generated concern and criticism.

Huckaby's explanations and her efforts to encourage former students to read her book did not appease many of Central High's white alumni. From their perspective, the school administrator and the television writers had exaggerated Central High's problems with desegregation and deemphasized the successes of the year. In service of a carefully crafted narrative of local and national progress, the white students of Central High felt they had been unfairly portrayed in order to underscore the bravery of school administrators and the Little Rock Nine and to demonstrate how far the city and nation had come from the controversy surrounding the crisis. In protest, alumni insisted that they too had adopted a moderate position that privileged their education over taking a stand on the question of civil rights. Like Hays and Huckaby, they had abided by the law and tried to forge a path between the extremist forces that beset their school. Former *Arkansas Gazette* editor Harry Ashmore embraced these students as representative figures, who in their desire to "simply get on with their education . . . reflected the submerged views of the community at large." Their position, like that of Elizabeth Huckaby, revealed that the "segregationist crusade was an aberration that ran counter to the basic good sense, and good feeling, of the majority of Arkansans of both races."[73]

In the early 1980s, the accounts of Southern white moderates Hays and Huckaby were widely read and watched, and broadly discussed. Book publishers and broadcasters promoted the narratives of figures they believed readers and viewers could relate to and respect. The most publicized criticism of these works was articulated by members of Little Rock's white community, who suggested that the "moral" position of these "hero-martyr[s] of moderation" was more widely shared than the authors allowed. In the controversy surrounding this debate, few questioned the elevation of white moderates to the center stage of Little Rock's civil rights story or the inattention paid to the Little Rock Nine, their families, their mentors, or the broad range of opinion in the city's black community. This preoccupation with the perspective of Little Rock's white citizens shaped academic scholarship related to the school desegregation crisis as well. It was not until years later that the historian John A. Kirk would publish his definitive study of black activism in Little Rock, *Redefining the Color Line* (2002). As Kirk noted, for more than thirty years, "the only black perspective on the school crisis was the memoir of Daisy Bates." In contrast, firsthand accounts as well as secondary works "focused on Governor Faubus, massive resistance and the White Citizens' Councils, local white clergymen, local white women, the local white business elite, white judges, and the interaction of (largely white-dominated) national and local political and legal issues."[74]

This elevation of white moderates and related efforts to reclaim Little Rock's progressive reputation occurred at a critical juncture in the city's history. As the city's newspapers and political figures celebrated the historical contributions of Little Rock's silent majority, the city was experiencing demographic changes and accelerated "white flight" that would soon result in racial imbalance and the resegregation of its schools. In the decades that followed, calls for the local control of schools, an end to cross-town busing and court oversight, the proliferation of private schools, and the creation of specialized magnet programs would become the new grounds for white resistance to school integration. In this context, Little Rock's transcendence and triumph over the past would be called into question with more and more frequency. In the midst of public debate about the future of the school system, the Little Rock school district stood at a critical crossroads. Although some school officials and advisors called for a continued commitment to systematic school desegregation, others called for a return to the pragmatic moderation of minimal compliance. Increasingly, busing was framed as a "failed" policy and district officials and public opinion makers fell back on "moderate" approaches to school desegregation that would be accepted by white school patrons. In doing so, these actors relied on the same logic and arguments that animated the first-hand accounts of Huckaby and Hays.

Although the introduction of district-wide busing in 1971 did not produce a precipitous drop in the number of white students enrolled in Little Rock's public schools, each year the proportion of black students in the district climbed by two or three percent. White families who had previously avoided desegregation by relocating to the city's predominantly white West End moved even further west to the suburbs or enrolled their children in private schools. Enrollments in the Pulaski County Special School District (PCSSD), which serviced the suburbs just outside the city, increased by 80 percent over the course of several years. PCSSD included all students not enrolled in the Little Rock or North Little Rock school districts in the county, as well as students living in predominantly white sections of Little Rock that had not been deannexed as the city expanded. In Arkansas, school district annexation and consolidation required joint agreement between the two districts involved. Following implementation of the Little Rock's district-wide desegregation decree in the 1970s, PCSSD refused to deannex additional territory to the city. By the early 1980s, 40 percent of the city of Little Rock lay outside of Little Rock school district's boundaries; 87 percent of the nearly 5,000 students that lived in Little Rock but attended schools in Pulaski County were white. As a result of these trends, by the 1980s, school officials in Little Rock were increasingly concerned that the Little Rock school district was reaching a crucial tipping point: many feared that when the percentage of white pupils in the system dipped below 30 percent, white flight would accelerate so quickly that the district would become virtually all black. It had become increasingly apparent that white parents of young children and new arrivals were reluctant to enroll their children in Little Rock's public schools. While secondary schools like Central High remained relatively well balanced throughout the 1970s, the percentage of black students in grades 1–3 had climbed to 72 percent by 1981.[75]

During this period, Little Rock Superintendent of Schools Paul Masem expressed growing concern about the resegregation of the city's schools. Masem held his predecessors, like Virgil Blossom, partially responsible for conditions in the school district a generation later. For nearly two decades, Masem asserted, school administrators and school board members had "established a climate that was negative toward desegregation." The school district had fought nearly every desegregation initiative in the courts, members of the school board had repeatedly stated their commitment to segregated schools, administrators had implemented desegregation remedies with the intent of limiting rather than extending their effects, and the system had failed to close achievement gaps between black and white students. In his doctoral dissertation, Masem noted, "The behavior of the Board and the administration during this period did nothing to eradicate the perceptions of whites concerning blacks' intellectual and social inferiority. On the contrary, the Board's behavior tended to reinforce those views." The school board had done nothing to mitigate white concerns about the quality of education in the desegregating school district, nor had officials taken any action as white families fled for suburban institutions and private academies.[76]

In contrast to his predecessors, Superintendent Masem urged the school board to develop a "planned response" to the problem of white flight. He proposed a slate of programs designed to stave off further resegregation, improve the public image of the city's school system, and develop better communication with school patrons, newcomers, and the general public. The school board created a Patrons Organization Committee to study the various white flight prevention proposals offered by the administration, while also asking the longstanding Biracial Advisory Committee to consider the impact the various alternatives would have on the court-ordered desegregation plan. Significant divisions between these two committees, and white and black patrons of the school district, emerged during this process. The Patrons Committee tended to favor approaches that accepted the inevitability of some racially identifiable schools. In their view, it might be possible to stabilize white flight if Little Rock was able to reduce the number of students bused and return some pupils to neighborhood schools. The Patrons Committee acknowledged that this approach would create some all-black schools in eastern parts of Little Rock, but suggested that it would also result in more evenly balanced racial ratios in other city schools that would be more appealing to white parents. Understandably, the Biracial Advisory Committee, charged with the task of assessing the impact these plans might have on desegregation in the district, looked on such proposals unfavorably. The Biracial Advisory Committee and most, but not all, African American community leaders rejected proposed intradistrict reorganization plans and favored interdistrict solutions that sought to bring more white students into the system through an effort to consolidate city and suburban school districts.[77]

At this critical crossroads, the school district decided to explore the viability of both of these approaches simultaneously. Superintendent Masem urged the school board to consider the possibility of a merger with the surrounding PCSSD either through voluntary cooperation or forcible intervention through the courts. Given the high legal threshold the school district faced in achieving these objectives, however, Masem encouraged board members to consider other options as well. "The political mood, and the enormity of the task to be undertaken, not to mention the social and financial cost, dictate caution," he warned. In order to meet the heavy burden of proof required in interdistrict cases, the school board "would be unwise to leap ahead and seek an interdistrict remedy without doing all its legal and political homework." Consequently, Masem simultaneously encouraged the school board to consider alternative student assignment procedures that might offer "more hope" of keeping white students in the system.[78] The school district's attorney Hershel Friday also warned the school board that a lawsuit designed to restructure the district's boundary lines would be "long and costly" and extremely contentious. Obtaining proof of an interdistrict constitutional violation with ongoing effects would require time and money. In Friday's opinion, "the chances for success within a meaningful time frame" were not strong.[79]

By the 1970s, political resistance to systemic school desegregation had reshaped jurisprudence in the federal courts, eroding support for sweeping intervention and rigorous court oversight. Increasingly, appointed judges placed limits on the scope of court-ordered remedies. In *Milliken v. Bradley* (1974), the Supreme Court established a high legal threshold for city-suburban consolidation suits and held that school district boundaries were more than "arbitrary lines on a map drawn 'for political convenience.'" Given the "deeply rooted" tradition of local control of schools, the Court decreed that district lines should not be breached unless plaintiffs demonstrated that the discriminatory actions in one district had caused segregation in an adjacent district or that boundary lines had been drawn or redrawn to segregate students. Four of the five justices who signed on to the majority opinion in the *Milliken* decision had been recently appointed by the Nixon administration during the controversy surrounding school busing. In a stinging dissent, Justice Thurgood Marshall suggested that the Court's opinion was shaped by "public opposition" to systemic desegregation rather than legal precedent and "neutral principles of law." Marshall argued that the court had not "limited" the scope of the remedy, but had provided children in urban school districts with "no remedy at all," guaranteeing that they would continue to receive a "separate and inherently unequal" education.⁸⁰ Nevertheless, in the wake of *Milliken,* the heavy burden of proof now required of plaintiffs in interdistrict cases made them almost prohibitively expensive to litigate.⁸¹

In this context, the Little Rock school board decided to approach PCSSD about the possibility of a voluntary merger. Their overture was not well received. The Pulaski County school board passed a resolution prohibiting school personnel from engaging in "cooperative efforts" with officials from the Little Rock school district.⁸² With this avenue closed, the Little Rock school board began to experiment with internal "reorganization" plans that accepted the inevitability of some schools with nearly all-black student bodies and promised to return more white students to neighborhood schools. Frustrated with the board's vacillation, attorney John W. Walker announced his intention to file an interdistrict lawsuit on the behalf of plaintiffs representing the city's African American students. While he acknowledged that the Little Rock school board was also considering similar legal action, Walker pledged to file an independent suit. "We don't know just how far they want to go," he explained. Moreover, he noted, a "partial basis" for his suit would be the "complicity" of both the Little Rock and Pulaski County school boards in the resegregation of the city's schools.⁸³

With this suit pending in the courts, the Little Rock School District (LRSD) decided to move ahead and formally file a suit against the PCSSD, the North Little Rock School District (NLRSD), the State of Arkansas, and the State Board of Education, charging that the defendants were responsible for the maintenance of a dual, racially segregated public school system in the county and calling for the reorganization or consolidation of the school districts with the assistance of the state.⁸⁴ LRSD's status as a plaintiff in this case would have important implications in future iterations of school desegregation litigation in the district. School officials pursued an interdistrict remedy by arguing in court that Greater Little Rock's racial politics and housing patterns continued to be shaped by Jim Crow–era practices and statutes, but they distanced themselves from this legacy.

Despite the high legal thresholds established in interdistrict consolidation suits, in 1985 Federal District Judge Henry Woods determined that PCSSD, NLRSD, and the state of Arkansas had "contributed to the continuing segregation of the Little Rock schools and that an interdistrict remedy was appropriate."⁸⁵ As Woods later recalled, "LRSD demonstrated beyond all peradventure that the Housing Authorities, real estate operators, school board members in the defendant districts, and the State of Arkansas had all collaborated to produce a decided trend toward an all-black Little Rock School District."[86] Woods found that school district lines had been drawn and redrawn within greater Pulaski County on the basis of race and determined that the suburban and rural areas surrounding Little Rock had been defined as a safe haven for whites seeking to avoid school desegregation. Indeed, for nearly a decade following the 1957–59 school desegregation crisis, the state paid to transport students across district lines to facilitate the transfer of students from desegregating schools in Little Rock to segregated institutions in surrounding areas. Judge Woods determined that the only long-term solution to these interdistrict violations was consolidation of the three school districts, insisting that the problems facing the Little Rock school district were so dire they could not "be avoided by equivocation or half measures." What was at stake in the case, he believed, was "the collapse of support for public education."[87] The defendants in the case immediately filed an appeal.

The controversy surrounding school consolidation in Little Rock had an immediate impact on local politics. Tommy Robinson, a former sheriff from Pulaski County, was elected to the House of Representatives on promises that he would introduce legislation to Congress designed to prevent federal courts from mandating consolidation. Former governor Frank White also used the issue to position himself in a bid for reelection against incumbent Bill Clinton in 1986. White warned that consolidation would trigger a "mass exodus" of students from the public schools, and he took a position similar to that of his "moderate" predecessors in 1957 by asking for compliance with the federal court order but calling on parents "to speak up for their children" and make their opposition known to lawmakers and political leaders.[88]

Indeed, White joined a delegation of representatives from the defendant school districts who asked Justice Department officials to file an *amicus curiae* brief in support of their legal position in the case. In the 1980s, the politicization of resistance to school desegregation continued to impact litigation in federal courts of law. The Reagan administration opposed many mandatory desegregation measures, including busing, and favored "parental choice" mechanisms such as voluntary student transfers, magnet schools, selective school closings, and "modest" adjustments to attendance zones. Assistant Attorney General for Civil Rights William Bradford Reynolds maintained that the federal government's responsibility for attacking segregation was limited to removing "remaining state-enforced barriers to open student enrollment." However, even as the administration touted the promise of magnets, it slashed federal funding for them by 94 percent in the president's first term. During the Reagan administration, the Justice Department did not file additional desegregation lawsuits. Rather, the civil rights division filed briefs in support of some of the same school districts the government had formerly sued for intentional segregation, approving their appeals to return to racially identifiable neighborhood schools.[89] Unsurprisingly, the Justice Department agreed to intervene in *Little Rock v. Pulaski County*. However, given the strength of the evidence, it did not challenge the court's findings of fact in relation to the interdistrict violations at issue in the case. Instead, government officials argued that consolidation would be "disastrous" for the area's schools and that the proposed remedy exceeded the scope of the constitutional violation.[90] Ultimately, the Eighth Circuit Court of Appeals affirmed this aspect of the Justice Department's position.

Based on a narrow reading of *Milliken*, the Eighth Circuit Court of Appeals sustained the district court's findings but determined that other "less intrusive" remedial measures were "better designed to restore the victims of segregation in the Pulaski County Schools to the position they would have occupied absent discriminatory conduct."[91] The interdistrict remedy approved by the appeals court was limited to boundary adjustments designed to make the Little Rock school district coterminous with city boundaries, the development of voluntary majority-to-minority interdistrict transfer programs, and the creation of special interdistrict magnet schools open to all students in the region. All three school districts were also directed to provide compensatory and remedial educational programs to racially isolated black students.[92] Although this limited interdistrict remedy had the potential to bring over 4,000 white students into the Little Rock school district, many school officials were pessimistic about whether these children would enroll and stay in the city's public institutions and anticipated continued white flight to the surrounding the suburbs.[93]

Despite the Eighth Circuit's claims that these provisions were "better designed" than Woods's consolidation decree, subsequent developments demonstrated that this limited remedy ultimately prevented the school districts involved from eliminating segregation and perpetuated the existence of racially isolated schools in greater Little Rock. In the wake of the court's decision, school officials argued with increasing confidence that "moderate" rather than systemic approaches to desegregation offered the system the only viable course forward. In their embrace of voluntary integration strategies, many civic leaders and white residents of Greater Little Rock rearticulated the principles that figures like Brooks Hays had stood for in the 1950s as the solution to the problems the district faced a generation later. However, while gradualism, tokenism, and minimal compliance had been advanced as legal postures designed to limit school desegregation and to undermine the constitutional rights of African American children in the mid-twentieth century, they were advanced in the 1980s as "integration" procedures that provided the only means of preserving some racial diversity in the city's schools. Just as Hays had reframed his historic legacy over the intervening years, "moderate" approaches to school desegregation were presented to the public and the federal courts in a new light.

Indeed, even as the school board solicited proposals from attorneys on how to proceed with its interdistrict lawsuit, it implemented policies designed to reduce busing and concentrate the remaining white pupils in the school district in a smaller number of schools. Despite doubts about the legality of the options under discussion and the pending interdistrict litigation, the majority of the board supported these measures in an effort to appease white school patrons and stem the tide of white flight. For example, as early as 1981, the school board approved a plan designed to cluster white students in grades one through three in homeroom classes until they made up at least 35 percent of students in a classroom. The plan would create seventy-nine homeroom classes composed entirely of black students. In proposing this plan, board member Peter Sherrill expressed interest in a "long term" strategy to merge city and suburban school districts, but stated his conviction that LRSD had reached a critical tipping point and faced the threat of "accelerated" white flight if it did not act immediately to alleviate the concerns of white parents that their children would be racially isolated in the city's schools. John W. Walker, attorney for the black plaintiffs, went to court to stop the plan the day after it was approved. After a brief hearing, the federal district court rejected what it described as "hurriedly conceived stopgap measure to appease white parents."[94]

The Little Rock school board, however, did not abandon its efforts to secure more white patrons in the city's schools and next adopted the Partial K-6 Plan over the objections of Superintendent Masem, the district's Biracial Advisory Committee, and civil rights leaders. The plan reestablished some neighborhood elementary schools and had the effect of creating four schools in African American neighborhoods that were 99 percent black while concurrently reducing the black student population in six other schools in white or integrated areas. This time, the school board hoped to circumvent the opprobrium of the federal courts by claiming that the plan was not motivated by a desire to appease white parents, but rather had been designed to "preserve" better racial balance in the majority of the district's schools. Although at least one public school official told the *New York Times* that after nearly three years of defeated school tax levies and the threat of insolvency, the measure was designed to "provide a few more carrots" to potential white patrons and taxpayers, the school district's attorneys adopted the official position that the plan was an "affirmative step taken to minimize resegregation." The district argued that its plan offered the best "hope of maintaining quality integrated education" and suggested that its current proposal was not designed to discriminate against black students.[95]

The federal courts accepted this argument on its face. While the school district could not propose a "reorganization" plan baldly designed to appease white parents, it could present a plan to create four racially identifiable elementary schools in black communities in Little Rock as an "integration" measure. The Eighth Circuit Court of Appeals accepted the district's contention that the plan was not designed to make the school district more attractive to white parents, but rather was designed to mitigate the effects of white flight and maintain a semblance of integration in some institutions by concentrating white students in a small number of schools. As the court held, "Although the possibility of white flight and . . . resegregation cannot justify a school board's failure to comply with a court order to end segregation, it may be taken into account in an attempt to promote integration."[96] Strikingly, this assertion seemed to ignore the fact that the Little Rock school district was still under court orders to eliminate its dual system of education and had never been declared unitary.

Under the Partial K-6 Plan, nearly 20 percent of African American students in Little Rock attended racially identifiable institutions. Despite the fact that *Brown v. Board of Education* had declared that segregation was inherently unequal, the federal court required the school board to monitor the isolated schools to "ensure that equality is actually maintained" and to adopt measures designed to reduce achievement gaps in black and white student performance in the district. The Eighth Circuit attempted to mitigate the effects of racial isolation by restoring elements of freedom of choice and insisting on a measure in the plan that provided transportation for black children that requested transfers to integrated institutions.⁹⁷ As the programs were implemented, substantial numbers of African American students experienced increased racial isolation. Nevertheless, Elizabeth Huckaby's successors in Little Rock's school administration defended their policies and the resegregation of these students by suggesting they were doing the best they could to preserve support for public education in the face of intransigent white resistance. Just as Huckaby had justified administrative policies that were not "morally right" a generation earlier, her successors insisted that pragmatic compromises were required to keep the school system operable and solvent.

Indeed, when the district tried to implement a new student assignment plan in 1986–87 that complied with the interdistrict desegregation decree, it encountered continued resistance from white school patrons. In his report on the state of desegregation in the city's schools on the thirtieth anniversary of the 1957 crisis, Robert L. Brown found that many white parents in the district expected the district "to bargain with or cater to white patrons in exchange for keeping their children in the public schools." "As a diminishing quantity," he observed, "whites were used to having their way." Some white parents categorically refused to send their children to predominantly black schools and enrolled their children elsewhere. White parents in Little Rock who were unable to transfer their children to magnet schools accused the district of holding their children "hostage" and asked school officials to fill vacancies in the interdistrict magnets reserved for suburban students with their own children.⁹⁸ Although LRSD argued that the interdistrict magnets would lose their "interdistrict" character if they did so, the Eighth Circuit Court of Appeals ordered school administrators to fill the vacancies. Consequently, by the next school year 17 percent of white children enrolled in Little Rock's non-magnet schools had either transferred to the interdistrict magnets or left the system for private schools.⁹⁹ The percentage of African American children in the district's non-magnet schools continued to climb.

In 1988 and 1989, the Little Rock, Pulaski County, and North Little Rock school districts filed settlement plans in the interdistrict lawsuit that accepted the inevitability of some resegregation and the existence of racially isolated schools. Each school district submitted an intradistrict desegregation plan and signed onto an interdistrict agreement. Little Rock's long-range "desegregation" plan designated one-fourth of the district's traditional elementary schools as all-black "incentive schools." In an effort to provide compensatory education for the enrolled students' racial isolation, the district promised to provide the "incentive schools" with twice as much funding as other schools in the system and expressed the hope that special programs would attract voluntary white transfer students. The remaining schools in the school district were identified as "elementary academies" that would be racially balanced. Under the plan, sold as "controlled choice," white students were permitted to transfer to incentive schools if they desired, and black students could opt to attend one of the elementary academies.[100] In 1990, the Eighth Circuit Court of Appeals upheld the proposed plans as "reasonable, good-faith efforts to solve seemingly intractable problems, efforts involving give and take on the part of all concerned." Although a "perfect" desegregation plan would not contain all-black schools, the Constitution merely required districts to "achieve integration to the maximum practicable extent." In order for majority black districts to maintain some well-integrated schools, the court found that it was "necessary to tolerate a small number of all-black schools."[101] Notably, in approving the settlement plans, the Eighth Circuit failed to acknowledge how the limitations of its own decree overturning school district consolidation had established parameters for what was "practicable" and had contributed directly to the resurrection of racially isolated schools. Instead of recognizing that their narrowly tailored remedy was insufficient, the court's opinion reflected the federal judiciary's retreat from the mandate outlined in *Green v. New Kent County* to eliminate segregation root and branch.[102]

The Little Rock school district struggled with the legacy of generations of segregation and discrimination throughout the 1980s. By suing PCSSD, NRLSD, and the State of Arkansas for interdistrict relief, the district accused others of fostering and maintaining racial discrimination but did not accept its own full measure of responsibility. This distance enabled school board members and district attorneys to argue that proposals put before the courts that knowingly created racially identifiable schools in historically black neighborhoods were not a return to the segregated practices of the past. Although many black school patrons read these developments as the natural byproduct of the school district's longstanding preoccupation with appeasing white parents and their children at the expense of their African American counterparts, district officials seemed to believe that a decade of compliance with court-ordered busing and their own determination to pursue an interdistrict remedy in the courts inoculated them against such charges. Indeed, they argued that the creation of virtually all-black "incentive schools" and compensatory education programs designed to make these separate institutions "more equal" were an indication of their commitment to integration and racial diversity.

At this same moment, cultural gatekeepers and opinion makers in Little Rock sought to reclaim the city's dormant reputation as a racially moderate and progressive Southern city. In the 1980s and 1990s, filmmakers and television producers routinely elevated the profile of white moderates in their portrayals of the civil rights movement in an effort to maximize their demographic appeal with white audiences. However, the appearance of these stories reflected deeper and broader cultural trends as well. In the 1970s, activists opposed to systemic desegregation purposefully sought to separate the accomplishments of the civil rights movement from the historical processes, actors, and mechanisms that made those achievements possible. This allowed white moderates like Huckaby to dismiss efforts to draw meaningful connections between the controversies surrounding token integration and those related to busing a generation later. It also allowed the vice principal to assert in the closing pages of her memoir that the "successful" integration in the district and the racial balance at Central High was not the product of sustained civil rights litigation, but the "fortitude" of the institution's predominantly white student body and administrative staff as they endured the crisis unleashed by "extremists" in their community. Public controversy surrounding the elevation of "hero-martyr moderate(s)" revolved primarily around the claim that Little Rock's "silent majority" and the city's traditional civic leadership also deserved credit for restoring the community's equilibrium and allowing Little Rock to transcend the calamity precipitated by "outsiders," segregationists from the Arkansas delta, and opportunistic politicians like Governor Faubus. In this narrative, it was the pragmatic face of white moderation that set Little Rock back on the path to progress. In the late twentieth century, school administrators and other public officials would continue to argue that Little Rock's tradition of pragmatic moderation and minimal compliance also charted the best course for its future as both the school district and the federal courts turned away from systemic desegregation strategies.

— CHAPTER FOUR —

Displacing Blame

During his 1997 State of the State address, Arkansas governor Mike Huckabee announced his intention to use the fortieth anniversary of the Little Rock School desegregation crisis as an opportunity to "make amends" and to reclaim the mantle of moderation for the Arkansas capital. Declaring 1997 the "year of reconciliation," Huckabee made note of plans in the city to mark the anniversary through the development of a visitor's center near Central High School and a commemorative ceremony. As he affirmed his support for these initiatives, the governor also shared his vision of the role he would play in these events: "On that day in September, as the 'Little Rock Nine' come back to Central High School, they will not be met by a governor who says, 'You can't come in,' but met by a governor who says, 'Please, come in and accept our sincere apologies and give us your forgiveness for ever allowing such a thing to take place among enlightened, supposedly God-fearing people.'"[1] This stark contrast was designed to distance Governor Huckabee from his predecessor Orval Faubus and to symbolize the evolution of political leadership and public opinion in the state of Arkansas.

Throughout the region, civic leaders and political figures pointed to the creation of civil rights museums in the 1990s and the observance of commemorative ceremonies as tangible evidence of racial progress. As Owen

Dwyer has noted, civil rights memorials offered "state actors seeking to solidify (quite literally in granite and marble) the discursive foundations of their office ... a way to clearly separate themselves from the past and project a progressive image into the future."[2] Likewise, commemorative ceremonies were designed to facilitate the "symbolic renunciation" of overt racism. As Renee C. Romano found in her study of the prosecution of civil rights cold cases in the 1990s, these "civic rituals" afforded communities with the opportunity to define racism as the individual expression of racial hatred and to publicly reject it while evading a broader recognition of systemic discrimination and oppression in the past or present. Indeed, in the final decade of the twentieth century, the construction of civil rights museums, the prosecution of decades-old murders, and the public recognition of civil rights anniversaries provided the palliative reassurance that the struggles that marked the 1950s and 1960s had been resolved. As such, they promised what Romano described as a "relatively painless redemption, one that did not require white Americans to fully confront, let alone admit, the nature of, the legacies of, or their responsibility for racial violence."[3]

In Little Rock, the fortieth anniversary of the school desegregation crisis offered the city's power brokers the opportunity to recast the 1957 standoff, reshaping it as a symbol of the transformative changes that had swept the city and the South in the intervening decades. As the city dedicated a new visitor center designed to interpret this history, Central High was promoted as a symbol of successful integration, equality before the law, and racial reconciliation. However, for some, this shining rhetoric and powerful symbolism obscured ongoing resistance to meaningful racial justice and desegregation in the Little Rock school district. As plans to observe the anniversary and establish a museum dedicated to the 1957–59 school desegregation crisis unfolded, some community leaders and African American activists argued that the commemorative efforts were little more than a public relations ploy designed to reshape the city's public image and to mask the real face of race relations in Little Rock. Although local neighborhood activists and civil rights organizations hoped to use the anniversary and the construction of the museum as an occasion to stimulate ongoing conversation about race relations in the city, they were frustrated by the efforts of civic leaders to use the occasion to "historicize" the events of the 1957–59 and disconnect them from the concerns of the present.

In federal courts of law, the city's celebratory civic narrative was deployed in the school district's attempt to secure release from federal court oversight. Indeed, the school district's petition to revise its desegregation plan moved forward in federal courts just one day after a fortieth anniversary commemorative ceremony held to honor the Little Rock Nine on the steps of Central High School. School officials, expert witnesses, and opinion makers in the city maintained that the district's problems had been resolved, and that persistent racial inequities were not the product of institutionalized racism or the vestiges of segregated education. Rather, they could be attributed to problems within the black community generated by a purported "culture of poverty."

Some contemporary activists contend that the way the civil rights movement is remembered has fed white denial and indifference in the "post-civil rights era." According to surveys completed at the turn of the twenty-first century, most white Americans believed that black-white integration and equality was an accomplished reality. Pointing to past civil rights victories, some respondents asserted that the nation had bent over backward to provide African Americans and other minorities with access to equal opportunity. In light of these findings, education activist Paul Street has argued that the public celebration of past civil rights victories "encourage[s] the illusion of racism's disappearance and the notion that the only barriers left to black equality in the United States are internal to the black community and that disadvantaged African Americans are personally responsible for their presence at the bottom of the US hierarchy."[4] In Little Rock and elsewhere, public celebrations of racial progress and reconciliation perpetuated the belief that persistent racial disparities in income, security, housing, health care, and education were the product of "self-sabotaging" behaviors in black communities rather than enduring racism and structural inequalities.[5]

The contradiction between Little Rock's stated intention to use the fortieth anniversary as occasion to foster racial reconciliation and the structural inequities built into the city's institutions led the local branch of the NAACP to boycott and picket the commemorative activities. NAACP officers, desegregation monitors, and attorneys for the African American plaintiffs in the school desegregation case asserted that the city was more interested in symbol than substance. They argued that this civic culture also shaped the school district's approach to fulfilling its responsibilities under the desegregation settlement agreement that had emerged in the late 1980s. School officials maintained that they had complied with the desegregation decree if they *implemented* programs designed to address recurrent problems in the district, regardless of whether or not those provisions had any demonstrable impact on reducing the racial isolation of African American students or resulted in improvements in student achievement. This "checklist mentality," some argued, was the legacy of Little Rock's culture of minimal compliance and belied public assertions that the city had transcended its past.

Interest in a building a museum or visitor center dedicated to interpreting the history of the 1957–59 desegregation crisis coalesced in Little Rock during the early 1990s and gained momentum as the fortieth anniversary approached. The effort to create the Little Rock Central High Museum and Visitor Center coincided with similar efforts in urban centers across the South relating to their own history during the civil rights era. In the space of a few short years, museums and institutes dedicated to preserving and interpreting local and national histories of the civil rights movement emerged in Montgomery (Southern Poverty Law Center's Civil Rights Memorial, 1989), Memphis (National Civil Rights Museum, 1991), Birmingham (Birmingham Civil Rights Institute, 1992), Selma (National Voting Rights Museum, 1993), Atlanta (Martin Luther King Jr. National Historic Site, 1996), and Savannah (Ralph Mark Gilbert Civil Rights Museum, 1996).[6]

Central High Museum Inc., a nonprofit 501(c)3 entity, was formally incorporated in September 1995. A variety of community groups, organizations, and individuals had a vested interest in shaping the history that would be presented to visitors touring the proposed facility. As the museum planning process unfolded, these constituencies advanced competing visions of the purpose of the museum, the historical narrative it would support, and its mandate in the present. The bipartite structure of Central High Museum Inc. ultimately functioned to contain and suppress these differences. Politically connected civic leaders on the organization's board were focused on quickly developing an interpretive exhibit focused on the events of 1957–58 in order to capitalize on the publicity surrounding the fortieth anniversary. In contrast, some local residents and community activists on the planning committee of the Central High Museum and Visitor Center advanced a more expansive vision of the role the center could play in the community as a vehicle for stimulating research and encouraging discussion of contemporary race relations. However, ultimately, the accelerated timeline of the project and decisions made by the board in relation to fundraising and site selection redirected the work of the planning committee, redefining and limiting their input into the broader project. The board's desire to capitalize on the full public relations potential of the fortieth anniversary overrode their interest in fostering community dialogue about the appropriate function of the center or the history it should encapsulate. In its final form, the small exhibit designed to commemorate the fortieth anniversary focused almost exclusively on the events of the 1957–58 school year and upheld Central High's status as a model of successful school desegregation.

In Little Rock, as elsewhere, interest in building a museum that focused on the city's civil rights history was supported by a diverse coalition of individuals and organizations pursuing a variety of agendas. According to Little Rock restauranteur Mark Abernathy, several white business leaders actively opposed the idea when he first proposed it in the 1980s, but by 1991 the alumni board of the Greater Little Rock Chamber of Commerce's Leadership Institute expressed interest in the project's potential. In the city of Little Rock, as many as six new museum projects were under development during the 1990s, including the Arkansas Museum of Science and History, the MacArthur Military Museum, and the Mosaic Templars Cultural Center, which was dedicated to preserving Arkansas's black history after Reconstruction. The *Arkansas Democrat-Gazette* referred to the proliferation of museum projects as the most visible manifestation of a movement it dubbed "Past Little Rock." The proponents of these projects not only viewed them as opportunities to "enlighten, enrich, and encourage" Arkansans to engage with their history, but also as tourist destinations and economic engines that could provide the city with a "gateway to its future" in a post-industrial economy.[7]

In communities across the South, civic leaders and business leaders who promoted the construction of civil rights museums often emphasized these pragmatic and profit-driven concerns. Real estate developers and urban planners embraced the projects as a means to revitalize decaying African American neighborhoods, which were frequently still suffering from the crippling effects of previous incarnations of urban redevelopment.[8] Tourism officials and entrepreneurs pointed to the potential of these sites to tap into a growing market for heritage tourism, particularly for African American travelers. In Little Rock, the museum project gained real momentum shortly after the city's weekly newspaper, the *Arkansas Times,* publicly endorsed the project. Editor Max Brantley directed attention to the popularity of civic rights museums in other Southern cities. Although Brantley acknowledged the effort of the Mosaic Templars Cultural Center to recognize the work of Daisy Bates, he characterized the planned African American history museum as a "poorly funded, obscure repositor[y]." Brantley urged city leaders to grasp the opportunity to push for the recognition of Central High School as a national historic site: the neighborhood surrounding the school would benefit from economic reinvestment, many of the prominent figures involved in the crisis were still available to share their stories, and additional support for the project might be garnered because Arkansas's Bill Clinton—a former governor who described the crisis as a watershed moment in the development of his own interest in social justice—was the current occupant of the White House. Brantley acknowledged that members of the white business establishment might once have balked at such a suggestion, but he urged the Little Rock community to see the crisis in another light. Little Rock "stands for something positive," he insisted. "It represents the federal government's commitment to the Constitution: the victory of law over the mob."[9] Several months later, Brantley extended this triumphalist narrative into the present, contending that Central High was already a "living monument to the civil rights movement, with its black principal, its majority black student body and its unparalleled record of academic achievement."[10] The city had nothing to fear and much to gain from the formal recognition of this accomplishment. This public appeal mirrored efforts to secure support for similar projects in other Southern cities, which sought to "turn a stigmatized past into a commercial asset." Professional reviews of early civil rights museums and exhibits constructed in the 1990s observed that many of these memorial sites offered visitors a "palatable," "constructive message" to "accompany the negative racial history" in effort to secure public support for their construction. In many of the civil rights exhibits built in the 1990s, exhibit developers placed an emphasis on the "moral righteousness of nonviolent protest," the "potential of interracial unity," and the "success of qualified integration" at the expense of a serious analysis of contemporary racial problems and contentious issues.[11]

Brantley's arguments resonated with Everett "Rett" Tucker III, incoming chairman of the Chamber of Commerce and son of one of the "moderates" on the Little Rock school board in the late 1950s and 1960s.[12] They also appealed to Skip Rutherford, a former Little Rock school board member and staffer for Senator David Pryor. Rutherford had become more familiar with the history of the 1957–59 crisis while negotiating a settlement with the state legislature to fund the 1989 desegregation agreement, and he found that elected officials were often completely unaware of the state's complicity in fostering segregation in the Little Rock school district. Both men noted that visitors to the city often sought more information about the crisis, and that the construction of a museum would provide a valuable service while enabling the city to tap into heritage tourism dollars that were currently being redirected to other cities like Memphis. Moreover, as supporters of public education with children who attended Central, both Tucker and Rutherford hoped to draw attention to the high school's long-standing record of graduating national merit semi-finalists and sending students to elite universities around the country. Tucker acknowledged that many in his father's generation might have thought that the less said about the crisis the better, but he believed the construction of a museum would be a productive way to acknowledge the city's progress while recognizing that the community still had "room to grow." Although some felt the crisis gave Little Rock a "black eye," Tucker recalled that "the people, the organizers and promoters of this idea believed it was something we needed to own. We needed to make sure we could tell the story correctly and learn from it."[13]

These well-connected civic leaders recruited the support of Little Rock mayor Jim Dailey as they pursued the idea of opening a museum in conjunction with the fortieth anniversary of the school desegregation crisis. Dailey, who was enthusiastic about the project's potential to rehabilitate the reputation of Little Rock, created a "Central High School Celebration Committee" to coordinate citywide events. Tucker was named co-chair of this body in order to ensure seamless coordination between the museum planning and the commemorative calendar. Dailey tasked the committee with developing appropriate events to mark the anniversary, preparing the school and its surrounding neighborhood for worldwide attention and promoting a positive picture of progress and racial healing in Little Rock.[14] Throughout the South, local and state politicians of various political persuasions threw their support behind the construction of civil rights museums, not only because of their ability to attract tourism and encourage investment in local businesses, but also out of a desire to distance their communities from the overt racism of the past. As Birmingham Mayor David Vann put it in relation to the development of a civil rights institute in his city, "The best way to put your bad images to rest is to declare them history and put them in a museum."[15]

Business leaders and political figures, however, were not the only members of the community interested in creating a visitor center at Central High School. Even before Brantley, Tucker, and Rutherford mobilized political support for the project, restauranteur Mark Abernathy engaged African American community leaders in informal discussions about the development of a museum, including NAACP president Dale Charles, the editor of the resurrected *Arkansas State Press* Janetta Kearney, and the Reverend Wendell Griffin, an Arkansas judge. The civil rights activist Annie Abrams and Central High School Neighborhood Association president Ethel Ambrose were also interested in exploring the project's potential.[16] Across the region, many movement activists and their allies supported the creation of civil rights museums not only as a means to memorialize the movement, but also as a vehicle to critique contemporary racial relations and to inspire future activism. In previous decades, this "memory for the future" had been sustained and perpetuated by African American civil rights organizations, civic groups, churches, alumni associations, and black history museums. As Andrea Burns has observed in her study of the black museum movement, these institutions "transformed the 'hidden' stories of African American history into *public* history," challenging Eurocentric narratives that had been used to justify and legitimize racial discrimination. Although Max Brantley dismissed the work of the fledgling Mosaic Templars Cultural Center as "obscure," this institution's efforts to preserve the history of the African American experience in Arkansas reflected this longstanding tradition. The appearance of civil rights museums on the public landscape in the 1990s was a measure of the increased political influence of African American communities and their sustained efforts to reshape and restructure public cultural institutions.[17]

As support for the creation of the Central High Museum and Visitor Center gained momentum, members of these two groups merged, but the alliance was an uneasy one from the outset. White business leaders were committed to an accelerated timeline for the museum's completion in order to capitalize on the publicity associated with the fortieth anniversary, while grassroots activists engaged in discussions related to the museum project had their own priorities and concerns. In February 1995, Central High

Neighborhood Association president Ethel Ambrose secured some leverage for grassroots activists when the group applied for and received a $5,000 community planning grant from the Arkansas Humanities Council related to the project. The conditions of the grant stipulated that humanities scholars and members of the community had to be involved in project planning and evaluation. The money could not be used for construction, renovation, or preservation, nor could it be used to promote the fledgling museum organization. Rather, it was provided to facilitate the development of the museum's purpose, design, and interpretation of the 1957–59 crisis.[18] Ambrose used these requirements to carve out space for community involvement. In June 1995, residents of the Central High School neighborhood that she represented, African American community leaders and political figures, and historians and museum professionals, as well as school district and city officials, were formally invited into the museum planning process. With the guidance of Arkansas Humanities Council granting agent John Matthews, Central High Museum Inc. was incorporated and work related to the establishment of a museum was divided into committees. Although Rett Tucker was appointed president of the new organization and director of the board, the contributions of the grassroots group were acknowledged with the appointment of Ethel Ambrose as vice president and chair of the planning committee. Moreover, the role of the planning committee was formally written into the organization's bylaws, providing it with substantial influence over the future direction of the museum. In the early stages of the museum's development, the board was primarily focused on raising money to make the project a reality, soliciting private and public support, and acquiring a facility to house the museum, while the planning committee discussed the vexing issue of exhibit content and design.[19]

As the museum planning process unfolded, however, it quickly became evident that the board's control over fundraising and decisions related to site selection, as well as efforts to broker political support for the establishment of a national historic site, placed constraints on the planning committee's expansive vision and narrowed the proposed scope of the visitor center's exhibit considerably. While most planning committee members acknowledged the need to open a facility for visitors before the fortieth anniversary of the 1957 crisis, many felt that this effort should only be the first phase of a two-part process. A small visitor's center could serve as an introduction, but committee members felt that the significance of the Little Rock school desegregation crisis merited the development of a much larger museum or even a civil rights institute that encouraged research and discussion of race relations. The historian Elizabeth Jacoway recalled that members of the planning committee were "encouraged at every meeting to 'think big' and plan a museum that could be a model of its type."[20]

While Tucker, the Central High Museum Inc. president, acknowledged these more ambitious plans, he insisted that the organization stay focused on its immediate goals and its impending deadline. According to news reports, Tucker estimated that it might take as long as five years and two to three million dollars to develop a large museum. The Chamber of Commerce chairman argued that it would be difficult to raise sufficient funds to realize the planning committee's vision—not only were six new museums under development within Little Rock itself, but civil rights museums in other cities like Birmingham, Savannah, Atlanta, Selma, and Memphis had already exhausted potential streams of revenue. Although Central High Museum Inc. secured modest support from a city community grant program and the state of Arkansas, the effort to build a facility dedicated to telling the story of the Little Rock school desegregation crisis was not universally embraced in the city. The nonprofit received some donations from Little Rock residents and local businesses, but others rejected fundraising appeals with hostility, indifference, or expressions of ambivalence. With these considerations in mind, some members of the board believed it was more realistic to raise enough funds to open a small visitor's center and operate it for a few years with the hope of turning control of the facility over to the state or even the federal park system.[21]

With Arkansan Bill Clinton in the White House and longtime senator Dale Bumpers approaching retirement, board members hoped both men might see the designation of Central High School as a national historic site to be an important part of their legacies. They approached Bumpers about introducing the appropriate legislation and also solicited support from local and state leaders. Governor Mike Huckabee endorsed the proposal and promised to help secure state funding to help operate the center while the organization pursued federal recognition. By the spring of 1997, Democratic congressman Vic Snyder announced that the National Park Service was considering the site as a federal park, and Rett Tucker confidently told reporters, "Our goal all along has been to open the doors with no debt and two years' operating funds in the bank." The board was not particularly concerned about funding or developing the planning committee's ambitious

FIGURE 9. The original Central High Museum and Visitor Center was located in a former Mobil gas station directly across the street from Central High. When the school became a national historic site, the National Park Service built a new visitor center to accommodate the need for more space. (Carol M. Highsmith Archive, Library of Congress)

vision for project, anticipating that federal officials and public funds would shape the site in the future.[22]

Instead, the board focused on opening a modest visitor center before the fortieth anniversary of the crisis. After raising sufficient funds, Central High Museum Inc. purchased a decaying Mobil gas station immediately across from the high school to house the museum. Nearly forty years earlier, members of the press used the pay phones at the station to file their reports as the crisis unfolded. The building was one of the only historic commercial structures still standing in the residential neighborhood surrounding the school. The board secured support from Mobil Oil to help refurbish the building and complete an exterior restoration. The architect selected to work on the project envisioned transforming the 900-square foot interior into a small visitor center, with the two service bays functioning as exhibit space and the rest of the facility accommodating a book store and gift shop. A small addition in the rear allowed for the addition of restrooms and office space.[23]

Members of the planning committee were concerned about the cramped dimensions of the proposed museum and visitor center. Committee chair Ethel Ambrose described board president Rett Tucker's decision to purchase the gas station as "unilateral."[24] Rather than developing or defining a long-term vision for the site, the planning committee's focus had been effectively restricted to the effort to design a small exhibit within the service bay of a gas station. Even with this more limited mandate, members of the planning committee discussed and debated the history of the 1957–59 school desegregation crisis and its public presentation for several months, and continued to weigh the merits of "Phase II" of the site's development. By its very nature, the planning committee represented diverse points of view on the crisis, and its conversations were shaped by decades of contested memory about what had transpired in 1957–59. Participants privileged their personal memory and perceptions over the history of the crisis as it had been presented by scholars and other actors.

This was a source of frustration for the two historians invited to participate in the group under the conditions of the Arkansas Humanities Council grant—Dr. Elizabeth Jacoway, an independent scholar who had studied and written about the crisis for two decades, and Dr. Johanna Miller Lewis, a University of Arkansas at Little Rock (UALR) professor who directed the university's public history program and had recently completed an exhibit with the alumni organization of Little Rock's historically black high school. For public historians and academic scholars, civil rights museums offered an opportunity to reshape the memorial landscape. Early preservation efforts and interpretations of the American experience in the nineteenth and twentieth centuries had largely revolved around the lives and homes of the white elite. With the advent of the new social history, a new generation of scholars attempted to shift the focus to the diversity of the American experience and the lives of average citizens. Civil rights museums provided public history professionals and academics with a unique opportunity to chronicle the development of a social movement from the bottom up. Instead of valorizing social and economic inequities, civil rights museums afforded public historians with the opportunity to reshape their field by challenging rather than reifying the foundations of white supremacy.

This transformation was not without its critics. In the early 1990s, curators and historians found themselves in the crosshairs of the culture wars. Vocal conservatives charged public historians with sacrificing traditional historical narratives in service of a "politically correct" version of the nation's past shaped by a liberal "revisionist agenda." Within this context, museums became battlegrounds, and exhibitions like the National Museum of American Art's "The West as America" and the National Air and Space Museum's interpretation of the Enola Gay and the atomic bombing of Japan became sites of symbolic power.²⁵ However, public history institutions also faced criticism from community activists and grassroots organizations who expressed reservations about the efforts of traditional museums to interpret their marginalized histories. As mainstream institutions took what Andrea A. Burns has described as "inconsistent and tentative" steps toward addressing the African American experience, a new front emerged in the culture wars. For example, in 1994, public controversy erupted when Colonial Williamsburg announced its intention to stage a slave auction reenactment. Representatives of the NAACP and SCLC who protested the event expressed their reservations within the context of the museum's traditional neglect of African American history and the lack of outreach and consultation with descendant communities.²⁶ Likewise, as civil rights exhibits proliferated across the region in the early 1990s, some critics and civil rights veterans complained that public history sites framed the movement within a traditional political narrative, emphasizing prominent leaders, institutions, court cases, and legislative victories at the expense of highlighting the importance of grassroots organizing, the diversity of opinion and perspective within the movement, and the cultivation of a vibrant culture that sustained and nurtured participants.²⁷

On the planning committee in Little Rock, Lewis noted that "the amount of passion people displayed about their ideas and memories increased as they moved along a continuum from being alive in '57, a Southerner, an Arkansan, a resident of Little Rock, or a viewer/participant in actual events." Little Rock natives on the committee questioned whether outsiders could "truly understand what had happened." Some believed that the Eisenhower administration's enforcement of the *Brown v. Board of Education* decision had a positive impact in relation to African American civil rights, while others believed that the crisis and federal intervention had a negative impact on public education. Lewis wrote, "Committee members showed no deference towards us [professional historians] in terms of expressing their opinions on what type of facility the museum should be, or exactly why and how the 1957 crisis occurred." From Lewis's perspective, planning committee members showed "little interest . . . in knowing the facts," and at times expressed "outright hostility to the historiography of the crisis." Lewis recalled that one committee member dismissed academic scholarship outright: "We don't care what the historians say."²⁸

Planning committee member and historian Elizabeth Jacoway attempted to redirect the energy of the group by distributing a list of secondary sources written by academic scholars with the hope that committee members would read these materials and familiarize themselves with the political, legal, economic and social issues related to the crisis that concerned professional historians like herself.[29] Repeatedly, she urged other members of the group "to consider the background and context!" She found herself "stewing about the shortcomings of the planning committee" and the "misperceptions, justifications, distortions, and oversimplifications" that marked its deliberations. "[As] the lone southern historian in the group," she wrote, "it was a humbling experience for me to realize that everyone on the committee had their own interpretation of the Little Rock crisis—replete with their own set of information and experiences—and that my perspectives on the past carried no more weight than anyone else's . . . I could see from the outset that what we were about was not the kind of historical reconstruction I had learned about in graduate school."[30] In an effort to build a bridge between these two different ways of knowing, Jacoway organized a professional conference designed to provide the city of Little Rock with a "crash course in southern history and race relations" in conjunction with the fortieth anniversary.[31]

Johanna Miller Lewis was also frustrated with the "overwhelmingly democratic" nature of the committee's conversations and the endless debate about the public memory of the crisis. From Lewis's perspective, members of the planning committee seemed to think that their "ideas about the crisis alone were enough to fill the exhibit." In order to provide a strong foundation for the committee's work, Lewis directed students in her History Museum Interpretation course at UALR to research the history of the crisis and construct a detailed timeline based on materials located in archival collections throughout the state, historical newspapers, and scholarly accounts. Students streamlined this information into a planning document that contained the information they thought should be included in the proposed exhibit and presented their work to the planning committee. Lewis also shared copies of the timeline and the bibliography with the board.[32] Lewis reported that the board was "*very* pleased" with the students' work and developed an appreciation for the role the university and its public history program could play in translating its ideas into reality. The board recognized Lewis's professional credentials as a public historian and her experience curating and fabricating exhibits as an asset, and asked her to become the exhibit's curator and to serve as Central High Museum Inc.'s liaison with the designer selected to fabricate the exhibit. Public history graduate student Laura Miller and Ronnie Nichols, a board member and the director of Arkansas's Old State House, also joined the exhibit team.[33]

The team was charged with developing an exhibit that fulfilled the mission of the Central High Museum and Visitor Center: "To empower, inform, enlighten and challenge people by interpreting, documenting, discovering and preserving the history of the 1957 Central High crisis and its context." As a professional historian, Lewis was primarily focused on informing her audience by interpreting the crisis. What she learned from listening to the planning committee's deliberations was that even this group, "composed of people who were somewhat familiar with the crisis," had little knowledge of "the facts" and "no patience for the nuances of historical interpretation." What was needed was an exhibit that informed members of the community about the "basics of the story" and "concentrated on the events and the major players of the crisis" in a clear and chronological narrative.[34]

According to Cathy Collins, planning committee member and executive director of Little Rock's Racial and Cultural Diversity Commission, some committee members embraced this emphasis on historical chronology but others "wanted to utilize the historical events as means for promoting current day racial healing."[35] Some members of the planning committee placed more emphasis on aspects of the mission statement that called for empowering and enlightening Little Rock residents through an active process of discovery. In their view, the construction of a chronological historical account was not as imperative. However, committee chair Ethel Ambrose later reflected that the professional historians involved with the project were "a bit unfamiliar with and perhaps uncomfortable with the grassroots approach we were taking to our work" and instead brought a "we've always done it this way" and "we know best" mindset to their interactions with other members of the group.[36] In October 1996, Annie Abrams, a neighborhood resident and civil rights activist, expressed her frustration with the development of an exhibit focused primarily on a chronological reconstruction of the crisis. In her view, the purpose of the museum was to "learn from but not return to" the events of the crisis years.[37] Jacoway rejected the notion that finding "solutions to the myriad problems of Little Rock's ongoing racial conflicts" was the committee's charge. Moreover, she found it difficult to understand how the community would be able to heal its wounds or learn from the events of 1957–59 without a "reasonably accurate historical understanding" of what had transpired.[38]

This distance between the professional historians on the planning committee and representatives of the community reflected different approaches to interacting and engaging with the past. In 1993 and 1994, a national telephone survey explored popular American attitudes toward "history making" and found that most respondents privileged intimate, personal, and eyewitness accounts of the past over interpretations they believed were "mediated" by political and cultural agendas or professional and commercial ambitions. The survey found that respondents trusted the stories of family members and eyewitness accounts more than historical narratives offered by college history professors, high school teachers, or textbooks. These trends were even more pronounced among African American respondents who criticized traditional histories and nurtured powerful counter-narratives focused on the black experience. In the broader survey, academic history fared better than popular or commercial history in terms of trustworthiness, but was often described as "dull" or "boring" because it failed to engage respondents. Those surveyed preferred the interactive experience of visiting museums or historic sites, which they also rated as the most trustworthy of historic sources. The surveyors found that "many respondents felt that the best of each of the other sources could be found in museums." Museums gave visitors "a sense of immediacy—of personal participation—that respondents associated with eyewitnesses; they evoked the intimacy of family gatherings; and they encouraged an interaction with primary sources that reminded respondents of independent research." Moreover, respondents seemed to be most attracted to historical narratives that were useful—that could be used to evaluate the present and chart a course for the future.[39] This emphasis on contemporary relevance was crucial for some members of the planning committee who were less concerned with recapturing the events of the 1957–58 school year in exhaustive detail.

In Little Rock, the exhibit team was caught between the countervailing views of the board and the planning committee. Although the team sought to satisfy both constituencies, Lewis found this increasingly difficult. As the exhibit moved toward production, the planning committee's role became even more tenuous since it did not control the funds required for fabrication and construction. While the exhibit team solicited feedback from the planning committee, it sought official approval of its ideas from the board; planning committee members served as sounding board or "audience focus group" for the exhibit team's ideas.[40] By December 1996, some members of the planning committee spoke frankly about their inability to influence the direction of the exhibit. Annie Abrams expressed frustration that the board continued to turn a deaf ear to the group's effort to discuss the long-term goals of the site. According to Cathy Collins, Janetta Kearney—editor of Little Rock black's newspaper—stated baldly, "We are not being included. We are being ignored." From Kearney's perspective, community representatives had been sidelined in the exhibit development process. The editor observed that there was "no color in anything that the group is doing" and suspected that the board intended to dissolve the planning committee.[41]

Kearney's prediction proved prescient. In January 1997, the board officially tabled discussion of Phase II of the project and redefined the role of the planning committee. The committee's conversations related to the exhibit planning process were perceived as contentious and unproductive. Committee chair Ethel Ambrose felt that many of her fellow board members were "not willing to accept" that the "grassroots" representatives involved in the project had any ideas "worth listening to."[42] Tucker characterized the conflict between the two groups differently. "The board consisted of people who wanted to get things done," the board president recalled, "and the planning committee consisted of people who wanted to plan . . . with no eye on results."[43] Moving forward, the planning committee would no longer determine its own agenda or operate independently of the board. Instead, the board would direct the actions of the planning committee and select board members to serve on it at the organization's annual meeting. In retrospect, committee member Cathy Collins believed the board's "power play" effectively strengthened its ability to "control and more effectively define the boundaries around the construction of the official memory of the desegregation of Central High School."[44] Not all actors involved in memorialization processes are able to leverage their influence, connections, and political resources as effectively as others. "The board was the board," Tucker recalled. As an adjunct of the board, the planning committee "had zero authority."[45] In Arkansas's capital, well-positioned business and civic leaders involved in Central High Museum Inc. steered and controlled the museum planning process, amplifying their own interpretation of the 1957–59 crisis, while defining its relevance and limiting the influence of other stakeholders.

The completed exhibit, "All the World Is Watching Us: Little Rock and the 1957 Crisis," installed in the former gas station's service bay, provided a streamlined interpretation of the 1957–58 school year. Within the limited space, the textual panels were brief and succinct.[46] Moreover, given the contested nature of the history of the crisis and the heated debates within the planning committee itself, Lewis was determined to make the exhibit as "historically accurate" as possible by utilizing quotes that "let the various participants tell their own story" while avoiding "potentially explosive and probably unanswerable question[s]." By focusing on documentable and widely known facts and representing the views of various parties through published quotes, the exhibit team navigated through the treacherous shoals of memory and public opinion about the crisis and mid-century race relations. The team was determined not to become embroiled in debates about minutiae and to "pick their battles carefully."[47] However, this focus on the documentable and unchallengeable foreclosed the opportunity to use the exhibit as an opportunity to generate deeper public discussion about the contested memory of the crisis and its relationship to ongoing school desegregation litigation in the city of Little Rock.

The exhibit framed the significance of Central High School's place on the memorial landscape in a manner that was in keeping with the broader themes of "reconciliation" that echoed throughout the fortieth anniversary commemoration. Unlike other civil rights museums built in the early 1990s, the visitor's center was not designed to educate visitors about the entire scope of the civil rights movement. From the beginning, the exhibit was dedicated to telling a local history that had national and global impact. Like many histories of school desegregation, the exhibit's narrative unfolded as a series of school board decisions, lawsuits, and court rulings, but the exhibit framed stiffening "political resistance to integration" within the context of the actions of Governor Orval Faubus and state legislators. "Opponents of desegregation," the exhibit explained, "argued that the Supreme Court and the federal government lacked the authority to impose its decisions on the states." Framing the crisis as a constitutional conflict rooted in arguments about state's rights shifted focus away from the ideology of white supremacy that undergirded organized resistance to desegregation not only during the crisis years but the decades that followed. Moreover, with its focus on the actions of political leaders and public figures, the exhibit adroitly avoided a potentially more controversial assessment of how average citizens in Little Rock felt about the Supreme Court's *Brown* decision.

The core of the exhibit, "A Time of Courage and Fear: 1957–58," focused on the events that captured national media attention and shaped public memory of the school desegregation crisis. The largest wall of the refurbished service bay was covered with oversized reproductions of historic photographs, and a 1950s-era television replayed the iconic scenes that unfolded outside of Central High School. These pictures included some of the most searing images captured during the crisis: the mob surrounding Elizabeth Eckford as she tried to enter Central High School, the 101st Airborne stationed outside the school, white students burning an effigy of a black male student, troops escorting the Little Rock Nine inside the front door of Central, Ernest Green dressed in his commencement robes on graduation day. As curator Johanna Miller Lewis observed, many of these images had become "ingrained in the nation's memory." Consequently, the team decided to utilize these resources to tell the story of the Little Rock desegregation crisis as much as possible.[48] Immediately below these iconic images, the events of the year unfolded in a dated timeline drawn from the research completed by Lewis's public history students. The timeline chronicled documented facts about the tension-filled days of September 1957—suits filed in court, public speeches made by the governor, the national media attention focused on the city as the students were denied entrance to Central High School, Faubus's conference with Eisenhower, the removal of the Arkansas National Guard, rioting outside the building while the Little Rock Nine attended their first day of classes, the deployment of the 101st Airborne, and the military escort provided for the African American students as they returned to classes. However, the exhibit team avoided speculation about the motives of various historical actors who participated in these events. For example, the exhibit did not attempt to explain why Governor Faubus deployed the Arkansas National Guard to prevent the Little Rock Nine from entering Central High School. Was it racism? Political expediency? Public safety? Or states' rights? Moreover, it hardly acknowledged the public discussion and heated historical debate over these questions.

While the first half of the timeline was dominated by well-known and publicly recorded events, the second half of the display turned its attention to the events that had unfolded inside the school outside of the view of reporters and cameras. The exhibit highlighted physical attacks, racial slurs, and vandalism directed at the Little Rock Nine throughout the school year. Although the events chronicled on the timeline were well documented in school records, much of the daily harassment experienced by the Little Rock Nine inside Central over the course of the school year was unrecorded. In the years that followed, white students and members of the Little Rock Nine advanced very different interpretations about what had happened inside the school and the number of students who bore some responsibility for the school's discipline problems. Many white students denied any involvement, and white student leaders resented and resisted suggestions that the student body was sympathetic to the segregationist cause. As Ernest Green noted wryly the year before the visitor center opened, "I can't find anyone that I went to school with now that was opposed to my being there . . . I go back to Little Rock and they're all my closest friends today."[49] This tension, while not directly acknowledged in the exhibit, shaped the Central High Museum and Visitor Center's development.

In advance of the visitor center's opening, the board and the exhibit team sent drafts of the exhibit script to the Little Rock Nine and Central High School student body representatives from 1957 and 1958 for comment. The exhibit team reported that feedback from the Little Rock Nine was generally positive, particularly in relation to the exhibit's acknowledgment that harassment continued inside the school during the 1957–58 school year.[50] However, this was precisely the part of the exhibit that provoked the most negative reaction from white members of Central's student body from that year. Craig Rains, 1958 class president, complained that the exhibit made the students "look bad" by focusing on the "ugliness" of the story. Sounding a familiar theme, Rains contended that the exhibit failed to illustrate that "95% of the white students took no part in it."[51] Rains was a sitting member of the city's fortieth anniversary commission and had been assigned the responsibility of working with the media. These duties were reassigned to Skip Rutherford, however, after Rains expressed his objections to the exhibit script and Tucker concluded he could not be a "team player" and stay on message.[52] In a public statement issued after the anniversary, Rains and 1958 student body president Ralph Brodie expressed their belief that the city and the state could and should take "pride in the attitude and conduct of Central's 1957–58 faculty and student body and their positive contribution to America's desegregation process."[53]

More immediately, Rains and Brodie threatened to organize a protest unless their perspective was included in the exhibit. The board tried to defuse this threat and address their concerns by inserting a panel entitled "View From Inside the School" that emphasized that most students obeyed the law and only "a handful . . . verbally and physically terrorized the

Nine."⁵⁴ The added text emphasized that the majority of Central's students adopted a guise of "sensible, peaceful neutrality" in the conflict between the African American students and their segregationist tormentors. Student government leaders "pledged to obey the law and asked the student body to follow their example." The panel underscored: "*Most students did.*" The relative lack of quotes from vocal white supremacists within the school, or white students resigned to obeying the law despite deeply ingrained and clearly stated segregationist beliefs, also implied that few white students opposed the presence of the Little Rock Nine. Although some involved in the exhibit planning process opposed the addition of the new panel, Johanna Miller Lewis defended the decision and suggested that "it did not detract" from the overall interpretation. Pragmatically, she argued that a "rigid or stubborn adherence to theoretical standards" without a "little diplomacy can doom a project from the beginning," but there was no question that planners made a significant change to the exhibit script at the request of the white students.⁵⁵

For their part, the African American students interpreted the "sensible, peaceful neutrality" of the majority of their peers much differently. To some degree, the concessions made to white students in the development of the exhibit were balanced by Elizabeth Eckford's poignant comments in a videotaped film that played in a constant loop at the end of the exhibit. As Eckford explained, the harassment the Little Rock Nine endured from a small "organized group" would not have been as pervasive without the "tacit cooperation" of the rest of the white student body. Eckford's comments drew attention to what some scholars have referred to as more "mundane and insidious forms of racism" that are often neglected at civil rights museums that focus on "white supremacy's most violent and widely scorned forms."⁵⁶ Nevertheless, Eckford's view of this issue was presented as her personal opinion, while the perspective of Central High's white student leaders was seamlessly and invisibly incorporated into the body of the exhibit text. The inclusion of the new exhibit panel enhanced the perception in some quarters that the museum represented an attempt by white business leaders to enhance the image of the city of Little Rock and capitalize on tourist dollars with a minimum of fuss.⁵⁷

Indeed, in its effort to address the aftermath of the 1957–58 school year, the exhibit called attention to the resurgence of "moderate" forces in the city and their efforts to reclaim control of the school board and administrative policies. The exhibit explained that Faubus closed the schools "pending a public vote on the issue of immediate integration of all grade levels," but did not explicitly state that the majority of Little Rock voters indeed ratified the governor's decision and voted to keep the schools closed rather than proceed with desegregation. Instead, the exhibit focused on the creation of the Women's Emergency Committee to Open Our Schools (WEC) and its efforts to reopen the public high schools by electing "moderate" candidates to the school board and recalling "segregationist" members. The exhibit did not reveal that the WEC refused to take a principled position in support of desegregation or admit African American women into its ranks. Nevertheless, unlike many narratives of the crisis that attribute the reopening of the public schools to the activism of this group of moderate white women, the exhibit did note that high school education in the city did not resume until the federal courts ruled that the state's school closing laws were illegal. Although the WEC is often credited with reopening the city's schools in public memory, it was court ligation filed by the NAACP that ultimately overturned the state statute in question.[58]

The exhibit did not elucidate the policies or positions of the city's moderates or their tolerance for token integration as a means of evading systemic desegregation. However, it did acknowledge that early desegregation initiatives were not "perfect": the progress of desegregation was "slow," the black community was "impatient," and further change required enforcement of the law by federal courts. The concluding panels of the exhibit briefly addressed contemporary issues, but their purpose, as curator Johanna Miller Lewis explained, was to demonstrate that "despite the crisis and some other racial problems over the years, integration did eventually take place."[59] The exhibit portrayed Central High School as a symbol of "academic excellence" and "the Constitution's guarantee of equal rights under the law." In his communication with the media, Skip Rutherford underscored Little Rock's progress and the investment in the community's future that the museum represented. "It was an easy story to tell about a high school that was working," he recalled. "It was an easy story to tell about neighborhood revitalization. It was an easy story to tell about African American tourism. It was an easy story to tell about public education."[60]

Within this framework, the Central High Museum and Visitor Center did not call attention to Little Rock's recurrent problem of white flight, the rising percentage of African American students in the city's schools, racial disparities in academic achievement, the persistence of academic tracking and social separation in Central High School, inequities in the application of disciplinary procedures, or the ongoing school desegregation litigation. As the historian W. Fitzhugh Brundage has noted, civil rights museums constructed in the early 1990s rarely addressed "the benefits that whites in recent times received from the maintenance of white supremacy," and topics like residential segregation, police brutality, or economic inequality were "seldom considered."[61] However, these were precisely the issues that members of the planning committee had hoped to address through their more expansive vision of a civil rights institute that would encourage research and public discussion of contemporary race relations. Committee chair Ethel Ambrose felt that the "spin" the board put on the project was imbued with "post-civil rights" rhetoric that did not compel the city to confront the "culture of segregation" that persisted in the community.[62] A reporter from the *Arkansas Democrat-Gazette* concurred with this assessment and described the exhibit's parting salvo as little more than a series of "platitudes" that did little to illuminate the evolution of race relations in the city.[63]

The Central High Museum and Visitor Center formally opened on 20 September 1997, in a dedication ceremony featuring Governor Mike Huckabee, Little Rock mayor Jim Dailey, the Central High Museum Inc. board and planning committee, members of the Little Rock Nine, and several hundred onlookers. After participating in the ceremony and cutting the ribbon to open the museum, Elizabeth Eckford carefully folded a piece of the gold and black ribbon as a keepsake. As the only member of the Little Rock Nine who still lived in Little Rock in 1997, Eckford had been approached early on about participating in the planning process. She walked out on an early meeting and later told reporters, "I perceived that these people were trying to use me." After some reflection, however, she decided to participate in fundraising efforts for the museum and was named to the board of directors in the hope that the legacy of Central High School and the events of 1957–59 would be preserved "with the kind of dignity it deserves." Nevertheless, as she prepared to see the exhibits for the first time, some of her ambivalence about the commemoration and visitor center resurfaced. She told reporters that she planned to avoid looking at the famous photographs taken of her walking through the mob outside Central forty years earlier by not wearing her glasses in the exhibit. "I plan to stay about four feet away, and it will be a blur," she remarked. And she had a very clear message for the museum's planners and its visitors: "This is a place where we can begin the process of reflection," she warned, "but this place is not an alibi for atonement."[64] During the invocation, planning committee member and African American activist Annie Abrams echoed these sentiments and prayed that the museum would serve as a "flagship" that would help guide the community of Little Rock through "the turbulent waters that we will encounter as we travel the long journey toward understanding our history in all its complexity." But she also implored God to provide museum planners with the "courage and strength to go forward from here to complete the wisdom of the Mission Statement" and to fulfill the planning committee's larger vision. A job, she implied, that was far from finished.[65]

Indeed, as the city prepared to welcome the Little Rock Nine, President Bill Clinton, and other dignitaries to Little Rock, discontent about the state of race relations in Arkansas's capital provoked strong opposition to the commemorative activities. Dale H. Charles, president of the Little Rock and Arkansas chapters of the NAACP, announced the organization's determination to picket the planned ceremonies on the steps of Central High School in order to call attention to the unequal distribution of city contracts to minority businesses, police brutality in African American neighborhoods, and ongoing problems with the school system. "With the focus on the Little Rock Nine and racial healing, everybody is talking about the new Little Rock," Charles observed, "but the new Little Rock is the same as the old Little Rock."[66]

Critics pointed to Little Rock's efforts to clean up the neighborhood surrounding Central High School in time for the fortieth anniversary as an example of the city's preoccupation with symbol rather than substance. The high school was freshened up with new paint and landscaping, and city director Joan Adcock created an adopt-a-house program to "spiff up the tattered, weather-worn facades" of the houses across the street. A disaster-cleanup crew from Michigan was brought in to tidy up vacant lots. Adcock insisted that this was about more than a "picture-taking" opportunity, and Mayor Dailey suggested that these efforts were merely a "springboard" for a "long-term" effort to revitalize the area. Planning Committee chair Ethel Ambrose chided city officials and fellow board members who supported this effort, contending that they were trying to create a "Potemkin Village" in the city's streets. Representatives of the Central High Neighborhood Association noted that little had been done to address the longstanding complaints of residents in the area for years. The organization had developed plans to make the neighborhood more hospitable to pedestrians, which included improved lighting, wider sidewalks, and better landscaping. Instead, a $28,000 donation from Nations Bank resulted in the creation of a brick logo in the middle of the intersection of Fourteenth and Park designed to give the neighborhood a "sense of place." The new Central High Neighborhood Association president, Cliff Riggs, described the addition as an "embarrassment" that did little to enhance the neighborhood for its residents. Annie Abrams, a local activist and museum planning committee member, told reporters that she hoped the damage from the city's efforts could be minimized. Just as the contributions of community representatives in the museum planning process had been sidelined, she felt this was another example of what "they do for us instead of do with us."[67]

John Walker, the attorney representing the black plaintiffs in the ongoing school desegregation litigation, described a starkly different reality from the image cultivated by the commemoration's planners through its carefully timed clean-up efforts. "We have something comparable to Johannesburg in South Africa during apartheid," he told reporters. "You have the black section and the white section, and you have a repressive police force that views its mission as keeping blacks in their place." The anniversary plans were a farce. "To establish Little Rock as a place that has overcome the bigotry and racism of the 1950s is a public-relations venture more than anything," Walker asserted. Over the last forty years the school board had operated in "bad faith" and had used the passage of time "to defeat the noble purposes of the *Brown* decision." Rather than being a symbol of success, Walker suggested, "those who said 'never' can point to Little Rock and see that the promised concept of unity likely will not be implemented and the concept of separate and ultimately unequal will continue to reign." Walker noted that black children in Little Rock were still fighting for their constitutional rights in court and they continued to "wait for the day when the city's actions measure up to its often stated good intentions." He warned that the issues surrounding the schools would never be resolved until a plan was mandated by the court "that delivers for black children."[68]

By the mid-1990s, it had become clear that many of the provisions outlined in the desegregation settlement that emerged from the interdistrict lawsuit were not working. The district had proposed to redress the problem of white flight by creating racially isolated incentive schools supported with compensatory educational programs and racially balanced elementary academies in other parts of the district. Although the city's specialized magnet schools attracted white students, the incentive schools located on the east side of the city with overwhelmingly black student populations did not hold the same allure. In 1994, district officials sent 10,000 letters to white parents in the district informing them about special programming available in the incentive schools, but only five families applied to enroll. Moreover, even with the concentration of black pupils in the incentive schools, the favorable racial mix of students promised in Little Rock's regular elementary academies failed to materialize as the percentage of white students in the district continued to decline. Test scores revealed that the compensatory education programs meant to address educational deficits among African American students in the city's poorest neighborhoods were failing to close the achievement gap between white and black children. Instead, the achievement gap was widening. At secondary schools, African American pupils continued to be tracked into remedial classes, while white students attended honors and advanced placement courses in disproportionate numbers.[69] Whether one viewed the incentive schools as a means of maintaining racial balance in the majority of the city's elementary schools, as super-magnets designed to attract white transfer students through special programs and extra resources, or as centers of education specifically designed to prepare the city's most disadvantaged students to compete on a more even playing field, the racially isolated schools were failing on all counts.

In this context, school desegregation monitor Joy Springer contended that the Little Rock school system was still segregated and that black students were systematically denied access to equal educational opportunities due to racial isolation, academic tracking, and inequitable disciplinary procedures. "What do we have to celebrate?" she asked. "They're still being treated differently. The idea was to provide equal education." The desegregation monitor insisted that the planned commemorative events were "not about race relations and reconciliation." Rather, they were an attempt by business leaders and civic officials to bring in tourist revenue that would shore up "the power structure." She asserted, "This is just hype, a public relations sort of thing, to say, 'We want to show the world that Little Rock is on the way to solving the problem' . . . They want you to believe that."[70]

Comments like these encouraged members of the press descending on Little Rock for the fortieth anniversary to take a closer look at the city's schools. Throughout the month of September, story after story made note of the academic disparities at Central: the low number of black students enrolled in honors and advanced placement courses, the persistent achievement gaps on standardized tests, and the disproportionate number of black students subject to disciplinary sanctions. Reporters also took note of the self-segregation and social isolation of students in the hallways and cafeteria.[71] Local columnist John Brummett acerbically noted that despite the attempts of city hall to dress up the neighborhood immediately surrounding Central for the media, reporters from around the country were not taken in by the "trumped-up phoniness."[72]

While attorney John Walker asserted that the persistent problems in the district were the result of the school system's failure to implement the desegregation settlement in good faith, school officials contested this claim. In response to public criticism, administrators argued that the desegregation settlement was poorly designed and its provisions too detailed to allow the school district to address the challenges it faced creatively. School administrators contended that they had been unable to integrate the incentive schools or meet the racial balance guidelines outlined in the settlement as a result of demographic shifts and persistent white flight; there were simply not enough white students left in the system by the mid-1990s to meet the benchmarks established half a decade earlier. School officials not only argued that the goals outlined in the plan were virtually unachievable, but they also asserted with increasing force that, in light of recent Supreme Court decisions, they were also unreasonable since they held the school district to a much stricter standard than other districts that had been declared unitary and released from court oversight. School officials contended that the district had desegregated the city's schools to the extent practicable in the absence of a broader city-suburban consolidation decree. More pointedly, they asserted that many of the remaining inequalities in the system were the product of external factors beyond their control.[73] Over the course of the 1990s, the district pushed for a relaxation of court oversight, arguing that officials had worked diligently to fulfil their obligations and that the school system was entitled to unitary or at least partial unitary status and the return of local control.

These arguments relied heavily on a trio of Supreme Court decisions issued in the 1990s. *Board of Education of Oklahoma City v. Dowell* (1991), *Freeman v. Pitts* (1992), and *Missouri v. Jenkins* (1995) revisited requirements for school districts seeking unitary status. As the ideological cast of the federal judiciary changed as a result of political appointments in the late 1970s and 1980s, courts turned away from systemic desegregation plans; the passage of time, the majority of justices on the bench agreed, made it less likely that persistent inequities were connected to the history of segregation. In this context, public discourse in Little Rock and elsewhere attributed persistent racial inequality to problems within the black community generated by a purported "culture of poverty." The Supreme Court affirmed arguments that discrepancies in student achievement could be attributed to "external factors" rather than administrative procedures and educational practices.[74] The Little Rock school district sought a declaration of unitary status, and an end to court-ordered desegregation in the city, on precisely these grounds in the 1990s.

In doing so, school officials explicitly relied on the logic of *Missouri v. Jenkins*, which held that school districts could only be held responsible for their efforts to implement the provisions outlined in their desegregation agreements, not their efficacy.[75] In Little Rock, this decision had a substantial impact on the way school officials viewed their obligations under the 1989 desegregation settlement. In preparation for compliance hearings, the Little Rock school district identified and assessed 2,097 desegregation obligations outlined in the 1989 settlement agreement. In July 1995, Dr. Ross Mayo, associate superintendent with oversight of desegregation, initially reported that the district had "completely complied" with 42 percent of its commitments; an additional 51 percent were "ongoing" efforts, such as efforts to maintain racial balance in non-incentive schools, and the remaining 7 percent had been added to the "district's list of things to do." But by the following April, Mayo's estimate had almost inexplicably climbed to 70 percent compliance. To reach this more optimistic statistic, Mayo had changed his measure from "complete compliance" to "substantial compliance." "We substantially comply when we implement a provision as required by the plan, but that doesn't always mean we get the results we want," Mayo explained. A mere month later, Little Rock's first African American superintendent, Henry Williams, stood in front of Central High School and enthusiastically proclaimed that the district had complied with 96.3 percent of its desegregation obligations. Williams asserted that the district had amassed "irrefutable evidence" that the district had "done all that we can do." In his view, the presence of racially isolated incentive schools and the widening achievement gap should not preclude the Little Rock school district from operating under local control. School board president Linda Pondexter was openly skeptical about the administration's claims. "This is nothing short of a miracle," she observed. "Six months ago we were told that we had an unworkable desegregation plan. Today, we have 96% compliance. I believe in Biblical miracles, but let's get real." In the district's defense, Mayo explained that reading the settlement agreement was "analogous to reading the Bible ... Your interpretation depends on your denomination."[76]

School district attorney Chris Heller told reporters that the motion he planned to file in court would demonstrate that the city's schools were more desegregated than others that had been released from court oversight. "It looked like the districts were failing to achieve certain goals, when, in reality, the problem was that unrealistic goals were set in the first place," he stated. "We believed when we developed the plans that certain things could be done. But no one in the country has been able to achieve them."[77] For district officials who advanced this perspective, ongoing inequities in the city's school system were not the product of local decisions, administrative actions, or educational policies. Rather, they were so widespread that Little Rock and other communities could be absolved of any legal responsibility to address them. Skip Rutherford, media liaison for the fortieth anniversary commission, deflected criticism of persistent inequities in the school district by noting, "Little Rock's disparity gap is America's disparity gap, no different than you find in Dallas, Detroit or Chicago."[78]

During the settlement plan hearings, the Little Rock school district's case was bolstered by the expert testimony of Dr. Herbert Walberg, an educational psychologist from the University of Chicago. Walberg testified that black student achievement was strongly correlated to the socioeconomic status of a student's parents rather than the degree of integration present in a school. While he acknowledged some benefits to having students from different socioeconomic backgrounds attending school together, Walberg also cautioned that disadvantaged students could become easily "frustrated" in such environments. Moreover, he suggested that educational institutions could only have a limited impact on reducing academic disparities, since students spent just 10 percent of the time between birth and age eighteen in school. Only "extraordinary measures" such as strong teaching methods, a longer school year and day, a high-quality curriculum, and homework could narrow the achievement gap. When asked if he knew of any school district that had successfully reduced the achievement gap, Walberg claimed that he knew of none. In short, Walberg suggested that if school districts had no hope of ameliorating the "external factors" that impinged on black student achievement, they should not be obligated to do so.[79]

In the area of student assignment, Dr. David J. Armor, a research professor at George Mason University, testified that it was "counterproductive" to try to establish racial balance in majority-minority school districts. As a proponent of voluntary desegregation programs, Armor spoke favorably of magnet schools and neighborhood schools with compensatory education programs, like those established in Little Rock. However, he suggested that it was unreasonable to apply racial balance standards to the district's remaining traditional elementary and secondary schools. To ensure that individual schools mirrored the racial diversity of the community with a variation no larger than 20 percent, it was necessary to mandate student assignment, a technique Armor insisted led to white flight. Moreover, Armor suggested that such a policy had virtually no benefits and that mandatory integration had no impact on black student achievement. Armor claimed that Little Rock's goals were more "stringent" than the norm—these "unrealistic and unobtainable" benchmarks made it difficult for the school district to comply with the plan's standards. Armor reported that other school districts had been released from court supervision without meeting racial balance requirements after they were exempted from compliance due to "extenuating circumstances."[80]

However, the third school desegregation expert to testify in the case, Dr. Gary Orfield of Harvard University, provided a different perspective on Little Rock's persistent problems. He characterized Walberg and Armor as "resegregationists" and countered their claims that integration had a limited impact on student achievement, noting that the test scores of black students had improved across the nation in the previous generation. He also rejected their arguments that educational programs in Little Rock could not continue to build and improve upon this success. As the *Arkansas Democrat-Gazette* summarized his testimony: "Students learn in school . . . otherwise there would be no use for education." Orfield urged the school district to eliminate programs that did not produce results through an ongoing evaluative process. He also encouraged the Office of Desegregation Monitoring to measure student achievement instead of focusing on the mere implementation of promised programs.[81]

Despite Orfield's appeal to the district to recommit itself to the principle of integration and educational excellence for all students, school officials continued to insist that the remaining inequities in the system could not be resolved through administrative policy. Superintendent Henry Williams asserted that Walberg and Armor's testimony substantiated his belief that the district was more desegregated than other school systems that had already been released from court supervision.[82] Their claims were also widely supported by influential opinion makers in the city at large. A UALR task force report entitled *Plain Talk: The Future of Little Rock's Public Schools* asserted that the major cause of "resegregation" and white flight from the district was not persistent racial prejudice but unpopular federal court orders. If achievement gaps persisted, the task force concluded, it was because the specificity of the school desegregation settlement constrained administrators and educators by not allowing them to dismantle ineffective programs and try alternatives. Moreover, the report asserted that the school district provided equal educational opportunity to all children. Consequently, the test score gap could not be attributed to differences in instruction, facilities, budgets, or curricula, but instead was the product of collective decisions made by "parents and students" and discrepancies in "motivation and learning," presumably among students of color.[83]

Robert McCord, senior editor and columnist at the *Arkansas Gazette*, also insisted that the school district had taken affirmative action and had made measurable progress toward eliminating discrimination. Remaining inequities and persistent disparities between black and white students in the district were the product of social problems beyond the reach of school administrators, like "poverty, crime, segregated neighborhoods, unemployment, [and] shortages of minority teachers."[84] While McCord attributed the low test scores of black students to broader environmental and cultural conditions, the rhetoric of other opinion makers was explicitly racialized. In 1995, John R. Starr, the managing editor of the *Arkansas Democrat-Gazette*, urged his readers to consider "the possibility that the gap in performance is not the fault of the schools" and could not be closed there. Black and white students in the city were being offered the same educational opportunities. Consequently, he argued, the "real reasons" for achievement disparities were "either hereditary or environmental." Starr acknowledged that some observers claimed that poverty put black students at a disadvantage, but he dismissed these arguments as "convenient excuse[s]" that had not been accepted when he was in school. This left readers to consider hereditary deficits. In this regard, Starr suggested that it would be "futile" to advance an argument that black students were genetically inferior to their white counterparts, not because it was incorrect but because anyone who dared to do so would be "trashed" and people in positions of power refused to "consider that possibility."[85]

During the fortieth anniversary commemorative ceremony that unfolded on the steps of Central High School in September 1997, this public debate animated the addresses delivered by the three keynote speakers: President Bill Clinton, a Democrat; Governor Mike Huckabee, a Republican; and Ernest Green. All three acknowledged the 1957–59 Little Rock school desegregation crisis as an important milestone in the struggle for African American civil rights and publicly recognized the city's progress, but offered divergent perspectives on American race relations, structural inequity, and the role of government and public policy in addressing the movement's unfinished business.[86]

President Clinton embraced the anniversary as an opportunity to launch his "Initiative on Race" with the stated purpose of sparking a national conversation about race relations. As he spoke to the large crowd gathered in front of Central High School, the president recalled that watching the events in Little Rock unfold as a young man fifty miles away had forced him and his white peers to ask themselves, "Where did we stand? What did we believe? How did we want to live?" As Clinton addressed his audience, it was clear he hoped to use the anniversary to pose these questions once again. Forty years after the desegregation crisis at Central High, Clinton emphasized, "There is still discrimination in America." Access to academic excellence and education was still not equal. In 1997, children at Central and schools across the nation were tracked into different academic programs. "Children of every race walk through the same door but often walk down different halls . . . They sit in different classes," Clinton said. The president pointed to the self-segregation that marked students' social lives and the "enclaves of ethnic isolation" that marked American life more generally. Throughout the nation, Clinton asserted, "segregation is no longer the law, but too often separation is the rule." The stubborn persistence of these trends had prompted many Americans to abandon the pursuit of integration, but the eruption of civil wars and genocide around the globe illustrated that Americans turned away from the vision of a *United States of America* at their peril. "The alternative to integration is not isolation or a new separate but equal," Clinton warned. "It is disintegration."

Clinton insisted that the crisis in the fall of 1957 had illustrated that the federal government must act to protect the constitutional rights of its citizens. The nation needed strong civil rights laws upheld by the courts and enforced by the executive. All Americans should embrace "the *vision* of a color blind society," the president said, "but recognize that we are not there yet and we cannot slam shut the doors of educational and economic opportunity." In direct contrast to the rhetoric surrounding achievement gaps in Little Rock, Clinton urged communities to set high academic standards for all school children so that they would not replace "the tyranny of segregation with the tragedy of low expectations." Clinton's Presidential Initiative on Race was primarily an appeal for "a candid conversation" on the state of race relations, in hope of creating a national dialogue that would inspire citizens and public figures to take action. Ultimately, however, the White House offered no concrete policy initiatives designed to address the problems the president highlighted in his address. To many, it seemed like an anemic response to organized efforts to unravel civil rights victories won in the 1950s and 1960s.[87]

In contrast to Clinton's gestures toward government action and federal enforcement, Governor Huckabee contended that systemic inequality had been effectively eliminated from American institutions. In her analysis of racial discourse in the 1990s, the media studies scholar Jennifer Fuller noted that "proponents of racial reconciliation" frequently described the state of American race relations from this perspective. "In this view," she observed, "the era of civil rights legislation was past; at best, changing racial attitudes was beyond the scope of the law, and at worst, such policies violated individual rights."[88] In his commemorative address, Huckabee suggested that there was no further role for government in the arena of race relations—the work that remained was moral and personal, and could not be addressed through structural or institutional changes. "Let me remind us," Huckabee cautioned: "government can do some things but only God can change people's hearts." Government could put children in the same classrooms, "but government can't make classmates go home and be friends when school is out."

Huckabee obliquely acknowledged the controversy surrounding the public ceremony and the remaining inequities in the Little Rock school district, but he tried to turn public objections to his own advantage. To those who said that the event was little more than a public relations ploy designed to burnish the image of local politicians, Huckabee suggested that he and Mayor Jim Dailey had been aware that people might view the event that way from the start. "We had a great anxiety and fear," he said, "that we would end up with little more than simple ceremonies and testimonies of those of us who are politicians coming to congratulate ourselves for all the things we had done." However, Huckabee insisted that none of the political figures sitting on the platform would claim that they were the ones who had "moved this generation." For those who objected to the notion that Little Rock had something to "celebrate," Huckabee noted that the official name of the event had been changed from a celebration to a commemoration.[89] In his view, Little Rock could "celebrate progress" and the "long way" it had traveled in forty years but still acknowledge that the city and the state were "not home yet."

Huckabee contended that the city would have to grapple with the legacy of the school desegregation crisis until Dr. Martin Luther King's dream that "we will judge people by the character of their hearts and not by the color of their skin" lived within each citizen. As the historian Renee C. Romano pointedly noted in her examination of the cultural politics of the 1990s, public figures that promoted this "individualistic model" of change charted racial progress by measuring the "changed hearts and minds of whites" rather than "the economic status of or educational opportunities for blacks." Those who espoused this point of view frequently framed racism as "a psychological problem with a therapeutic solution."[90] Huckabee expressed hope that the new exhibit in the Central High Museum and Visitor Center would be a catalyst for this kind of internal change, and would serve as a call to stand up against overt expressions of racism and violence so that no one could ever ask again, "Why didn't somebody do something?"

In his address before the gathered crowd, however, Ernest Green, the first African American graduate from Central High School, challenged Huckabee's framing of the relationship between past and present. The lesson to be drawn from the events of 1957 was not, as Huckabee had suggested, that people did not speak out and act against racial injustice in the past, but that the Little Rock Nine, their parents, and supportive members of the black community did. As the courts reconsidered Little Rock's desegregation plan in the months leading up to the fortieth anniversary, school administrators and various experts had testified that there was nothing that could be done about disparities in black and white student achievement and persistent patterns of residential segregation. Green acknowledged that the current "general consensus" among many scholars and social scientists was that the "chasm that exists between the races . . . is so great in length, breadth, and scope that no one can offer real or viable solutions to bridge that gap, at least not any time soon." Green, however, rejected this perspective, boldly stating, "I believe they are unequivocally wrong." Drawing a parallel between past and present, he noted that his parents and his peers had rejected the claims of "recognized experts" forty years earlier who claimed that the structure of American society could not be changed. "They were wrong," Green said, implying that those who made similar claims in 1997 were mistaken as well. "What we needed was the same thing to which all young people are entitled," he asserted, "a community that wanted to see us blossom not bleed, a society that encouraged us to reach for our dreams and recognized us as whole persons." He pointed to the importance of individual action and personal responsibility, but he also urged his audience to address the structural inequities and injustices that continued to mark American society.

For Green, the fortieth anniversary was not an opportunity to talk about talking about race, or to await changes in people's hearts and minds, but an opportunity to recruit the next generation of social activists. "Power concedes nothing without a struggle," Green reminded his audience. His own journey toward justice had been painful but rewarding. He hoped the lesson the young people in the audience would learn from his story was "the belief that he or she can open a door, succeed against the odds, dream the impossible dream, turn no into a yes, or navigate uncharted waters." The anniversary was an occasion to turn the Little Rock Nine into "Little Rock ten, ten-hundred, ten-thousand, ten-million" as Little Rock and the nation at large confronted the challenges of the present. Public prognosticators who claimed that nothing further could be done to address the systemic inequality that continued to shape American institutions obscured, perpetuated, and naturalized racial injustice, just as claims about an immutable and unchangeable "southern way of life" had forty years earlier.

Despite Green's poignant appeal, the fortieth anniversary commemorative ceremony was not designed to inspire the next generation of challenges to educational inequity. In Little Rock, as school district officials prepared their petition for unitary status, the ceremony and publicity surrounding the fortieth anniversary celebration was designed to historicize the events of 1957–59 and underscore the city's racial progress. The triumphant narrative that undergirded the commemoration implicitly suggested that the city had redressed racial discrimination as much as possible, connecting this "good faith" effort to the passage of time. At the conclusion of the ceremony, as

FIGURE 10. President Bill Clinton, Governor Mike Huckabee, and Mayor Jim Dailey usher the Little Rock Nine through the doors of Central High at the conclusion of the fortieth anniversary commemorative ceremony. Mike Huckabee had envisioned this historic moment months earlier during his State of the State address. (Getty Images)

Governor Huckabee envisioned, the Little Rock Nine mounted the steps of Central High School and were ushered inside the school by both President Clinton and the governor himself. As the audience stood and provided a standing ovation, a voice intoned, "Ladies and Gentleman, history is again made at Central High School." This was the symbolic image that civic leaders and others who had shaped the commemorative ceremony hoped would speak louder than public criticism of the city's schools. The occasion was "historic" in its own right.

This triumphal symbolism undergirded the Little Rock school district's presentation of a Revised Desegregation and Education Plan the very next day in federal court. The district's motion seeking release from court oversight had not been received hospitably by District Judge Susan Webber Wright. Instead, she had urged the parties involved to renegotiate the terms of their agreement. The district's new plan proposed a reduction of busing, a return to neighborhood schools, and the elimination of satellite zones that facilitated the integration of students from noncontiguous residential areas. Ironically, the only school that would retain a satellite zone was

Central High. In order to maintain the school's celebrated integration and withstand the recurrent scrutiny of the media, white students from western Little Rock would continue to be bused into the predominantly African American neighborhood surrounding the city's flagship institution. In the rest of the district, integration would be maintained entirely through voluntary mechanisms like transfer requests and enrollment in magnet and interdistrict schools. School officials continued to hope that a turn away from mandatory measures and the abandonment of efforts to maintain racially balanced schools would reduce white flight. District officials argued that their proposal turned the "focus back to education" and was rooted in the premise that "excellent education programs" rather than integrated student bodies provided "the best (if not only) opportunity for meaningful long-term desegregation." In exchange for the relaxation of racial balance requirements, school officials promised to improve minority student achievement, equalize educational opportunities, and reduce racial disparities in discipline.[91] However, the district's programs aimed at achieving those goals in the incentive schools had proven ineffective to date.

In presenting this plan, school officials suggested that the use of satellite zones had a negligible impact on school desegregation, but when the district implemented the proposal, it quickly became clear that their abolishment had a significant effect. Before the satellite zones (and the busing associated with them) were eliminated, only four of the district's schools had enrollments that were more than 90 percent African American. With the return to neighborhood student assignments, nine of the district's schools had enrollments that were predominantly black, and an additional four elementary schools had enrollments that were predominantly white.[92] The district continued to maintain voluntary desegregation mechanisms, including magnet schools, incentive or specialty schools, and student transfer programs. Nevertheless, despite these provisions, almost 70 percent of the city's middle and elementary schools fell outside the 40/60 ratio the district had formerly used to determine if a school was "truly desegregated."

District officials maintained that the return of racially identifiable schools did not signify the return of "inherently unequal" schools because they were committed to distributing resources equally to every campus regardless of its racial composition. But the *Brown* decision had maintained that segregated schools were inherently unequal, regardless of whether facilities or other tangible factors were equalized because of the stigma associated with racial isolation. And certainly the district's own statements suggested that they had adopted the revised plan in order to appease white parents who did not want to send their children to predominantly black schools. This suggested that the district implicitly recognized that, at least for these white parents, there was a stigma associated with predominantly black and increasingly isolated institutions.[93]

Despite President Clinton's warning that there was no "new separate but equal," and that abandonment of the integration ideal would only lead to national "disintegration," district officials accepted the "general consensus" rejected by Ernest Green and insisted that many of the district's persistent problems could not be resolved through school policy. Rather, they attributed racial inequity in the district to poverty, low motivation, crime, unemployment, and the racial isolation of black communities. School officials pointed to the same national trends Skip Rutherford's public relations team had used to deflect criticism of Little Rock's schools. "Little Rock's disparity gap is America's disparity gap," they reasoned. Persistent residential segregation, white flight, and other factors that undermined stable racial balance in the school system were beyond their control or the control of other government officials. Like Governor Huckabee, they argued that local government had done everything it could to address segregation and discrimination in education. Further progress in the field of race relations would depend on individual changes of heart. The majority of Little Rock's residents, like the majority of white students at Central High School forty years earlier, maintained a position of "peaceful neutrality" in relation to the school district's proposed plans. They too stood in silent witness as the city presented a "desegregation" plan designed to accommodate persistent resistance to school integration and appease white parents.

For some observers, the position of the Little Rock school district suggested that the city had been more interested in talking about talking about race, and racial progress, than actually working toward it. From this perspective, the school system's effort to escape court oversight confirmed the charges of the NAACP that the fortieth anniversary had been little more than a public relations venture designed to escape the past rather than learn from it. Like Birmingham's Mayor David Vann, Little Rock seemed convinced that "the best way to put your bad images to rest is to declare them history and put them in a museum."

— CHAPTER FIVE —
Resisting Historical Erasure

ittle Rock Central High School was recognized as a national historic site in 1998. Formally established through an act of Congress, the site's purpose was defined in the context of Little Rock's role as a "catalyst" in the effort to integrate public schools throughout the United States.[1] Over the next decade, the National Park Service developed a new visitor center designed to replace the facility created by Central High Museum, Inc. At the dedication of the new building in 2007, Elizabeth Eckford spoke to an audience of hundreds gathered for the occasion and a block of empty seats reserved for white members of the Class of 1958 who boycotted the event. "I started walking through the painful past in the late 1990s when I began to hear things that were totally outside my experience," she explained. "Today I talk to students extemporaneously and I try to be accurate, because I've read the books written by the historians *of late,* I read the biographies *of late,* I read all kinds of tales." In her view, the history of the crisis had become a kind of "mask ritually colored . . . a fraud agreed upon." Efforts to commemorate the events of the 1957–58 school year placed recurrent emphasis on racial reconciliation, but Eckford insisted that this rhetoric was hollow without a direct acknowledgment of her reality. "I know the difference between an apology and someone who's just trying to make themselves feel good," she asserted. *"If you can't name what you did, it's not an apology.* We can never have true reconciliation until we honestly acknowledge our painful but shared past."[2]

For Eckford, Little Rock's public history functioned as a "great dust heap"—a "terrible mill in which sawdust rejoins sawdust." Certainly, the triumphal narrative of passive progress that has shaped the public memory of the Little Rock school desegregation crisis sought to minimize the impact of past discrimination, to contain the expansive goals of mid-century civil rights advocates, and to obscure the historic actors and mechanisms that made meaningful systemic change possible. The effects of this narrative are not only felt in memorial spaces, but resonate in contemporary life as well. The delusion that racial discrimination has been eliminated from American life naturalizes persistent inequities and actually fosters cultural racism as a tool for explaining or justifying them. The rising ascendance of "colorblind" racial ideology has been actively deployed to rollback federal enforcement and court oversight of school desegregation despite persistent inequity and racial isolation in the nation's educational institutions.

However, in her remarks before the assembled guests at the dedication of the Little Rock Central High School National Historic Site Visitor Center, Eckford also noted that history could function as a "voice sounding forever across the centuries the laws of right and wrong," and acknowledged that historical actors like herself carried important memories that enabled them to act as "witness to the times."[3] Indeed, in recent years, Eckford and other members of the Little Rock Nine have collectively sought to make a number of interventions in the public memory of the Little Rock school desegregation crisis, challenging key tenets of the triumphal narrative of passive progress and reanimating counter-narratives that frame their legacy as a call to action in the present. In Little Rock and elsewhere, civil rights activists have persistently called for systematic and sweeping change, drawn meaningful historical parallels between past and present, and chronicled the unbroken chain of organizing and activism that has animated efforts to address racial inequity in American education. This sustained effort should remind us that collective memory is contested and is shaped not only by cultural elites and political leaders but also by activists, intellectuals, and other concerned citizens.[4] As the French historian Pierre Nora has argued, while public memory is "vulnerable to manipulation and appropriation," it also remains in "permanent evolution," and public memories that have been marginalized are perpetually "revived."[5] In this spirit, the Little Rock Nine have challenged the way the Little Rock school desegregation crisis has been

FIGURE 11. The Little Rock Nine have engaged directly with the public memory of the 1957 school desegregation crisis, challenging Arkansas and the nation to confront its history. The power of their personal testimony is symbolically evoked in the Testament monument, in which bronze statues representing the Little Rock Nine stand on the lawn of the Arkansas State Capitol, visible from the same governor's office once occupied by Orval Faubus. (Raymond K. Cunningham, Jr.)

framed through memoirs, films, and countless speaking engagements. In doing so, they have resisted the processes of historical erasure that support "Won Cause" mythology and have worked toward preserving a "memory for the future" designed to build and sustain a more equitable society.

The contest over the public memory of the school desegregation crisis has deeper implications and broader social effects. The reification of the triumphal narrative of progress into Supreme Court jurisprudence at the turn of the twenty-first century demonstrates that our public histories matter. The logic undergirding the Court's recent school desegregation decisions has been rooted in an effort to define racial discrimination as narrowly as possible, minimizing its effects in the past and its persistence in the present. In this context, contemporary racial inequality has not been attributed to systemic racism or institutionalized white privilege, but rather to "natural" preferences or cultural deficiencies within black communities. Moreover, the triumphal narrative of progress has enabled a "rearticulation" of the functional *meaning* of racial equality. With the purported elimination of systems of privilege, discrimination has been redefined as a practice that impacts individuals rather than social groups. As a result, white litigants opposing race-conscious remedies have appropriated the legacy of the civil rights movement for themselves in an effort to advance their own claims of "reverse discrimination." In this context, historical arguments first advanced in the field of public memory through memoirs, retrospective media accounts, documentary and feature films, museums, and commemorative ceremonies have been transformed into legal "findings of fact," and the "burden of proof" required to challenge their dominance has shifted back onto the shoulders of civil rights organizations and their clients.

In his analysis of colorblind racial ideology, the sociologist Eduardo Bonilla-Silva argues that this effort to historicize racism and place it in the past functions as a foundational myth in American discourse. "This myth," Bonilla-Silva contends, "is the central column supporting the house of color blindness." It functions both to "deny the enduring effects of historic discrimination as well as to deny the significance of contemporary discrimination."[6] In the late 1950s and early 1960s, the architects of passive resistance maintained that minimal compliance, gradualism, and tokenism fulfilled the mandate of the *Brown v. Board of Education* decision. For many of these actors, distancing themselves from the forces of massive resistance and overt expressions of racism enabled them to justify the perpetuation of white privilege through pupil placement provisions and freedom-of-choice plans. Five decades later, their colorblind successors have capitalized on this strategy, distancing themselves from the racial demagogues of the 1950s and 1960s by historicizing the mid-century civil rights movement and celebrating its victories as a means of redirecting attention away from enduring structural inequities. Moreover, in contrast to the efforts of civil rights activists to foster an inspirational public memory focused on the impact of collective action, their opponents in courts of law sought to contain the movement's reach by attributing change to the passage of time itself and advancing their own race-neutral policies as a models for pragmatic rather than "extremist" change.

These arguments have been deployed to undermine race-conscious desegregation remedies as relics of a distant past that no longer have relevance in contemporary society. For example, in *Board of Education of Oklahoma City v. Dowell* (1991), the Supreme Court held that school boards were entitled to be released from court supervision if they had "complied in good faith" with their desegregation degree, and if they had eliminated "vestiges of past discrimination . . . *to the extent practicable.*"[7] A year later, the Court held in *Freeman v. Pitts* (1992) that districts could be released from their desegregation responsibilities "in incremental stages," provided that the relaxation of judicial supervision would not undermine a desegregation decree as a whole. In particular, *Freeman v. Pitts* established that district courts could relinquish control over student assignment in communities where school boards could demonstrate that racial imbalances and racially identifiable schools were not "traceable" to previous constitutional violations. Although school boards bore the burden of proof in this regard, the high court indicated that the bar would not be set very high. The court stated that "vestiges of segregation that concern the law in a school case may be subtle and intangible, but they must be so real that they have a *causal link* to the de jure violation being remedied." The court noted that a school board's case was strengthened by the *passage of time* and the intervention of demographic changes, which made it "less likely that a current racial imbalance in a school district is a vestige of the prior *de jure* system." Moreover, the causal link between past violations and current conditions was "even more attenuated" if the district could demonstrate that it had complied with its desegregation decree "in good faith."[8] When a school district is released from court oversight, it is declared "unitary"—this legal status indicates that the school system in question has eliminated the historical residue of the discrimination and segregation that were the hallmarks of the Jim Crow era.

The Court's decisions in the early 1990s led to a surge of unitary status petitions in communities like Little Rock that operated under court orders. However, as the school desegregation analyst Gary Orfield has noted, the assumptions undergirding the Court's decisions were grounded in the rhetoric of the triumphal narrative of progress rather than the reality of race relations in the United States. "If the problems of racial polarization and inequality that grew from a history of pervasive discrimination had been solved," Orfield noted, "one might expect that desegregated schools would continue without court orders or race-conscious plans by local school districts." However, more than twenty years of data have demonstrated that as schools were released from court oversight, racial isolation increased throughout the nation but particularly in the South, which had been the most desegregated region in the country for nearly three decades. Moreover, as desegregation and anti-poverty programs were replaced by educational policies that place an emphasis on testing and accountability, predicted improvements in student performance have not materialized. Rather, in the "post-civil rights era," racial achievement gaps between white students and students of color remain unaddressed.[9]

Even in the wake of this trend toward resegregation, celebratory narratives have proven to be remarkably resilient. Persistent school segregation and residential racial isolation are not attributed to systemic and institutionalized racism. Instead, they are ascribed to the vicissitudes of the real estate market, individual "preference," and the exercise of free "choice." The naturalization of persistent racial segregation, Bonilla-Silva argues, is rooted in the claim that the preference to "gravitate toward likeness" is "almost biologically driven and typical of all groups in a society." As he notes, "This claim requires ignoring the multiple institutional and state-sponsored practices behind segregation and being unconcerned about these practices' negative consequences for minorities."[10] In addition to denying the reality of contemporary racial discrimination, this rationale also obscures its historical roots, disregarding the long history of discriminatory federal mortgage guidelines, selective urban renewal programs, inequitable student assignment policies, and their reverberations in the present.

This naturalization of contemporary racial inequity has also been written into Supreme Court jurisprudence. In *Board of Education of Oklahoma City v. Dowell* (1991), the Court determined that after a district had been released and declared unitary, school boards regained authority over local school decisions and were not obligated to maintain patterns of student assignment or other measures that had previously been required by the courts. Moving forward, it was presumed that a school board's actions, such as a decision to return to racially isolated neighborhood schools, were racially innocent. Plaintiffs would bear the burden of demonstrating that any resulting resegregation was motivated by an intent to discriminate instead of other demographic or educational factors.[11] In this regard, a declaration of unitary status imposed a kind of willed historic amnesia on desegregation litigation in the school district in question. Looking to the future, courts would not consider the history of systemic discrimination in a community or its effects. Since a declaration of unitary status was formal determination that the vestiges of de jure discrimination had been eliminated, courts would proceed as if they had never happened.

The triumphal narrative of passive progress and the colorblind racial discourse used to support it are advanced as nonracist. However, their deployment in the public sphere may actually reinforce racist thinking in the United States. "If we say that race is of declining significance," the anti-racism educator Tim Wise has observed, "but at the end of the day serious inequities persist (given the race-specific injuries colorblind universalism cannot address) it will become almost *rational* to adopt racist views to explain those gaps."[12] Likewise, in their seminal text *Racial Formation in the United States,* the sociologists Michael Omi and Howard Winant contended that the triumphal narrative of passive progress "requires either that one deny the ubiquitous evidence of everyday life—its continuing segregation, its racially assigned poverty and privilege, its bigotry, fear, and nihilism—or that one engage in wholesale victim-blaming, a procedure that merely updates the racial prejudices of days gone by."[13] The prevalence of "culture of poverty" arguments in Little Rock and elsewhere to explain racial disparities in academic tracking, discipline, graduation rates, and student achievement suggests that this is not an either/or proposition. Indeed, efforts to displace the consequences of systemic inequity onto the purported "deficiencies" in black communities and their failure to transmit "values" that support academic success is a reflection of the resurgence of cultural racism *and* the widespread denial of the persistence of racial discrimination.[14]

Recent Supreme Court jurisprudence has also been shaped by this mythology. In *Missouri v. Jenkins* (1995), the Supreme Court held that states and school districts could be released from their obligation to provide remedial education programs (like those in place in Little Rock's incentive schools) even if students made no appreciable gains in achievement. The Court held that measurable improvement in test scores and minority achievement was not the "appropriate test" in determining whether the state had fulfilled its obligations. In *Freeman,* the Court had suggested that demographic factors independent of de jure segregation could affect the racial composition of schools. In *Missouri,* the Court held that "numerous external factors" that were beyond the control of school districts or state authorities could affect minority student achievement. Consequently, courts could not hold school districts and state authorities responsible for such deficits indefinitely. Rather, remedial programs should be tailored to address specific deficits attributable to de jure segregation to the "extent practicable." On remand, the majority's opinion noted that remedial education programs had been in place in Kansas City for seven years, suggesting that the appropriate test in such cases was the implementation of programs for a relatively brief period of time, after which remaining deficits could no longer be considered the "vestiges" of four centuries of discrimination.[15]

The triumph of this perspective in the federal courts is not an accident. The architects of passive resistance and their colorblind successors have actively cultivated and deployed this narrative of racial progress to derail or reshape the hard-won victories of the civil rights era and the legislative initiatives of the Great Society. Claiming the legacy of the movement for themselves, colorblind litigants have defined its singular objective as "the elimination of racial classification and the establishment of formal equality before the law." This rhetoric has been used to dismantle majority-minority voting districts, affirmative action, two-way busing, and the court-ordered integration of schools. According to colorblind litigants, these "race conscious" policies betrayed the movement, subverted self-reliance among African Americans, and created special group privileges, making some people "more equal" than others.[16] "Won Cause" mythology is deployed in support of these claims. If persistent inequities are the product of individual action rather than enduring structural inequality, then issues like racial discrimination must be addressed at the individual level. As Omi and Winant observed, this denial of the broader racial social order has effectively redefined the meaning of racial discrimination to "the curtailment of individual rights." Significantly, this was "a distinction that could apply to whites and non-whites alike."[17]

This rearticulation of the meaning of racial inequality laid the essential groundwork for claims of "reverse discrimination" in federal courts of law and has reshaped the landscape of school desegregation litigation. In December of 2006, the Supreme Court considered cases from Louisville and Seattle that involved student assignment plans that took race into some consideration along with other factors when assigning students to schools in order to maintain diversity. The white plaintiffs in these cases argued that any voluntary consideration of race in student assignment that had not been mandated by the courts in order to remedy de jure segregation was unconstitutional. Regardless of the intent of school districts, such plans violated the individual rights of white students under the equal protection clause of the Fourteenth Amendment. In districts that had never been found guilty of de jure violations or had been declared unitary, only a "colorblind" student assignment policy that ignored race altogether was appropriate.[18]

The Louisville school district involved in the case had been under court orders to desegregate its schools for twenty-five years and had pursued many of the same policies as its counterpart in Little Rock.[19] Initially, the city had adopted geographic attendance zones and a freedom-of-choice plan, but these limited efforts did not effectively dismantle the dual system of schools. During the course of litigation, the Louisville school system was consolidated within the predominantly white Jefferson County school district, and was ordered to adopt an extensive busing program that enabled it to maintain racial balance. By the late 1980s and early 1990s, the district sought to reduce the disruption produced by this plan and to curb white flight. A plan titled "Project Renaissance" weakened the district's racial balance guidelines, redrew school assignment areas to reintroduce geographic attendance zones, permitted majority-to-minority student transfers at the elementary level, created magnet middle schools, and encouraged "open" high school enrollment that introduced school choice within broad racial guidelines. These adjustments were similar to those made in Little Rock during the same time period, and had the effect of reducing the significance of a student's race in school assignment. In 1999, several parents brought a lawsuit petitioning for the dissolution of the desegregation order. The Louisville school board opposed dissolution, arguing that the system still suffered from "demographic imbalance" that was the product of de jure segregation. However, the federal court ruled in the parents' favor, taking the school board's argument as "overwhelming evidence" that the district had fulfilled the "underlying purposes" of the desegregation decree—it was clear the Louisville school board had "treated the ideal of an integrated system as much more than a legal obligation—they consider it a positive, desirable policy and an essential element of any well-rounded public school education." The court seemed to express confidence that the board would maintain this commitment and granted the district unitary status. After attaining unitary status, the school district retained its student assignment policies in order to ensure that its schools would not revert to their formally segregated state. However, a few years later, the school district found itself standing before the Supreme Court trying to preserve the remnants of a system that had once been mandated by law.

These cases produced a split decision under the title *Parents Involved v. Seattle* (2007). The Court reviewed the Louisville and Seattle plans under the "strict scrutiny" test to determine whether the use of individual racial classifications was "narrowly tailored" to meet a "compelling" government interest. A plurality of the court—including Chief Justice John Roberts, and Justices Antonin Scalia, Clarence Thomas, and Samuel Alito—argued that consideration of race in student assignment, regardless of the intent of the school board, was unconstitutional and precluded by Supreme Court precedent, including *Brown v. Board of Education*. In *Parents Involved*, the Supreme Court held that unitary school districts cannot consider a student's race in determining school assignments or distributing resources. A school district, like Little Rock, that was required to bus white and black students to different schools in order to maintain some semblance of racial desegregation while under federal court oversight, is prohibited to do so once declared unitary.[20]

The plurality held that the true intention of *Brown I* was to eliminate the consideration of race in student assignment. Regardless of the intent of the school district—segregation or integration—any program that makes race a determining factor in a student's assignment fails to pass constitutional muster. The Court determined that the racial classifications used to assign students to schools and retain diversity were "inherently suspect," because the use of such classifications "demeans the dignity and worth of a person" and promotes "notions of racial inferiority and leads to a politics of racial hostility." Citing the implementation order in *Brown II* and the NAACP's oral arguments in the case, the plurality contended that the intent of the *Brown* decision was to "achieve a system of determining admission to the schools *on a nonracial basis*." They concluded, "Before *Brown*, schoolchildren were told where they could and could not go to school based on the color of their skin. The school districts in these cases have not carried the heavy burden of demonstrating that we should allow this once again—even for very different reasons." If the districts and other members of the Court were concerned about racial discrimination, they argued, "the way to stop discrimination on the basis of race is to stop discriminating on the basis of race."[21]

This remarkably limited and curiously *ahistorical* reading of the *Brown* decision has had enormous import for school districts and students all over the country. The four Supreme Court justices who dissented from the plurality's opinion emphasized the importance of historical context in weighing the use of race-conscious student assignment. Justice Stephen Breyer argued that the "colorblind" test applied in the case was a "cruel distortion of history," and that the plurality's opinion ignored "the terrible harms of slavery, the resulting caste system, and 80 years of legal racial segregation" that shaped and informed previous Supreme Court decisions related to school desegregation:

> The plurality pays inadequate attention to [fifty years of school desegregation] law, to past opinions' rationales, their language, and the contexts in which they arise. As a result, it reverses course and reaches the wrong conclusion. In doing so, it distorts precedent, it announces legal rules that will obstruct efforts by state and local governments to deal effectively with the growing resegregation of public schools ... and it undermines *Brown's* promise of integrated primary and secondary education that local communities have sought to make a reality. This cannot be justified in the name of the Equal Protection Clause.

Citing precedent, Justice Breyer argued that it was "not surprising" that the Court had previously drawn distinctions between racial classifications used to promote inclusion and those used to enforce exclusion because this practice was "predicated upon a well-established legal view of the Fourteenth Amendment." The amendment sought to bring "into American society as full members those whom the Nation had previously held in slavery" by "forbidding practices that lead to racial exclusion." The plurality's opinion effectively discarded this understanding of the history of systemic racism and dismissed the relevance of institutionalized white privilege. As a result, Justice John Paul Stevens asserted, the Court's decision in *Parents Involved* "rewrites the history" of the *Brown* decision by failing to note that "the history books do not tell stories of white children struggling to attend black schools."[22]

The plurality's opinion in *Parents Involved* drew directly upon the logic of the triumphal narrative of passive progress and the colorblind rhetoric it supports. Yet if the dissenting opinions in the case provide a roadmap for future challenges to the Court's decision, it is clear that reanimating alternative public histories that preserve a record of systemic discrimination in the United States, the long struggle to achieve educational equity, and the uneven processes and practices of school desegregation is essential work. As Leigh Raiford and Renee Romano noted in their introduction to *The Civil Rights Movement and American Memory*, "The struggles over the memory of the civil rights movement are not a diversion from the real political work of fighting for racial equality and equal rights in the United States; they are key sites of that struggle."[23] In the face of recent setbacks in the federal courts, memorial spaces may enable civil rights advocates and their allies to preserve and incubate oppositional histories of the mid-century black freedom struggle as they look toward the challenges of the future.

At the turn of the twenty-first century, Little Rock's schools continued to face substantial challenges related to race. In a city that was majority white, the city schools were predominantly black. The 2000 census revealed that 48 percent of white students in the city attended private schools, placing Arkansas's capital among the top ten cities in the nation with the highest percentage of white children opting out of the public system. The city continued to suffer from residential segregation, and with the end of racial balance guidelines and the use of satellite zones, white students in the district were concentrated in as few as twelve schools. Hall High School, built in order to provide the city's wealthiest families with the means to escape token integration in 1957, was 92 percent African American five decades later. Fifty years after the school desegregation crisis, while 86 percent of white juniors at Central High School passed their proficiency tests, only 28 percent of their African American peers could say the same. Magnet programs, enriched classes, and advanced placement courses were predominantly white, while regular or remedial classes were predominantly black. Brandon Love, student body president in 2006-7, captured the isolation of his experience as one of a few African American students registered in advanced placement classes at Central High in his college admissions essay entitled "A Tale of Two Centrals."[24]

Despite these statistics, in 2001, the school district renewed its petition to be released from court oversight and declared unitary. As the court weighed the merits of the school district's petition, the attorneys for the African American intervenors involved in the longstanding litigation asserted that far from actively addressing racial inequity in the school system, the district's policies actually exacerbated it. When the district courted white families and encouraged them to enroll their children in the public schools, officials, they maintained, "promised a different education for . . . white students." Because white students were a minority in the school district, they were more likely to be admitted to magnet schools and other special programs. Moreover, two-thirds of white students in the district were enrolled in enriched or advanced placement classes. The intervenors argued that guidance counselors did not encourage African American students to take advantage of the same programs, and noted that regular and remedial sections were primarily black: "The district is thus one of substance for white students and staff, especially those who are within the sphere of influence of the economic and political activities of the area, and one of *show* for the Black students and much of its staff." The intervenors argued that the district's policies actively worked against narrowing the achievement gap between black and white students. "The gap starts off wide and gets wider with the active aid of district officials," they noted. "Clearly, the longer the Black students stay in the Little Rock School District, the farther behind they get."[25]

Dr. Terrence Roberts, one of the Little Rock Nine, supported this position in his testimony before the court in the unitary status case. In the late 1990s, Roberts lent his expertise to the Little Rock school district as a desegregation consultant and clinical psychologist. The Revised Desegregation Plan required the district to hire a professional like Roberts, and although he suspected that the district's decision to hire one of the Little Rock Nine was "strictly public relations," Roberts took the position in the hope of generating change from inside the system. After visiting schools throughout the district and speaking with administrators, Roberts concluded that "racist attitudes were widespread" among school personnel. He developed workshops to help district employees cope with difference and understanding their own attitudes toward diversity, but he later reported that many of the 500 to 600 workers who participated in the program "were openly resistant throughout" and that administrators who participated were merely going "through the motions." As the school district petitioned for release from court oversight on the grounds that it had fulfilled its obligations under the Revised Desegregation Plan, Roberts publicly refuted this contention and testified that district officials were not truly committed to redressing racial inequities in the district but rather continued to operate under the "compliance" mentality that had marked the Little Rock school district's approach to school desegregation from the outset. The preoccupation with fulfilling the requirements of the settlement agreement, in lieu of a deeply rooted commitment to addressing problems facing students of color, raised concerns for Roberts about how the district would proceed once it had attained unitary status and was no longer required to actively work toward addressing racial discrimination. Roberts predicted that he would no longer be asked to serve as a consultant in the absence of a court mandate.[26]

As he prepared to testify in the unitary status case, Roberts reflected on the long history of school desegregation litigation in the district. For him, the proceedings carried an undertone of traditional southern justice, where white defendants (in this case plaintiffs) were put on trial and absolved of wrongdoing. Roberts recalled, "As I waited my turn to testify in the district's case, my eyes wandered around the room, and suddenly it hit me: I was staring into the faces of all the past justices of the court. Their portraits were arrayed along the walls, and they all stared back at me in silent monochromatic assent that this was *their* court room, not mine." Roberts concurred with attorney John Walker's assessment that the courts were only willing to go so far as to extend due process to the African American intervenors in the case, not equal protection of the law. He fully expected the Little Rock school district to be found "NOT GUILTY!!!"[27]

After reviewing the briefs, testimony, and evidence in the case, Judge William Wilson granted the Little Rock school district partial unitary status in 2002, releasing it from court supervision in all areas except its obligation to assess and modify programs related to improving African American student achievement. Wilson acknowledged Roberts's testimony, accepting his observations, but rejected his interpretation of the district's "compliance mentality." He wrote, "It is one of the bedrock principles of school desegregation litigation that a school district can only emerge from federal court supervision after it has carefully dotted all the I's and crossed all the T's necessary to establish that it is operating in unitary and constitutional fashion." The compliance mentality Roberts observed, Wilson concluded, was not due to indifference. Rather, it was an "inevitable negative long-running byproduct" of the litigation itself. Removing the district from court supervision would allow teachers and administrators to focus on the education of their students.[28]

When negotiating the terms of the Revised Plan, attorneys for the African American intervenors had accepted the burden of proving that the school district had not fulfilled its obligations successfully. While Wilson acknowledged that this was unusual, he suggested it was appropriate because of the circumstances surrounding this phase of the litigation, noting that the particular case under consideration—*Little Rock v. Pulaski County*—had originally been filed by the district itself after it became alarmed that it would not be able to retain racial balance in its schools due to a shrinking pool of white students. When the case was filed in the 1980s, the Little Rock school district initiated it as a plaintiff in order to pursue the consolidation of all three districts in Pulaski County. "In this case," Wilson wrote, "LRSD has never been adjudicated to be a 'constitutional violator.'" Instead, as a plaintiff, the district had "voluntarily agreed" to commit itself to a Revised Plan, which went well beyond commitments that had been mandated by the Supreme Court. "There can be no question," he wrote, "that LRSD administrators, principals, and teachers took their responsibilities under the Revised Plan seriously and exercised their best efforts to comply with each section of the document." Wilson found that the district had operated in "good faith" and expressed confidence "that LRSD can be trusted, in the future, to operate the Little Rock school system in compliance with the Constitution, without the need for federal court supervision in those areas in which I decide it is unitary."[29]

Wilson's decision drew directly on some of the hallmarks of the triumphal narrative of passive progress. Here, successful desegregation was defined within the boundaries of minimal "compliance" rather than an assessment of the school district's ability and commitment to provide equal access to educational opportunity for all students in the system. Likewise, civil rights litigation and the "negative" byproducts associated with "long-running" court oversight were defined as problems rather than solutions to persistent inequity in the district that distracted educators from the business of educating students. Indeed, the Little Rock school district was even absolved of carrying the label of "constitutional violator" and instead was praised for its moderate position and "voluntary" commitment to addressing racial discrimination.

Within four years, the impact of the district's release from court oversight in student assignment was significant. Given the shifting legal climate, Little Rock school administrators devised a "race-neutral" system of student assignment, in which a student's race could be considered in school placement but would no longer operate as a "key factor." The school district hoped to "retain school choice and student diversity to the extent practical," by including other measures of diversity such as socioeconomic status and standardized test scores.[30] However, enrollment figures indicated that schools in the district became less diverse as a result of these changes. King Magnet Elementary had been 53 percent black in 2003–2004, but was 77 percent black in 2007–8. Likewise, the percentage of black students at Rockefeller Elementary climbed from 58 percent to 82 percent; from 66 percent to 80 percent at Romine Elementary; and from 62 percent to 92 percent at Washington Elementary. At Dunbar Middle School—located in what had once been Little Rock's premiere African American high school—the percentage of black students rose from 58 percent to 73 percent. When these changes became public, Assistant Superintendent Junious Babbs admitted,

"We are not totally taken aback by what's happened." He acknowledged that it was difficult for some district administrators who had worked for years to maintain racial diversity to change the "paradigm" under which they operated. "We've been so entrenched but we're gradually working out of it," he said. As required by the Supreme Court, the district had to embrace a much "broader" definition of diversity.[31]

Civil rights attorneys engaged in the litigation expressed their dismay in the wake of these developments. "Our position is the schools have become resegregated, with the approval of persons in positions of responsibility," John Walker explained. "You cannot have a desegregated school district when black students are treated differently."[32] Dale Charles, president of the Little Rock and Arkansas NAACP, described the changes in the district as "The Second Crisis in Little Rock Public Schools." From Charles's perspective, African American students found themselves in a worse position than their predecessors in 1957. "In 1957 we could rely on the courts for some relief," he said, "but today we cannot depend on the courts to enforce the law." The low test scores of black children in the district refuted claims by the school board and the courts that "everything is fine." He called on voters to elect school board members who would be committed to closing the achievement gap with or without the help of the courts.[33] In 2006, voters in Little Rock elected a majority-black school board for the first time in the city's history, increasing the number of African American representatives on the seven-person board from two to four. Several of the new board members campaigned on issues related to the school desegregation litigation and civil rights attorney John Walker actively supported their election.[34] Robert Daughtery, the board's president, told the *Arkansas Democrat-Gazette* that these electoral victories indicated that the community was "looking for change" and had elected a board capable of opening a dialogue with the city's civil rights community. "In the near future, you'll see the district working more closely with the other stakeholders in the city," he promised.[35]

However, in the first decade of the twenty-first century, it became clear to the reconfigured board that the achievement of unitary status in areas like student assignment did not mean that they could necessarily do the "same, before and after" the system was recognized as desegregated. Before a declaration of unitary status, the Little Rock school district had been required to adopt a variety of racial balance guidelines, transportation strategies, magnet and incentive schools, and student transfer programs. However, after a declaration of unitary status, these very same mechanisms—which were once constitutionally required—became constitutionally suspect precisely because they considered a student's race when making school assignments. Under the weight of the Supreme Court's decisions, unitary status signified more than the return of local control; it also curbed local school boards' ability to utilize race-based strategies designed to maintain diversity.[36] In this context, some members of the Little Rock school board began to question whether pursuing a final declaration of complete (rather than partial) unitary status was a desirable goal. Indeed, all four African American members of the board testified *against* the school district as administrators filed their Final Compliance Report and sought an end to decades of litigation.[37]

Nevertheless, in 2007, the Eastern District Court of Arkansas declared the Little Rock school district unitary, a decision that was affirmed by the Eighth Circuit Court of Appeals in 2009. Although Little Rock, like so many other school districts around the nation, continued to be afflicted by achievement gaps on standardized test scores and "black" and "white" schools in racially identifiable neighborhoods, this decision amounted to a formal finding that those problems could no longer be attributed to the legacy of discrimination in the city. The *Arkansas Democrat-Gazette* embraced the decision, parodying Martin Luther King's "I Have a Dream Speech" and proclaiming, "Free at last, thank God almighty free at last!" With seemingly little regard for the constitutional rights of African American schoolchildren, the paper's editorial board suggested that the "principal function" of the case had been "to support generations of lawyers" rather than an effort to secure equal protection under the law for all of the district's pupils. With the "legal detritus" cleared away, the paper asserted, the district could finally focus on education.[38] In announcing his decision, Judge Wilson placed an emphasis on the return of local control. "LRSD's Board can now operate the district as it sees fit; answerable to no one except LRSD's students and patrons and the voters who elected them to office," he averred. "I want to express my heartfelt best wishes as LRSD begins to operate, as our Founders intended, under the control of the citizens of the City of Little Rock."[39] Yet in the wake of Supreme Court's decisions and the changes they required, unitary status and the return of "local control" meant that Little Rock's majority-black school board would not necessarily be able to retain policies it believed benefitted African American school children.

Indeed, to date, local control has proven to be a chimera. In 2015, shortly after several newly elected board members pledged to address the growing inequality in the city's schools, Little Rock's school board was dissolved in a hostile state takeover. The Arkansas State Board of Education voted to take over the Little Rock school district after six of the district's forty-eight schools failed to demonstrate that 50 percent of their students were proficient in reading and math. Many civil rights advocates noted that the takeover occurred almost immediately after the city elected a majority-black school board for only the second time in Little Rock's history and that other districts with a higher percentage of schools in academic distress were not similarly targeted. Congressman John Walker, the longstanding attorney in the school desegregation litigation, filed a federal lawsuit claiming that the state's actions were racially motivated. Many supporters of public education in the city contended that dissolution of the school board disenfranchised Little Rock's voters and was part of a larger campaign driven by white business elites in Arkansas (most notably the Walton family) to undercut the fiscal stability of the public schools by promoting the rapid expansion of charters. The Little Rock School District Civic Advisory Committee protested the State Board of Education's decision to more than double the number of charter seats in the district after compiling data that revealed that charter schools were disproportionately serving high-income and white students, resulting in higher concentrations of poverty and more racial isolation in the city's traditional schools.[40] While the denouement of this next chapter of Little Rock's school desegregation story has yet to be written, these developments demonstrate that despite a declaration of unitary status, the self-determination of the district's patrons has not materialized. On the cusp of the sixtieth anniversary of the school desegregation crisis, the politics of the Little Rock school district continued to be fraught with racial tension.

Despite the recent pronouncements of the Supreme Court and their application in communities across the country, civil rights advocates like the Little Rock Nine continue to challenge and resist the implications of the triumphal narrative of racial progress. As one of the students who first breached the boundaries of racial segregation in Arkansas's capital, Terrence Roberts urged the nation to "confront the past" and "learn from it," rather than promote and foster a version of history more to its liking. In his memoir *Lessons from Little Rock* (2009), Roberts pointed to a number of indicators that institutional and systemic racism continued to shape life in America, including the disproportionate number of black males housed in prisons, disparities between black and white income, and the racial isolation of the nation's schools. For Roberts, these indicators were a sign that the nation had not radically reshaped society in the wake of the *Brown v. Board of Education* decision or undone a political, legal, and social system based on centuries of discrimination. "We should not be deluded that we have reached some kind of racial equality in our culture," he wrote. "We must not entertain the wishful thinking that racism is a thing of the past."

Roberts observed that those invested in maintaining the status quo had been unremitting in their efforts to undercut *Brown,* and, in Roberts's view, "The 'old' school voices" continued to be "much more strident and demanding than any speakers of the new gospel."[41] Indeed, a careful excavation of the public memory of the Little Rock school desegregation crisis reveals that the "old school voices" have framed their public rhetoric carefully. Rather than deriding or dismissing the accomplishments of the mid-century civil rights struggle, they have endeavored to carefully circumscribe the movement's impact and even redefine the movement's legacy in their own image. Several members of the Little Rock Nine, however, have spoken publicly about their desire to advance a "new gospel" designed to challenge the dominant public memory of the school desegregation crisis.

From the perspective of many of the former students, the triumphal narrative of progress not only prevents a forthright engagement with the city's—and indeed, the nation's—history, but also obscures persistent racial inequity in American society. Moreover, in its relative inattention to the collective action of civil rights organizations and the mechanisms of social change, it also fails to empower citizens to confront social injustice. In this regard, the Little Rock Nine have utilized their own lived historical experience to contest the public representation of the Little Rock school desegregation crisis and to critique its broader implications. They have done so by countering efforts to minimize discrimination and its effects, confronting stereotypes designed to naturalize persistent inequities in the present, and challenging attempts to frame the mid-century civil rights movement as a relic of the distant past.

Over the course of more than half a century, many historical actors and scholars weighed in on the history of the Little Rock school desegregation crisis, but for decades, nine of the most important voices were relatively absent from this public discussion—those of Melba Pattillo Beals, Elizabeth

Eckford, Ernest Green, Gloria Ray Karlmark, Carlotta Walls LaNier, Terrence Roberts, Jefferson Thomas, Minnijean Brown Trickey, and Thelma Mothershed Wair. Even in the midst of the media attention that accompanied the crisis in 1957, the Little Rock Nine were encouraged to maintain a certain level of silence about their experience. NAACP State Conference president Daisy Bates, for example, urged them to minimize their accounts of harassment inside Central High School. As an experienced journalist, she feared that too many negative comments about conditions inside the school might provide segregationists with the ammunition they needed to end integration in Little Rock.[42] Melba Pattillo Beals later recalled in her memoir *Warriors Don't Cry* (1994) that she kept Bates's instructions in mind when speaking with reporters: "Accentuate the positive—don't complain too much."[43] Some members of the Little Rock Nine even withheld information from their own families, not only to spare them the pain of knowing about the daily abuse but also because they feared their parents would not let them return to Central if they were aware of the extent of the harassment.[44]

For some members of the Little Rock Nine and their families, the trauma associated with the school year prevented them from speaking candidly about it with their closest loved ones for decades. Minnijean Brown Trickey never revisited the 1957–58 school year with her mother, and was reluctant to discuss the crisis with her children. "You can't talk about inhumanity to somebody who is sweet and innocent. You don't even want them to know that exists," she explained. "I didn't want to discourage them at a young age, so I didn't tell them."[45] Trickey's daughter, Spirit, later worked at the Little Rock Central High School National Historic Site as a park ranger and recalled that she first learned about her mother's role in the civil rights movement when the family traveled to Little Rock to participate in the NAACP's thirtieth anniversary commemorative activities.[46] Likewise, Carlotta Walls LaNier did not speak directly to her husband about the crisis or her role as a member of the Little Rock Nine for the first decade of their marriage, and never revisited her years at Central High with her mother. She spoke to her children about it when the television docudrama based on Vice Principal Elizabeth Huckaby's *Crisis at Central High* was scheduled to air, but the subject did not come up again for many more years. "The wounds opened in Little Rock," she observed, "are deep, and in some cases, still raw."[47]

Given this reticence to speak about the events of 1957–59 with even the closest family members and friends, many members of the Little Rock Nine declined to make public comments about their experience for three decades or more. When reporters and journalists were able to track the former students down, the pain of reliving the school desegregation crisis could be traumatic. Elizabeth Eckford's solitary walk in the midst of the mob gathered in front of Central High School was captured and immortalized in a photograph that drew the world's attention to events unfolding in Arkansas's capital. She was also the only one of the nine students who continued to live in Little Rock for many years. Consequently, she was frequently sought out by reporters even as she battled with depression and anxiety stemming from her experience at Central High School.[48] When she did not feel like talking, she told her sons to tell persistent reporters that she was dead. Even fifty years later, Eckford told *Vanity Fair* writer David Margolick that the long conversations they were having in preparation for a feature article and his upcoming book were too taxing. According to Margolick, Eckford told him, "Those calls cause some backwash in my life that's hard to deal with ... I'm having trouble sleeping at all."[49]

However, when the history of the Little Rock school desegregation crisis began to be recognized on a much larger and public scale, several members of the Little Rock Nine started to work toward coming to terms with the events of the 1957–58 school year. In the introduction to her memoir *Warriors Don't Cry*, Melba Pattillo Beals noted that she began writing about her experience at Central High shortly after she left Little Rock, but she "could not face the ghosts" that her diary and collected news clippings called forth. "During intervals of renewed strength and commitment," she wrote, "I would find myself compelled to return to the manuscript, only to have the pain of reliving my past undo my good intentions." After thirty-five years, Beals found that "enough time has elapsed for healing to take place, enabling me to tell my story without bitterness."[50] Beals may have been the first of the nine students to publish a retrospective account of her experience, but she was certainly not the last. The turn of the twenty-first century was marked by the release of a series of retrospective accounts that placed the Little Rock Nine, their families, and the city's black community at the center of the story. This transition was reflected in the production of Walt Disney's *Ernest Green Story* (1993) and the publication of Melba Pattillo Beals's *Warriors Don't Cry*, both of which focused on the turbulent events of the 1957–58 school year and were marketed to young adults. It was also manifest in the filming of *Journey to Little Rock: The Untold Life of Minnijean Brown* (2001), as well as the release of

Terrence Roberts's *Lessons from Little Rock* (2009) and Carlotta Walls LaNier's *A Mighty Long Way* (2009). These latter works addressed the impact of the 1957–59 school desegregation crisis on the students later in life, and drew more explicit connections between the historical events associated with the 1957–59 school desegregation crisis, the persistence of racial inequity in the twenty-first century, and the need for continued activism. Despite these differences in emphasis, in 1997 the former students collectively trademarked the name the "Little Rock Nine" and launched the Little Rock Nine Foundation, a non-profit organization dedicated to educating youth about their experience and promoting the importance of academic excellence. In establishing the foundation, Carlotta Walls LaNier urged her peers "to stop complaining about people using us" and to seize the opportunity "to take as much control as possible of our own legacy."[51]

In recent years, the Little Rock Nine have attempted to force the city of Little Rock to look its history squarely in the face. Over the last six decades, a vocal portion of the city's population has argued that Little Rock and Central High School suffer unfairly under the burden of history. Following a script first penned by Superintendent of Schools Virgil Blossom and others, the 1957–59 Little Rock school desegregation crisis has been described as an aberration that did not reflect the racially progressive and moderate character of Arkansas's capital. According to this perspective, the events that captured the nation's attention were the product of the political machinations of Governor Faubus's race-baiting reelection team, or the result of the outside agitation from groups such as the NAACP and the segregationist Citizens' Councils of America. A variety of evidence is offered to support the claim that the crowds outside the school were largely composed of individuals from outside of Little Rock. To the extent that locals participated in the mobs outside or the harassment of children inside the school, these individuals represented a small portion of the citizenry drawn from working-class "hard core" segregationist sections of the city. In this narrative, the vast majority of Little Rock residents accepted *Brown v. Board of Education* as the law of the land, were taken by surprise by the vehemence and violence that overtook their community, and remained silent for fear of economic reprisals and social ostracization. As the historian Karen Anderson observed, this narrative permitted "locals to deny any responsibility for events occurring in their midst and to project racism and violence onto people from another place, social class, or political standpoint . . . This view not only enabled Little Rock residents to save face, it also allowed them to believe that their actions and political commitments were not at issue."[52]

The triumphal narrative of passive progress continues to utilize the 1957–59 Little Rock school desegregation crisis as a benchmark against which all other manifestations of injustice in the city's school system are measured. In their effort to historicize the mid-century civil rights movement and contain its impact, the "old school voices" advanced a narrative that associated the racialized violence of 1957 with the nadir of race relations in the city and framed the moderation of minimal compliance as progress. In this context, progress was defined as the elimination of overt expressions of racism and the defeat of massive resistance. However, racial inequality in the Jim Crow South was not only sustained through the threat of extralegal violence, but also was built on a bedrock of structural and institutional racism that enabled white moderates who sought to contain the spread of school desegregation to advance their strategy of passive resistance—or as they framed it, minimal compliance—as a legal, practical, and reasonable alternative. Although white moderates frequently presented themselves before federal courts of law and in retrospective accounts of the crisis as allies rather than obstructionists, Terrence Roberts challenged this characterization of the city's civic and business elite in his memoir. Roberts noted that racism was not the sole province of the forces of massive resistance. "It was the most upstanding citizens," he observed, "who, through their actions, both overt and covert, presented the most formidable barrier to our full, equal participation in the state."[53]

Most of the Little Rock Nine reject the notion that Little Rock was a progressive or moderate city, noting that the rules of segregation were pervasive and firmly enforced. Carlotta Walls Lanier learned to "follow them like I learned to walk, by observing those closest to me and following their guidance until I knew the steps well enough to venture out on my own."[54] While much has been made of the fact that Little Rock peacefully integrated its buses before the school crisis erupted, Jim Crow reigned almost everywhere in the city. Public accommodations, including restaurants, lunch counters, movie theaters, swimming pools, and restrooms were rigidly segregated. African Americans were denied employment opportunities and membership in local unions. In his study of black activism in Little Rock, the historian John Kirk has characterized the racial change that preceded the school desegregation crisis as "little more than a tokenistic tampering with segregation." Moreover, the concessions that were made were designed to preserve the system of segregation by allowing local white leaders to maintain control over the pace of change.⁵⁵

Some of the former students have also chafed at the suggestion that Governor Orval Faubus was solely responsible for the mobs that gathered outside Central High. From Terrence Roberts's perspective, the governor acted "with the complicity of the people" when he provoked the crisis in 1957 and closed public high schools in the city in 1958–59. Certainly, the majority of Arkansas's voters did not reject Faubus's racial politics when they reelected him to another four terms of office. Faubus, Roberts contended, "did not act alone in blocking our admission to Central; he was simply the identified leader of the opposition . . . If the Guard had not stood in our way, then most certainly the angry, shouting, deranged mob of white protestors assembled in front of the school would have fulfilled that assignment." For those who might suggest that the mob itself was composed of undereducated, "hillbillies" from rural parts of Arkansas, Roberts replied, it was "the average white citizen," not "some demented, deluded interloper, who filled the ranks of the mobs surrounding Central High."⁵⁶

While making the case that the harassment they experienced in 1957–58 was an outgrowth, and not an aberration from the state of race relations in Little Rock, the nine former students have also pointed to the fact that resistance to integration continued once they were inside Central High School and attending classes with teenagers who had been steeped in the region's social mores. "Getting inside Central," Carlotta Walls LaNier recalled, "was just the beginning of a brand new struggle."⁵⁷ In their written work and public addresses, the Little Rock Nine refer to themselves as "soldiers," "warriors," and "comrades," who entered into a daily "war" or "battle" to claim the rights the Supreme Court had declared theirs in 1954.⁵⁸ In their accounts, they endured constant torment and suffered under the threat of even more extreme violence. A group of committed segregationists inside the building "was willing to do whatever they could think of to persuade us to reconsider our decision to come to Central," Roberts maintained. "They hit, kicked, pushed, shoved, slapped, tripped, scratched, spat on, and verbally abused us constantly."⁵⁹

For their part, some white student leaders from the Class of 1958 reject this characterization of the school year. An integral part of the defense of Little Rock's reputation for "good race relations" is the contention that the harassment reported inside Central High School has been "exaggerated" by news reporters seeking headlines, historians casting the crisis as a black and white morality play, and, more recently, the Little Rock Nine themselves. In the 1990s, sociologist Beth Roy documented the reaction of some white students to Melba Pattillo Beals's *Warriors Don't Cry*. In her interviews with Central High alumni immediately after the book was released, Roy noted that white students dismissed and discredited Beals's account. According to her informants, the physical abuse the Nine characterized as racial would more accurately be described as harmless adolescent pranks, and the social ostracization they experienced was common for new students, white or black. Some contended that Beals's account of harassment in the school was an outright lie, others suggested it was an exaggeration, and many asserted that they never witnessed any of the events described. Some simply suggested that Beals's account could not possibly be true because they could not imagine that any American teenager could have endured such torment. In Roy's words, the alumni argued that "Melba's book was a strategic construct designed to discredit the white students, many of whom . . . deserved credit for human kindness to the black students." A few informants suggested that Beals had lied because "she was hurt and resentful that she was ignored."[60] Some of the white students who attended Central High in 1957–58 advanced this alternative perspective in an anthology entitled *Central in Our Lives* (2007). According to the contributors, while the majority of students may not have heroically defied their peers and befriended the Little Rock Nine, they should not be held responsible for the decisions and behavior of a handful of hard-core segregationists.[61] In response to this claim, Carlotta Walls LaNier reminded the readers of her own memoir that even the white students who stood by silently had an impact. By turning their backs, LaNier asserted, they failed to acknowledge the humanity of their black peers or their suffering. This was devastating in itself.[62]

The Little Rock Nine endured this harassment in order to secure access to educational opportunities that were unavailable to black students in segregated institutions. When describing the decision-making process behind their decision to attend Central High, several of the Little Rock Nine stressed that in doing so they were not rejecting the all-black institutions that had nurtured them through grade school, nor were they acting out of an overriding desire to attend classes with white students. Indeed, several of the Little Rock Nine had family members that worked in the city's all-black schools. These institutions had their own strong educational tradition, despite the fact that the city's African American teachers had to cope with outdated course materials, fewer resources, and lower pay.[63] As Gloria Ray Karlmark recalled, "Back then, we looked up to our teachers who taught us out of professionalism and love, but also with the disgracefully disproportionate public means at their disposal in the public schools in our community. The community relied on their skills, their dedication to make up for what our school lacked in publicly funded resources. It was difficult for us, but we would show that despite the discrimination that we could excel."[64] In Little Rock's black schools, African American students learned important survival skills that would enable them to succeed even in the segregated South. Even so, most observers were aware that students at Central were given more access to resources, including laboratory equipment and instruction in classes that were not offered at Horace Mann. Several of the Little Rock Nine believed that Central's national reputation would provide them with access to a wider field of choices in higher education.[65] "Access to options," Roberts explained, "gives you more ways to respond to life's demands, more ways of understanding what is happening around you, more information about how to realize the potential that is yours to develop."[66] This fundamental promise of access to opportunity was embedded in the *Brown v. Board of Education* decision, and as Carlotta Walls LaNier has noted, at fourteen she was "old enough to understand the historical significance of . . . enrollment in Central."[67]

In the city's schools, Little Rock's self-image as a racially moderate and progressive city led some to believe that only modest changes were needed to provide opportunity to "exceptional" black students like the Little Rock Nine and to bring the school district into compliance with federal court orders. The effort to define "successful integration" within the context of minimal compliance, the flexible application of federal law, and tokenism not only shaped the Little Rock school district's arguments before federal courts of law for nearly five decades, but also influenced the public memory of the Little Rock school desegregation crisis. Moderates framed their pragmatism in juxtaposition to the extremism of ardent segregationists and civil rights advocates, and advanced their agenda as the only viable strategy for preserving support for public education.

However, the Little Rock Nine have collectively rejected this constrained and limited definition of successful integration and its failure to address systemic inequality and institutionalized white privilege. Speaking on behalf of the group of former students at the "People's Celebration" organized by the historically black Philander Smith College on the occasion of the fortieth anniversary of the crisis, Terrence Roberts addressed this issue directly. "In this national dialogue about . . . whether desegregation is still important, the Little Rock Nine are firmly committed to the desegregation of schools." Roberts called for efforts to promote meaningful diversity throughout the district and renewed attention and commitment to improving the access to educational opportunity for all students. "We are talking about total access," he clarified. "We want it all. We don't just want a taste."[68]

Melba Pattillo Beals, a journalist and public relations executive, also made it clear that the Little Rock Nine did not view commemorative activities as a victory celebration. Central's relatively balanced racial ratios meant little if black students were not participating in the institution's celebrated advanced placement and honors courses, were graduating several grade levels behind their white counterparts, and if the majority of students in the district were continuing to attend racially isolated schools. Beals insisted that the battle for integration was always about more than putting black and white students together in a classroom. "Does anybody really think we wanted to go to Central High School because we wanted to sit next to white people?" asked Beals. "We wanted to go to Central High School because they were getting Rhodes Scholarships there. We wanted equal access to opportunities."[69]

In this regard, the city's moderate self-image continued to blind some civic officials to the systemic and structural inequality that continued to shape education in the district. "Discrimination never derived its main strength from individual actions or prejudices," according to the sociologists Michael Omi and Howard Winant. Rather, "its most fundamental characteristic was always its root in the racially organized *social* order."[70] In Arkansas's capital, the failure to recognize the structural and historical roots of discrimination has laid the foundation for the naturalization of racial inequity in the present. Opinion makers and expert witnesses in Little Rock attributed current conditions to a "culture of poverty" and deficiencies within underprivileged populations. At the turn of the twenty-first century, the argument that "external factors" like poverty, neighborhood violence, and lack of parental investment were the primary drivers of low African American student achievement was successfully deployed by school districts across the country to escape court oversight.

The pervasiveness of this rhetoric among administrators, teachers, and students in Little Rock was captured with startling clarity in the HBO documentary *Little Rock Central: 50 Years Later* (2007). Brent and Craig Renaud, two white brothers who graduated from Central High in the 1990s, returned to Central fifty years after the school desegregation crisis to chronicle conditions in the school and illuminate the barriers that continued to stand between white and black students at one of the district's most diverse institutions. The filmmakers documented racially identifiable academic tracks in the high school, directing attention to predominantly white advanced placement classes and largely black remedial courses. They also illuminated the stark socioeconomic disparities within the student population, following both white and black students home and asking them to reflect or comment on the color line at Central and racial disparities in academic achievement. The majority of students depicted in the film explained contemporary conditions in the school as the byproduct of differences in internal motivation and family upbringing. This rhetoric had been internalized by African American students as well as their white counterparts. "Most African-American students do not want to try," said one of the few black students enrolled in the high school's advanced placement classes. As the *New York Times* described it, "Students and teachers alike spoke blithely or painfully of the low educational aspirations and achievements of many black students." Teachers and administrators expressed frustration with the persistent disparities in achievement at the school and demonstrated their commitment to working with individual students, but Principal Nancy Rousseau rejected the notion that it was within the power of school officials to "fix" these issues on a broader systemic basis. School officials highlighted the relative success of a handful of underprivileged students in an effort to demonstrate that the system provided access to equal educational opportunity for those motivated to seek it out.[71] This rhetoric echoed the logic of the Little Rock school board's defense of tokenism nearly half a century earlier. "The proper measure of progress in desegregation is not the number that have exercised a right," they had maintained, "but the number to whom this right is available."[72]

As students attributed low African American student achievement to a "culture of poverty" or low motivation, these sentiments were not questioned or challenged even during class discussions facilitated by teachers. The only adult who challenged the students to think outside of this paradigm was Minnijean Brown Trickey. As she addressed a self-segregated classroom, she urged the students to see their own actions and the broader forces that shaped their experience inside Central within the context of institutionalized racism—"ideology, process, and practice."[73] In public forums, Trickey referred to the scenes captured in the film as an indictment not only of Little Rock but the nation at large. "The black kids in this documentary believe in their intellectual inferiority and the white kids believe in their intellectual superiority," she told the *New York Times*. As the only member of the Little Rock Nine featured in *Little Rock Central: 50 Years Later*, Trickey noted that the perceptions the filmmakers captured on camera were pervasive in her encounters with black students participating in her nonviolence training sessions and antiracist workshops. Brent Renaud asserted that the students were merely sharing "their experience" and "the way they're seeing the world" and that the film's primary value was its illumination of these "different perspectives." However, Trickey asserted that the students' perceptions should not be understood as a reflection of reality, but should be framed within the context of internalized stereotypes. In the *Brown v. Board of Education* decision, the Supreme Court held that segregation was inherently unequal because racial isolation generated a "feeling of inferiority" among schoolchildren "that may affect their hearts and minds in a way unlikely ever to be undone." At a screening of the film at Harvard, Trickey insisted that it was critical to continue to challenge misconceptions that African American students were uninterested or incapable of learning. Students' self-perception was shaped by these "embedded concepts in our society" and the persistence of racialized academic tracking; educators and others had an obligation to help students "dismantle" and challenge internalized stereotypes.[74] As Terrence Roberts reminded readers in his memoir, "It simply isn't true that black people are somehow unable to compete equally because they are racially inferior, or that they are more criminally inclined than white people, or that they simply don't take advantage of opportunities to build wealth." Rather, these pervasive stereotypes were a means of continuing to justify and perpetuate racist inequity by obscuring its systemic and institutional roots.[75]

Through their memoirs, antiracist workshops, and countless speaking engagements, the Little Rock Nine have resisted the historical erasure and willed amnesia that sit at the center of the triumphal narrative of passive progress. "History cannot be rewritten in the face of overwhelming evidence to the contrary," Roberts observed, "but that does not seem to deter those who seem convinced that things were not at all what they seemed to be."[76] The determination that the Little Rock school district was unitary was a legal finding that it no longer maintained a dual system of education and had successfully eliminated all "vestiges" of racial discrimination. In his memoir, however, Roberts rejected attempts to sharply demarcate the civil rights movement as an epoch of a distant past. "History, all of history, is but the antecedent action to all we find around us today," he explained, and the stakes involved in establishing an accurate historical record were high. "I write not as one who wishes to 'live in the past' but as one who wishes to understand how the past is manifest today," Roberts insisted. "I choose not to join the chorus of those who say that we must forget what happened and get on with life. I am firmly convinced that we will fail to accomplish our goal of creating a truly integrated and equal society if we continue to avoid facing the truth about who we are and have been."[77]

The former students have called attention to the deeply rooted cultural mores and social expectations that sustained and continue to sustain systemic racism and institutionalized white privilege in the United States. Moreover, they have directly refuted the idea that racism has or will disappear naturally with the passage of time. In their experience, as Roberts put it, "time itself is neutral, and without concentrated, sustained effort by human beings, change will not occur."[78] The former students reject the fatalism that imbues most discussions of racial inequality in the nation's schools today, especially arguments that all "practicable" actions have been taken to address persistent double-digit achievement gaps and racially isolated schools. The decision not to act in the face of injustice is a decision in favor of maintaining the status quo. "We have to remember that justice is a perpetual struggle, and we've got to keep doing it, and keep on doing it forever," Minnijean Brown Trickey asserted at the fiftieth anniversary of the school desegregation crisis. "That's our responsibility and we must take that responsibility seriously."[79]

In their effort to craft an empowering history of the Little Rock school desegregation crisis, the Little Rock Nine have challenged us to remember that even the most unequal educational systems, including those that operate as an entrenched part of the social fabric, are vulnerable to challenge. In doing so, they have sought to preserve an alternative history of the mid-century civil rights movement written in active rather than passive voice, and translated from past to future tense. The echo of this "voice sounding forever across the centuries the laws of right and wrong," as Elizabeth Eckford put it so poignantly in the 2007 dedication of the National Park Service visitor center, may be increasingly critical in a nation where the pervasiveness of what she called "a fraud agreed upon" has had real and concrete consequences for students in Little Rock and across the nation.

— CONCLUSION —

In a reflective area overlooking Park Street, visitors to the Little Rock Central High School National Historic Site are prompted to reflect on what they might have done to address racial injustice if they had been present in Little Rock during September 1957 and to consider the history presented at the site in light of current conditions. "Although Park Street is quieter today than it was in September 1957, the hostility and prejudice that surfaced then are still a part of our lives today, and still challenge us to stand up and respond to injustice," a panel positioned under a large picture window notes. As they consider the cultural and historical landscape surrounding the high school, visitors are urged to contemplate thought-provoking questions such as, "Is equal education a right? Do the events of 1957 affect my life today? Would I have had the courage to fight for my rights in 1957? Do I have the courage now?" These questions evoke the potential of memorial spaces to incubate alternative histories capable of challenging the nation to question the triumphal narrative of racial progress, and to connect struggles against social injustice in the past to efforts to create a more equitable society in the present.

As our only national historic site that is also a functional school, the Little Rock Central High School National Historic Site sits at the intersection between public memory and educational policy, and it is uniquely positioned to help visitors interrogate the chasm between the rhetoric of the "post-civil rights" era and the reality of persistent racial inequality in

American education. In creating a new visitors' center to replace the facility housed in the Mobil gas station, National Park Service interpretive planners recognized the site's potential to challenge passive constructions of social change and placed a renewed emphasis on the actions of civil rights pioneers and their allies. This focus also continues to drive special programming, including a ground-breaking social consciousness gathering hosted at the site in 2015 under the leadership of Superintendent Robin White that brought together activists from across the country to explore strategies for fostering social justice.[1]

However, the full promise of the Little Rock Central High School National Historic Site has not been realized in its permanent exhibit space. In an effort to help a broad spectrum of visitors identify with the story of the Little Rock Nine, the exhibit connects the experience of these civil rights pioneers to other social movements in the United States that sought to reshape constitutional law. But this shift away from a focus on school desegregation does not illuminate persistent resistance to the mandate of the *Brown v. Board of Education* decision or contextualize the challenges facing contemporary educational institutions like Little Rock Central High School. These topics may be raised by visitors or park rangers in the more interactive environment of ranger-led interpretive tours, particularly as they stand in front of the school's famous façade or tour the interior of the building on the rare days when this opportunity is available.[2] However, as an interpretive experience that is available to all visitors, the permanent exhibit space affords the park with an unrealized opportunity to challenge, question, and problematize dominant narratives of progress in relation to school desegregation.

In the visitor center dedicated in 2007, the Park Service continued to present Little Rock as a symbol of federal enforcement of the *Brown* decision and the nation's commitment to addressing educational inequity. In planning documents, the historical significance of the Little Rock school desegregation crisis was framed as a "monumental test" of the nation's commitment to live up to the promises inscribed in the Declaration of Independence in a battle that pitted "federal upholding of constitutional civil rights against states' rights of self-governance." Interpretive planners highlighted Eisenhower's use of executive power as a demonstration of the "national commitment to enforce civil rights" in the mid-twentieth century. The exhibits installed in the visitor center framed the *Brown* decision and its implementation in Little Rock as

FIGURE 12. Commissioned for the fiftieth anniversary of the school desegregation crisis, this image draws connections between past and present. The youthful figures of the Little Rock Nine and the segregationists who sought to keep them out of Central High School are preserved in the school's reflecting pool, but the civil rights pioneers are surrounded by a diverse student body fifty years later. As a functioning high school and a national historic site, Central High is uniquely positioned to inform visitors about transformations in American education over the last five decades. However, the racial inequities that continue to shape student experience today are not fully illuminated in the historic site's exhibits. ("Reflections" by Lyuba Bogan. © 2007 all rights reserved)

pivotal turning points in the nation's effort to become a "more perfect union."[3] As Leigh Raiford and Renee C. Romano noted in *The Civil Rights Movement in American Memory*, the mid-century civil rights movement is perpetually "held up as a shining example of the success of American democracy," proof of "the vitality of America's legal and political institutions, and evidence of the nation's ongoing quest to live up to its founding ideals of egalitarianism and justice."[4] In Little Rock, the interpretive exhibits inside the visitor center placed a spotlight on active federal intervention and sutured the story of the civil rights movement into a broader national narrative of progress by focusing on the expansion of civil and political rights, not only for African Americans but other groups as well.

This interpretive emphasis drew directly on a long legacy of federal efforts to define the significance of the crisis in these terms and to redress negative public opinion at home and abroad in its aftermath. If Little Rock is frequently presented today as a symbol of the federal government's commitment to protecting civil rights, the crisis was not always framed that way. In 1957, Little Rock functioned as a symbol of American hypocrisy and a standing rebuke to the United States' efforts to project itself as a beacon of freedom, democracy, and equality around the world. As the civil rights movement and the Cold War unfolded concurrently, questions and concerns about American race relations acquired increased importance. International pressure provided an incentive for the American government, particularly the executive branch, to support limited changes in the field of civil rights. Government officials and politicians frequently framed their support for federal intervention and reform by stressing the significance of this issue around the world, especially for newly independent nations in Asia and Africa.[5] In his televised address explaining his decision to send the 101st Airborne to Little Rock, President Eisenhower recognized the international implications of the crisis and its negative impact on global public opinion when he emphasized the importance of resolving the crisis in order to "restore the image of America" around the globe. The president contended that the nation's enemies were "gloating over this incident and using it everywhere to misrepresent our whole nation." Eisenhower maintained that America could only redeem itself in the "eyes of the world" by restoring the city of Little Rock to its "normal habits" and preserving and respecting the law.[6] It was not only Little Rock, but the nation at large, that needed to rehabilitate its reputation.

Despite Eisenhower's forceful action, public affairs officers, American diplomats, and foreign-service agents reported that fallout from Little Rock had an immediate impact on American foreign policy objectives. By December 1958, the State Department determined that the conflict had created a "solid target for anti-American propaganda." The department concluded that the crisis had the effect of "weakening . . . our moral position as the champion of freedom and democracy, and in raising and reinforcing doubts as to the sincerity of our professions of concern for the welfare of others particularly in the non-white world."[7] In its public information campaigns, the United States Information Agency (USIA) recognized that reshaping negative perceptions of American race relations abroad was the "information agency's most challenging policy problem."[8] However, instead of responding defensively to criticism of American practices, the USIA carefully cultivated an image of progress that reframed developments in civil rights as an inspirational American success story and presented the struggle for racial equality as an example of democracy in motion. As Mary L. Dudziak has noted, in doing so the agency attempted to neutralize a "potential threat" to American relationships abroad and turn it into an "asset."[9]

For example, as early as 1964, the US government produced a retrospective account of the Little Rock school desegregation crisis that adopted this approach. In *Nine from Little Rock,* a propaganda film produced by the USIA, the agency chose to highlight the forceful intervention of the federal government and the nation's commitment to the rule of law. The film's carefully scripted and edited vignettes were meant to demonstrate that the nine students, the city of Little Rock, and America itself had transcended the 1957–59 school desegregation crisis. In this context, the violence outside Central High School was defined as the "rare misdeed" of a "small minority," and Eisenhower's decision to send troops to Little Rock demonstrated that American laws were more than "just words in a book or idle talk in a classroom."[10] Supplementary materials printed and distributed with the film asserted that conflict developed in Arkansas because a tradition of segregation had taken root that was "alien to the older and greater traditions of American democracy."[11] In framing the past this way, the film pointedly ignored the United States' long and tortuous history of racial discrimination, white supremacy, slavery, as well as its pervasive system of legal segregation and extralegal violence.

The film also sought to assure international audiences that the United

States was making meaningful progress with school desegregation by revisiting several members of the Little Rock Nine and documenting their success as college students in 1964.[12] However, the former students themselves had no opportunity to challenge or question the way the government agency framed their experience. Although *Nine from Little Rock* won an Academy Award for Best Short Documentary, Congress did not permit the USIA to distribute its films within the United States. Few Americans, including the members of the Little Rock Nine who participated in the production, saw it at the time. Indeed, although filmmaker Charles Guggenheim maintained that the city's racial progress would only be "convincing if they say it is," the film's narrative did not reflect the impatience some of the students expressed to the production team about the glacial pace of racial change in the United States. Instead, in an act of ventriloquism, the USIA overlaid footage of the civil rights pioneers attending college with first-person narrative voiceovers recorded by actors in seventeen languages so that the film would "carry the freight" of their message to international audiences.[13] At a time when only 1.18 percent of African American school children in the eleven former states of the Confederacy were attending schools with their white peers, the use of this technique allowed the USIA to continue to frame developments in American race relations as they desired, while silencing the opinions and sentiments of the Little Rock Nine themselves and obscuring the reality of conditions in Little Rock.[14] Unfortunately, over fifty years later, the Little Rock Central High School National Historic Site continues to show this film to student groups as an introduction to the events of the 1957–58 with little or no explanatory context.[15]

The permanent exhibit gallery at the Little Rock Central High School National Historic Site also continues to frame the significance of the crisis within a narrative of progressive change, the nation's commitment to the rule of law, and the strength of American democracy. Crafted by the National Park Service, these interpretive themes served the needs of the US government. Despite the significant number of international visitors that came to Little Rock, the exhibit did not acknowledge the external international pressure that prompted Eisenhower to act in 1957 (and motivated the federal government to explain the crisis away in the years that followed). An interpretive focus on these kinds of diplomatic calculations might have suggested that the drivers of change did not lie within the democratic experiment itself. Instead, the site placed new emphasis on internal forces propelling the nation forward. Interpretation emphasized the capacity of citizens to effect change and to compel the state to recognize their constitutional rights through direct action and collective organization. In this regard, the site directly challenged passive constructions of social change and prompted visitors to reflect on their own responsibility to confront persistent injustice. One of the principles that guided interpretation at the Little Rock Central High School National Historic Site was the desire to engage the "attention and emotion" of visitors and to "provoke thought and reflection" not only in relation to the past, but also in relation to contemporary issues.[16] The site's enabling legislation directed the Park Service to preserve the site for the "benefit, education, and *inspiration* of present and future generations."[17]

From the outset, the Park Service exhibit encouraged visitors to view themselves—and not just the Little Rock Nine—as change agents. "Like the nine students who desegregated Little Rock Central High School in 1957, all citizens share the responsibility to shape this nation," an opening panel declared. The site challenged efforts to portray the Little Rock Nine as exceptional individuals who could be idolized but not emulated, and echoed a theme emphasized by the former students themselves. In 2007, Elizabeth Eckford acknowledged, "People tend to think we're unusual," but, she averred, "I am a most ordinary person." Eckford described herself as a "shy, submissive child" and an unlikely pioneer in the arena of school desegregation, but she assured her audience that "even that kind of person, can find steel."[18] In her memoir, Carlotta Walls LaNier also emphasized that the "determination, fortitude, and ability to move the world aren't reserved for the 'special people.'"[19]

In a departure from the ventriloquism of *Nine from Little Rock,* the voices of Eckford and LaNier and other members of the Little Rock Nine pervaded the exhibits at the visitor center through the use of multimedia touch stations and direct quotations from documents, interviews, and oral histories that highlighted their experience. Several members of the Little Rock Nine have argued that change begins with recognizing and embracing our individual capacity to act, and interpretation at the Little Rock Central High School National Historic Site was imbued with this same sensibility. By challenging the paradigm of passive progress, the former students hoped to empower others to take action on issues of concern to them and their communities. In her work with young people in antiracism workshops and nonviolence training sessions, Minnijean Brown Trickey frequently passed on a lesson she borrowed from Gandhi: "Our challenge today and tomorrow and forever is to be the change we want to see in the world."[20]

Given this emphasis, even as the interpretive exhibits inside the center continued to position Little Rock as a symbol of federal enforcement of African American civil rights, the National Park Service framed this development within the context of persistent social activism that pressured government officials to deliver on the promises inscribed in the country's founding documents. "The Constitution of the United States clearly expresses the importance of justice and liberty. In the early days of the nation, it did not protect everyone's rights," the exhibit observed. "Throughout the history of the United States, ordinary people have brought about change. Individuals like the Little Rock Nine relied on the promises of the 14th Amendment to the Constitution in seeking an equal education. They and others have taken action to force the country to live up to its founding principle that 'all men are created equal.'"[21] While the contributions of civil rights litigators, black plaintiffs, and their parents received scant attention in other official repositories of memory, these historical actors were placed at the center of the narrative in the visitor center's exhibits.

In its attention to the history of the crisis years 1957–59, the exhibit challenged historical narratives that focused on the racial moderation of Little Rock's citizenry. Narratives that ascribed the cause of the crisis to outside forces—politicians, rabid rural segregationists, overbearing federal courts— and excused the inaction of the majority of the city's citizens did not have the power to motivate people in the present to recognize and understand what they might do to challenge the status quo in their own time. Interpretation at the site challenged characterizations of Eisenhower's intervention in 1957 as an unjustified federal "occupation." Moreover, exhibit panels focused on the crisis years did not mount a defense of the majority of students or white moderates who remained silent bystanders. Instead, they focused on the tension outside *and* inside Central High School and the persistent harassment of the Little Rock Nine by community members, segregationist organizations, and white students within the building. The site also noted that three-quarters of Little Rock residents voted in support of Governor Faubus's decision to close the city's high schools, an indication that the politics of massive resistance held widespread appeal. For those who questioned the veracity of these events, the exhibit noted that they were well documented in military reports and archival documents.

In an effort to help diverse audiences connect with the story of the Little Rock Nine, interpretation at the site also encouraged visitors to consider the role of individual agency in a wide array of movements for social change. Although park interpretation focused on the Little Rock school desegregation crisis and familiarized visitors with the historical context surrounding it, it situated these developments within a much broader historical framework and called attention to efforts to fight discrimination against native peoples, to demand rights for farm workers, to secure rights for American women and the physically disabled. These campaigns for social justice were connected to the Little Rock school desegregation crisis as examples of other social movements that challenged the United States to become a more equitable and just nation.

By expanding the exhibit's scope and national reach, however, the Park Service turned visitors' focus away from exploring the local impact and legacy of the school desegregation crisis in Little Rock today. If representatives of the Little Rock Nine have endeavored to use their story to challenge the historicization of the movement—to reconnect past and present—the exhibit was less successful in this regard. Despite the fact that the Little Rock School District was not declared unitary until the year the new National Park Service visitor center opened, the exhibit blithely asserted that the district "completed its desegregation plan in 1972." The difficulty the district faced in its efforts to "maintain integration" was not connected to persistent resistance to school desegregation. Instead, it was attributed to "demographic changes" such as the growth of suburbs and proliferation of private schools. Interpretive panels mentioned the persistence of residential segregation in large cities throughout the United States, but did not provide historical context that might enable visitors to understand why "African Americans, whites, Latinos, and other groups lived in separate neighborhoods" or neighborhood schools continued to serve only "one racial or ethnic group." Parental opposition to court-ordered busing was attributed to "organizational problems" rather than racial animosity. Interpretive panels emphasized the importance of provisions outlined in the 1964 Civil Rights Act and the Supreme Court's 1968 *Green v. New Kent County* decision holding that school districts were obligated to create school desegregation plans that were demonstrably effective. However, the tremendous ideological shift on the Court from the 1970s forward remained unaddressed. "Today," the exhibit noted, "many school districts continue to struggle to achieve racial balance, while other issues such as equitable funding and achievement gaps among different racial and ethnic groups compete for attention." Little historical context was provided that would help visitors understand the persistence of these issues, however. Framing the crisis and its relationship to the present within this framework may be reassuring and bolster the image of the federal government's role in enforcing school desegregation, but it obscures the historical roots of many of the seemingly intractable problems that face the nation's schools today and continue to influence conditions in Little Rock and elsewhere.

The architects of passive resistance cultivated the building blocks of the triumphal narrative of progress during the late 1960s and 1970s when their arguments fell out of favor with federal courts of law by working to disconnect the past from the present in public discourse. The effort to reconnect our collective understanding of the relationship between past and present is a profoundly historical endeavor. The interpretive space within the Little Rock Central High School National Historic Site might do more to help visitors understand the problems facing American educational institutions, to debate the merits of potential solutions, and to consider their own responsibilities as individual citizens by contextualizing the conditions at Little Rock Central High School immediately across the street. Our memorial spaces have the capacity to provide this vital historical context. Alternative histories that challenge the triumphal narrative of passive progress focus not only on dramatic confrontations between the forces of massive resistance and federal enforcement in the mid-twentieth century, but on the long struggle to desegregate the nation's institutions that has unfolded over the course of decades. Refusing to vacate this history illuminates the history of systemic discrimination and the institutionalization of white privilege that continues to animate resistance to meaningful school desegregation, and challenges racial stereotypes that ascribe racial inequity to deficiencies within communities of color.

Advancing this antiracist project is a choice, and in this regard the Little Rock Nine continue to remind of us our collective responsibility to be active agents of change by evoking their own historic challenge to racial inequality in the United States. "By doing nothing," Terrence Roberts wrote, "we would have prolonged the system of racial discrimination that restricted our lives simply because we were black people."[22] By extension, those who chose to do nothing were making their own choice to preserve the social system that had undergirded life in the city of Little Rock for decades. Likewise, the refusal to challenge the triumphal narrative of passive progress is a decision in favor of the status quo. "Sometimes it's not the people who do the deed," Minnijean Brown Trickey has asserted; "it's the people who stand by and do nothing" that do the most to perpetrate injustice.[23]

NOTES

Introduction

1. Gary Orfield, John Kucsera, and Genevieve Siegel-Hawley, UCLA Civil Rights Project / Proyecto Derechos Civiles, "E Pluribus ... Separation: Deepening Double Segregation for More Students" (September 2012), http://civilrightsproject.ucla.edu/research/k-12-education/integration-and-diversity/mlk-national/e-pluribus ... separation-deepening-double-segregation-for-more-students/orfield_epluribus_revised_omplete_2012.pdf.
2. Paul Louis Street, *Segregated Schools: Educational Apartheid in Post-Civil Rights America* (New York: Routledge, 2005), 50, 63.
3. See Michael Kammen, *Mystic Chords of Memory: The Transformation of Tradition in American Culture* (New York: Knopf, 1991); David Lowenthal, *The Past Is a Foreign Country* (Cambridge: Cambridge University Press, 1985); John Gillis, ed., *Commemorations: The Politics of National Identity* (Princeton, NJ: Princeton University Press, 1994); David Blight, *Race and Reunion: The Civil War in American Memory* (Cambridge, MA: Belknap Press of Harvard University Press, 2001); W. Fitzhugh Brundage, *The Southern Past: A Clash of Race and Memory* (Cambridge, MA: Harvard University Press, 2005); David Thelen, ed., *Memory and American History* (Bloomington: Indiana University Press, 1990).
4. For the theoretical foundations of this work see Antonio Gramsci, *Selections from the Prison Notebooks of Antonio Gramsci,* ed. Quintin Hoare and Geoffrey Nowell Smith (New York: International Publishers, 1990); Raymond Williams, "Base and Superstructure in Marxist Cultural Theory," in *Problems in Materialism and Culture: Selected Essays* (London: New Left Books, 1980); Stuart Hall, "Notes on Deconstructing the Popular," in *Cultural Theory and Popular Culture: A Reader,* ed. John Story (Athens: University of Georgia Press, 1997), 443–53; Frederic Jameson, "Reification and Utopia in Mass Culture," *Social Text* 1 (1979): 130–48.
5. Gillis, *Commemorations,* 5.
6. Jacquelyn Dowd Hall, "The Long Civil Rights Movement and the Political Uses of the Past," *Journal of American History* 91, no. 4 (March 2005): 1233–63.
7. For examples, see the following historiographies and bibliographies of the long civil

rights movement: Charles W. Eagles, "Toward New Histories of the Civil Rights Era," *Journal of Southern History* 66, no. 4 (2000): 815–48; John Dittmer, "The Civil Rights Movement," in *The African American Experience: A Historiographical and Bibliographical Guide*, ed. Arvarh Strickland and Robert J. Weems Jr. (Westport, CT: Greenwood Press, 2001); Hall, "The Long Civil Rights Movement"; Peniel E. Joseph, "Introduction: Toward a Historiography of the Black Power Movement," in *The Black Power Movement: Rethinking the Civil Rights-Black Power Era*, ed. Peniel E. Joseph (New York: Routledge, 2006), 1–26.

8. Michel-Rolph Trouillot, *Silencing the Past: Power and the Production of History* (Boston: Beacon Press, 1995), xix.

9. Hall, "The Long Civil Rights Movement," 1234. See also Owen J. Dwyer, "Memory on the Margins: *Alabama's Civil Rights Journey* as a Memorial Text," in *Mapping Tourism*, ed. Stephen P. Hanna and Vincent J. Del Casino Jr. (Minneapolis: University of Minnesota Press, 2003), 37–38.

10. In the final years of his life, King turned his attention to economic injustice, poverty, and the war in Vietnam. His struggle to "redeem the soul of America" increasingly led him to call for a "reconstruction of the entire society, a revolution of values" and "a radical redistribution of economic and political power." But this King has no place in the dominant memory of civil rights. In his essay, "Beyond Amnesia: Martin Luther King Jr. and the Future of America," Vincent Harding notes, "It appears as if the price for the first national holiday honoring a black man is the development of a massive case of national amnesia concerning who that black man really was" (Vincent Gordon Harding, "Beyond Amnesia: Martin Luther King Jr. and the Future of America," *Journal of American History* 74, no. 2 [September 1987]: 469). Malcolm X may be the only postwar leader who comes close to rivaling the dominance of King's memory in this arena. Even then, Malcolm X's memory is frequently evoked within the context of unflattering "Martin v. Malcolm" storylines that elevate King's "righteous" nonviolent philosophy at the expense of Malcolm X's legacy and teaching (Edward P. Morgan, "The Good, The Bad, and the Forgotten: Media Culture and the Public Memory of the Civil Rights Movement," in *The Civil Rights Movement in American Memory*, ed. Renee Romano and Leigh Raiford [Athens: University of Georgia Press, 2006], 137–66). See also Hall, "The Long Civil Rights Movement," 1234.

11. Quote from Clayborne Carson, "Civil Rights Reform and the Black Freedom Struggle," in *The Civil Rights Movement in America*, ed. Charles Eagles (Jackson: University Press of Mississippi, 2006), 28. See the collected essays in *The Civil Rights Movement and American Memory*, ed. Renee C. Romano and Leigh Raiford (Athens: University of Georgia Press, 2006) and *Civil Rights History from the Ground Up: Local Struggles, a National Movement*, ed. Emilye Crosby (Athens: University of Georgia Press, 2011). See also Owen J. Dwyer, "Interpreting the Civil Rights Movement: Place, Memory, and Conflict," *Professional Geographer* 52, no. 4 (2000): 660–71; Dwyer, "Memory on the Margins"; Dwyer, "Memorial Landscapes Dedicated to the Civil Rights Movement" (PhD diss., University of Kentucky, 2000);

Glenn T. Eskew, "From Civil War to Civil Rights: Selling Alabama as Heritage Tourism," in *Slavery, Contested Heritage, and Thanatourism,* ed. Graham M. S. Dunn and A. V. Seaton (New York: Haworth Press, 2001), 201–14; Joseph Tilden Rhea, "Memory of a Nation: The Race Pride Movement and American Collective Memory" (PhD diss., Harvard University, 1995); Allison Graham, *Framing the South: Hollywood, Television, and Race during the Civil Rights Struggle* (Baltimore: Johns Hopkins University Press, 2001); Brian Ward, "Introduction: Forgotten Walls and Master Narratives: Media, Culture, and Memories of the Modern African American Freedom Struggle" in *Media, Culture, and the Modern African American Freedom Struggle,* ed. Brian Ward (Gainesville: University Press of Florida, 2001). See also Harding, "Beyond Amnesia"; Joseph, "Introduction: Toward a Historiography of the Black Power Movement"; Hall, "The Long Civil Rights Movement."

12. Owen J. Dwyer has attributed this phrase to the historian Glenn Eskew in relation to Eskew's work on civil rights heritage tourism in Alabama. Owen J. Dwyer and Derek H. Alderman, *Civil Rights Memorials and the Geography of Memory* (Chicago: Center for American Places at Columbia College Chicago, 2008), fig. 40; Dwyer, "Memory on the Margins," 37. See Eskew, "From Civil War to Civil Rights," 201–14.

13. For example, see the United States Information Agency (USIA) film *Nine from Little Rock,* prod. and dir. Charles Guggenheim, 19 min. (Guggenheim Productions, Inc., 2005), DVD; Melinda M. Schwenk, "Reforming the Negative through History: The US Information Agency and the 1957 Little Rock Integration Crisis," *Journal of Communication Inquiry* 23, no. 3 (July 1999), 288–306; Michael Krenn, *Black Diplomacy: African Americans and the State Department, 1945–1969* (Armonk, NY: M. E. Sharpe, 1999), 104–5; Mary L. Dudziak, "The Little Rock Crisis and Foreign Affairs: Race, Resistance, and the Image of American Democracy," *Southern California Law Review* 70, no. 6 (September 1997): 1698–99; Mary L. Dudziak, *Cold War Civil Rights: Race and the Image of American Democracy* (Princeton, NJ: Princeton University Press, 2000), 142–44; Cary Fraser, "Crossing the Color Line in Little Rock: The Eisenhower Administration and the Dilemma of Race for US Foreign Policy," *Diplomatic History* 24, no. 2 (Spring 2000): 252; Kenneth Osgood, *Total Cold War: Eisenhower's Secret Propaganda Battle Home and Abroad* (Lawrence: University Press of Kansas, 2006), 282–83.

14. Tony Horowitz, *Confederates in the Attic: Dispatches from the Unfinished Civil War* (New York: Pantheon Books, 1998).

15. See Karen Anderson, *Little Rock: Race and Resistance at Central High School* (Princeton, NJ: Princeton University Press, 2010); Numan V. Bartley, "Looking Back at Little Rock," *Arkansas Historical Quarterly* 66, no. 2 (Summer 2007): 112–24; David L. Chappell, "Diversity with a Racial Group: White People in Little Rock, 1957–1959," *Arkansas Historical Quarterly* 66, no. 2 (Summer 2007): 181–93; Graeme Cope, "'A Thorn in the Side?': The Mother's League of Central High School and the Little Rock Desegregation Crisis of 1957," *Arkansas Historical Quarterly* 57 (Summer 1998): 160–90; Graeme Cope, "Honest White People of the Middle and Lower Classes? A Pro-

file of the Capital Citizens' Council during the Little Rock Crisis of 1957," *Arkansas Historical Quarterly* 61 (Spring 2002): 36–58; Graeme Cope, "'Marginal Youngsters' and 'Hoodlums of Both Sexes'? Student Segregationists during the Little Rock School Crisis," *Arkansas Historical Quarterly* 63, no. 4 (Winter 2004): 380–403; Adam Fairclough, "The Little Rock Crisis: Success or Failure for the NAACP?," *Arkansas Historical Quarterly* 56, no. 3 (Autumn 1997): 371–75; Tony A. Freyer, "Politics and Law in the Little Rock Crisis, 1954–1957," *Arkansas Historical Quarterly* 66, no. 2 (Summer 2007): 145–66; Tony A. Freyer, "The Little Rock Crisis Reconsidered," *Arkansas Historical Quarterly* 56, no. 3 (Autumn 1997): 361–70; Tony A. Freyer, *Little Rock on Trial: Cooper v. Aaron and School Desegregation* (Lawrence: University Press of Kansas, 2007); Sandra Gordy, *Finding the Lost Year: What Happened When Little Rock Closed Its Public Schools* (Fayetteville: University of Arkansas Press, 2009); Elizabeth Jacoway, *Turn Away Thy Son: Little Rock, The Crisis That Shocked the Nation* (New York: Free Press, 2007); *Understanding the Little Rock Crisis: An Exercise in Remembrance and Reconciliation*, ed. Elizabeth Jacoway and C. Fred Williams (Fayetteville: University of Arkansas Press, 1999); John A. Kirk, "Massive Resistance and Minimum Compliance: The Origins of the 1957 Little Rock School Crisis and the Failure of School Desegregation in the South," in *Massive Resistance: Southern Opposition to the Second Reconstruction*, ed. Clive Webb (New York: Oxford University Press, 2005), 76–98; John A. Kirk, "The Little Rock Crisis and Postwar Black Activism in Arkansas," *Arkansas Historical Quarterly* 66, no. 2 (Summer 2007): 224–42; C. Fred Williams, "Class: The Central Issue in the 1957 Little Rock School Crisis," *Arkansas Historical Quarterly* 56, no. 3 (Autumn 1997): 341–44.

16. Renee C. Romano, "Narratives of Redemption: The Birmingham Church Bombing Trails and the Construction of Civil Rights Memory," in *The Civil Rights Movement in American Memory*, ed. Renee Romano and Leigh Raiford (Athens: University of Georgia Press, 2006), 96–133. See also Renee C. Romano, *Racial Reckoning: Prosecuting America's Civil Rights Murders* (Cambridge, MA: Harvard University Press, 2014).

17. *Board of Education of Oklahoma City v. Dowell*, 498 US 237 (1991); *Freeman v. Pitts*, 503 US 467 (1992); *Missouri v. Jenkins*, 515 US 79 (1995).

1. Defining Successful Integration

1. Capital Citizens' Council, "'Mrs.' Daisy Bates: Little Rock's 'Lady' of the Year," folder 4, box 6, Mss 523, Daisy Bates Papers, 1946–66, Wisconsin Historical Society, Madison, Wisconsin (Mss 523, Bates Papers, WHS).
2. Reference files, White and Block Opposition, 1957–58, folder 13, box 5, Mss 523, Bates Papers, WHS; political advertisement paid for by Dewey Coffman, *Arkansas Democrat*, 4 December 1958, Reel 5, Micro 801 Daisy Bates Papers, 1946–66, Wisconsin Historical Society, Madison, Wisconsin (Micro 801, Bates Papers, WHS).
3. Roy Reed, "Daisy Bates Writes a Bitter Account," *Arkansas Gazette*, 4 November 1962, folder 4, box 4, Mss 523, Bates Papers, WHS.
4. John A. Kirk, "Massive Resistance and Minimum Compliance: The Origins of

the 1957 Little Rock School Crisis and the Failure of School Desegregation in the South," in *Massive Resistance: Southern Opposition to the Second Reconstruction,* ed. Clive Webb (New York: Oxford University Press, 2005), 76–98.
5. In his biography of Daisy Bates, Grif Stockley notes that Bates relied on as many as four ghostwriters when drafting *The Long Shadow of Little Rock.* Stockley contends that this was part of a longstanding practice and that Bates did little professional writing during her career, despite her frequent byline in the *Arkansas State Press.* Rather, Bates's practice was to dictate material to her secretaries. Stockley suggests that Bates adopted this practice because of her own insecurities about her lack of a formal education. Nevertheless, the sentiments expressed in the memoir are consistent with Bates's public speeches, addresses, and statements in other forums. Regardless of whether the written words were penned by Bates, the memoir published under her name is a reflection of how she wanted to frame the school desegregation crisis for public audiences (Grif Stockley, *Daisy Bates: Civil Rights Crusader from Arkansas* [Jackson: University Press of Mississippi, 2005]).
6. Kirk, "Massive Resistance and Minimum Compliance," 77–79.
7. Virgil T. Blossom, *It HAS Happened Here* (New York: Harper and Brothers, 1959), 77. School board member Harold Engstrom contended that Blossom's ambitions were broader than school administration and that he sought to increase his public profile in hopes of running for elected office (Elizabeth Jacoway, *Turn Away Thy Son: Little Rock, The Crisis That Shocked the Nation* [New York: Free Press, 2007], 85).
8. Blossom, *It HAS Happened Here,* 174.
9. Ibid., 49.
10. Ibid., 4.
11. Ibid., 199–201.
12. Ibid., 199.
13. Kirk, "Massive Resistance and Minimum Compliance," 76, 93.
14. Blossom, *It HAS Happened Here,* 29.
15. Ibid., 17–18.
16. Ibid., 14–16. For the full text of the Little Rock Board of Education's "Plan of School Integration" see *Aaron v. Cooper,* 143 F. Supp. 855 (Dist. Court, ED Arkansas, 1956). See also Numan V. Bartley "Looking Back at Little Rock," *Arkansas Historical Quarterly* 66, no. 2 (Summer 2007): 113.
17. John A. Kirk, *Beyond Little Rock: The Origins and Legacies of the Central High Crisis* (Fayetteville: University of Arkansas Press, 2007), 151–58.
18. Blossom, *It HAS Happened Here,* 17. Virgil Blossom's niece, the historian Elizabeth Jacoway, has noted that her uncle "reportedly advised numerous people . . . that if they wanted to keep their children in segregated [white] schools they should move to the Heights" to attend Hall High (Jacoway, *Turn Away Thy Son,* 57). See also Bartley, "Looking Back at Little Rock," 113; John A. Kirk, "The Little Rock Crisis and Postwar Black Activism in Arkansas," *Arkansas Historical Quarterly* 66, no. 2 (Summer 2007): 239.

19. Blossom, *It HAS Happened Here*, 17–24, emphasis added; *Aaron v. Cooper*, 156 F. Supp. 220 (Dist. Court, ED Arkansas, 1957). See also Kirk, "Massive Resistance and Minimum Compliance," 87; Wiley A. Branton, "Little Rock Revisited: Desegregation to Resegregation," *Journal of Negro Education* 52, no. 3 (Summer 1983): 257–58. Branton notes that none of the thirty-three original plaintiffs in *Aaron v. Cooper* was selected for transfer.
20. Blossom, *It HAS Happened Here*, xi.
21. Ibid., 4.
22. Ibid., 17–18.
23. Daisy Bates, *Long Shadow of Little Rock* (Fayetteville: University of Arkansas Press, 1986), 53; Kirk, "Massive Resistance and Minimum Compliance," 84–85.
24. Blossom, *It HAS Happened Here*, 28–29.
25. Tony Freyer, *The Little Rock Crisis: A Constitutional Interpretation* (Westport, CT: Greenwood Press, 1984), 49; Stockley, *Daisy Bates*, 84–85. White supremacist organizations were even more pointed than school officials in their claims about the outside influences driving the desegregation litigation. The *American Nationalist* distributed a leaflet in Little Rock contending that Daisy Bates was merely "serving as stooge for the New York Jews who control and run the NAACP." The circular proclaimed, "It is high time the people of Little Rock learned the identity of their *real* enemies: the trouble-making New York Jews who control the NAACP and who are responsible for the military occupation of their city! Neither Daisy Bates nor any other Negro in Arkansas was the *real* instigator of the Little Rock Crisis!" (Frank L. Britton, ed. "the Little Rock Story," *American Nationalist*, folder 10, box 5, Mss 523, Bates Papers, WHS).
26. Blossom, *It HAS Happened Here*, 28–29.
27. *Aaron v. Cooper* (Dist. Court, ED Arkansas, 1956). For the perspective of the NAACP, see Wiley A. Branton, "Little Rock Revisited," 250–69; Bates, *Long Shadow of Little Rock*, 51–53. See also Kirk, "Massive Resistance and Minimum Compliance," 94; Kirk, "The Little Rock Crisis and Postwar Black Activism in Arkansas," 239. For a comprehensive legal history of the litigation that came to be known as *Cooper v. Aaron* from the NAACP decision to initiate the suit in 1956 to its conclusion in 1958, see Tony A. Freyer, *Little Rock on Trial: Cooper v. Aaron and School Desegregation* (Lawrence: University Press of Kansas, 2007). This phase of school desegregation litigation in Little Rock was argued under the title *Aaron v. Cooper*, but the Supreme Court issued its final opinion in the case in 1958 under the title *Cooper v. Aaron*.
28. Blossom, *It HAS Happened Here*, 29.
29. Ibid., 49.
30. Ibid., 36–37.
31. Ibid., 2–4.
32. Ibid., 39, 44–45, 147.
33. Ibid., 29.
34. J.A.M. to Virgil Blossom, n.d., folder 1, box 2, series 1, Virgil Blossom Papers, Special Collections, University of Arkansas Libraries, Fayetteville (Blossom Papers).

35. Archie [House] to Virgil Blossom, n.d., folder 1, box 2, series 1, Blossom Papers.
36. Blossom, *It HAS Happened Here*, 3.
37. Michael Meyer, introduction to *It Can't Happen Here* by Sinclair Lewis (New York: New American Library, 2005).
38. Blossom, *It HAS Happened Here*, 48–49, 52.
39. Ibid., 77, 110–11.
40. Ibid., 70–71.
41. Ibid., 48–49.
42. Ibid., 53, 86–89, 124–25.
43. Ibid., 131.
44. Ibid., 201.
45. Ibid., 43–44, 64.
46. Ibid., 53–60.
47. Jacoway, *Turn Away Thy Son*, 84–100.
48. In his own memoir published nearly thirty years later, Faubus contended that the Thomason suit was Blossom's idea and that the superintendent himself delivered the petition "except for the names of the plaintiffs and attorneys" directly to the governor's mansion. Faubus was reportedly shocked when Superintendent Blossom distanced himself from the claims of impending violence in the petition, and testified that he had not heard of any threats of violence outside of Central. Faubus maintained that he had "been double-crossed and betrayed" by Blossom and other members of the board who had appealed to him for assistance, and left him vulnerable to the charge that he had "manufactured" the crisis for his own political gain. See Orval Faubus, *Down from the Hills* (Little Rock: Democrat Lithographing & Printing Press, 1980), 199–204.
49. Substituted Petition, *Aaron v. Cooper*, US District Court, Eastern District of Arkansas, folder 1, box 6, Mss 523, Daisy Bates Papers, WHS.
50. Blossom, *It HAS Happened Here*, 87–88.
51. Ibid., 88–89.
52. Fred L. Zimmerman, "Little Rock Revisited: Racial Calm Marks City Once Torn by Violence," *Wall Street Journal*, 17 December 1963; Reed Sarratt, *The Ordeal of Desegregation: The First Decade* (New York: Harper & Row, 1966), 89.
53. *Shuttlesworth v. Birmingham Board of Education*, 162 F. Supp. 372 (Dist. Court, 1958); *Shuttlesworth v. Birmingham Board of Education*, 358 US 101 (1958).
54. As noted in *Norwood v. Tucker*, 287 F. 2d 798 (8th Circ., 1961). The laws were upheld as "facially valid" in *Parham v. Dove*, 271 F.2d 132 (8th Circ., 1959) and *Dove v. Parham*, 282 F. 2d 256 (8th Circ., 1960). See also Adam Fairclough, "The Little Rock Crisis: Success or Failure for the NAACP?," *Arkansas Historical Quarterly* 56, no. 3 (Autumn 1997): 372.
55. "Little Rock Moves to Spur Integration," *New York Times*, 25 March 1964.
56. Little Rock School Board, Special Meeting Minutes, 8 July 1960, Little Rock School District Administration Building, Little Rock, Arkansas (LRSB); Little Rock School Board, Special Meeting Findings, 5 August 1960, LRSB.

57. Sarratt, *The Ordeal of Desegregation*, 89.
58. Central High student Sybil Jordan recalled being subjected to "psychological testing by someone in the Little Rock Public School system which included the Rorschach test followed by personal interviews with the school board members" (Sandra Gordy, *Finding the Lost Year: What Happened When Little Rock Closed Its Public Schools* [Fayetteville: University of Arkansas Press, 2009], 169).
59. *Norwood v. Tucker* (8th Circ., 1961); Stuart H. Loory, "Back in Little Rock—Now It's a Cold War," *New York Herald Tribune*, 27 August 1961.
60. Gertrude Samuels, "Little Rock Revisited—Tokenism Plus: Five years after the Battle of Central High, the school system is being desegregated as slowly as possible. But outside the schools the city is moving forward," *New York Times Magazine*, 2 June 1963.
61. Bates, *Long Shadow of Little Rock*, 47–48.
62. Daisy Bates, "Little Rock Integration Plan," Manuscripts and Drafts *Long Shadow of Little Rock*, reel 2, Micro 801, Bates Papers, WHS.
63. Bates, *Long Shadow of Little Rock*, 51–52.
64. "Depositions of the Witnesses, Rev. J. C. Crenchaw and Mrs. L. C. Bates," *Aaron v. Cooper*, US District Court Eastern District of Arkansas, folder 1, box 6, Mss 523, Bates Papers, WHS.
65. Daisy Bates, "Citizens Reaction to the 1954 Decision," Manuscripts and Drafts of *Long Shadow of Little Rock*, reel 2, Micro 801, Bates Papers, WHS.
66. Daisy Bates, "The Little Rock Integration Plan"; Kirk, "Massive Resistance and Minimum Compliance," 80, 84–85.
67. "Speeches and Statements of Daisy Bates," n.d., folder 8, box 3, Mss 523, Bates Papers, WHS.
68. Ibid. The historian John A. Kirk has concurred with this assessment, arguing that Blossom's policies "paved the way for the beginning of a movement toward outright defiance of the law and total opposition to school desegregation" (Kirk, "Massive Resistance and Minimum Compliance," 81, 90).
69. "Speeches and Statements of Daisy Bates," n.d., folder 8, box 3, Mss 523, Bates Papers, WHS. See also Bates, "The Embattled Nine," *Long Shadow of Little Rock*, 113–60.
70. "Speeches and Statements of Daisy Bates," n.d., folder 8, box 3, Mss 523, Bates Papers, WHS.
71. Bates, *Long Shadow of Little Rock*, 121–22.
72. Daisy Bates, Manuscripts and Drafts of *Long Shadow of Little Rock*, reel 1, Micro 801, Bates Papers, WHS.
73. Southern Research Council (SRC), "A Background Report on School Desegregation for 1959–60," 10 August 1959, in Desegregation, Schools General, 1959, box 101, Part III: A Administrative File, 1909–69, NAACP Papers, Library of Congress, Washington, DC (NAACP Papers).
74. The editorial board of the *Arkansas Gazette* applauded the pupil placement procedures. See Ben F. Johnson III, "After 1957: Resisting Integration in Little Rock,"

Arkansas Historical Quarterly 66, no. 2 (Summer 2007): 271; Bill Lewis, "Pupil Placement Laws Appear as Big Weapons for Saving Segregation," *Arkansas Gazette*, 28 June 1959; John A. Kirk, *Redefining the Color Line: Black Activism in Little Rock, Arkansas, 1940–1973* (Gainesville: University Press of Florida, 2002), 93, 101–3.

75. Gene Foreman and Tucker Steinmetz, "Looking Back at 'Little Rock': How Ten Years Have Changed the Perspective," *National Observer*, 1967.
76. Bates, *Long Shadow of Little Rock*, 222–25.
77. Ibid., xx. See John Kirk, "Daisy Bates, the National Association for the Advancement of Colored People, and the 1957 Little Rock School Crisis: A Gendered Perspective," in *Gender and the Civil Rights Movement*, ed. Peter J. Ling and Sharon Monteith (New Brunswick, NJ: Rutgers University Press, 2004), 19.
78. Bates, *Long Shadow of Little Rock*, 225.
79. Genevieve Fabre, "African American Commemorative Celebrations in the Nineteenth Century," in *History and Memory in African-American Culture*, ed. Genevieve Fabre and Robert O'Meally (New York: Oxford University Press, 1994), 72–73.
80. Daisy Bates, "Speech delivered to the Detroit Branch of the NAACP," 2 May 1958; folder 4, box 3, Mss 523, Bates Papers, WHS.
81. Bates, *Long Shadow of Little Rock*, 38.
82. Ibid., 52. This may be the case, but a number of observers have noted that local and regional NAACP officials were at odds about the best legal strategy to pursue in the case. The local branch preferred to push for full implementation of the geographic attendance zones (which would have had the effect of admitting more than 500 black students to Central High), while regional attorney U. Simpson Tate decided to argue the case on constitutional grounds (Freyer, *The Little Rock Crisis*, 56–57; Kirk, "Massive Resistance and Minimum Compliance," 84–85; Stockley, *Daisy Bates*, 88).
83. NAACP News Release, 19 October 1957, folder 10, box 4, Mss 523, Bates Papers, WHS.
84. Daisy Bates, "Address delivered by Mrs. L. C. Bates at FFF Program sponsored by Cincinnati, Ohio Branch, NAACP," 24 November 1958, folder 4, box 3, Mss 523, Bates Papers, WHS.
85. NAACP News Release, 19 October 1957.
86. Daisy Bates, Manuscripts and Drafts of *Long Shadow of Little Rock*, reel 3, Micro 801, Bates Papers, WHS.
87. Daisy Bates, "Address delivered by Mrs. L. C. Bates at FFF Program."
88. Daisy Bates, Manuscript and Drafts of *Long Shadow of Little Rock*, reel 2 and 3, Micro 801, Bates Papers, WHS.
89. Many reviews of the text followed the First Lady's lead and described Bates's text as a moving if bitter insider account of the crisis and its aftermath. For example, see Robert E. Baker, "Bitter View from Little Rock," *Washington Post*, 28 October 1962.
90. Irvine J. Spitzberg Jr., *Racial Politics in Little Rock, 1954–1965* (New York: Garland Publishing, 1987), 134, 150–51; Kirk, *Redefining the Color Line*, 150; Kirk, "Daisy Bates," 37; Stockley, *Daisy Bates*, 210–18.

91. Council on Community Affairs to Mr. Everett Tucker Jr., President of the Little Rock Public Schools Board of Education, 29 August 1963, as transcribed into the board's minutes, Executive Meeting, 21 November 1963 LRSB. See also "Little Rock Schools Quiet," *New York Times*, 31 August 1963.
92. Board of Directors of the Little Rock School District (4-2) to Dr. W-H Townsend, President of the Council on Community Affairs, November 1963, as transcribed in the board's minutes, Executive Meeting, 21 November 1963, LRSB. See also "White Schools' Negro Student Total Attacked," *Arkansas Gazette*, 1 September 1961, in Desegregation, Schools, Arkansas, General, 1956-64, box 98, Part III:A, Administrative File, 1909-1969, NAACP Papers.
93. For detailed statistics provided by the Southern Education Reporting Service on school desegregation by state in 1964, see Sarratt, *The Ordeal of Desegregation*, 359, table 1.
94. *Clark v. Board of Education of the Little Rock School District*, 369 F.2d 661 (8th Cir. 1966); Statistics provided by Floyd W. Parsons, Superintendent of Schools, "Desegregation Report: Little Rock School District," January 1968, filed in minutes of the Little Rock School Board, LRSB; "Little Rock Adopts a New School Plan Stressing, 'Choice,'" *New York Times*, 24 April 1965. See also Kirk, *Redefining the Color Line*, 174-75.
95. "'Little Rock Nine,' Now Adults, Proud of Integration Role," *Arkansas Gazette*, 30 January 1966.
96. *Clark v. Board of Education* (8th Cir. 1966). See also Kirk, *Redefining the Color Line*, 174-75.
97. *Green v. County School Board*, 391 US 430 (1968).
98. *Clark v. Board of Education of the Little Rock School District*, 426 F.2d 1035 (8th Cir. 1970).
99. Karen Anderson, *Little Rock: Race and Resistance at Central High School* (Princeton, NJ: Princeton University Press, 2010), 50, 229.

2. Obscuring Effective Mechanisms of Change

1. *Clark v. Board of Education of the Little Rock School District* 426 F.2d 1035 (8th Cir. 1970).
2. Peter Milius, "Apartheid in the City Schools: Boston Typifies Battle over Integration Goals," *Washington Post Times Herald*, 4 April 1971. See also Linda Matthews, "Why Just Us? South Asks on Desegregation," *Los Angeles Times*, 8 August 1971.
3. *Clark v. Board of Education* (8th Cir. 1970); US Commission on Civil Rights, *School Desegregation in Little Rock, Arkansas* (Washington, DC, June 1977), 2; Statistics drawn from University of Arkansas, College of Business Administration, Industrial Research and Extension Center, "Population Changes and Migration in Arkansas by Color, 1950-1970," Arkansas Population Analysis Series, no. 70-73 (Little Rock, July 1974), 6-7; Ben F. Johnson III, "After 1957: Resisting Integration in Little Rock," *Arkansas Historical Quarterly* 66, no. 2 (Summer 2007): 260-64; Karen Anderson,

Little Rock: Race and Resistance at Central High School (Princeton, NJ: Princeton University Press, 2010), 38–41; Roy Reed, "Resegregation: A Problem in Urban South," *New York Times,* 28 September 1970; Herbert H. Denton, "Race Issue Still Dogs Schools in Nation, Conference Told," *Washington Post Times Herald,* 2 February 1969; "Little Rock Office on Public Housing Sued by US on Bias," *New York Times,* 22 November 1968. The housing authority signed a consent order agreeing to desegregate public housing in December 1968 ("Little Rock to Desegregate," *Los Angeles Times,* 8 December 1968; James Scudder, "Two Separate Societies: The Population Shift in Little Rock . . . and Its Effects on the Schools," *Arkansas Democrat,* 18 April 1971).

4. *Clark v. Board of Education* (8th Cir. 1970). The student populations of Carver, Gilliam, Granite Mountain, Ish, Pfeifer, Rightsell, Stephens, and Washington were each 95 percent or more black. See also Scudder, "Two Separate Societies."
5. *Clark v. Board of Education* (8th Cir. 1970).
6. Little Rock School Board, Regular Meeting Minutes, 28 May 1970, Little Rock School District Administration Building, Little Rock, Arkansas (LRSB).
7. *Clark v. Board of Education* (8th Cir. 1970). Jerol Garrison, "LR School Zoning Is Turned Down; New Plan Ordered," *Arkansas Gazette,* 14 May 1970.
8. *Swann v. Charlotte-Mecklenburg Board of Education,* 91 S.Ct. 1267; 402 US 1; 28 L. Ed. 2d 554 (1971); "Supreme Court Rules Busing Can Be Required: But Ratio Formula Rejected," *Arkansas Democrat,* 20 April 1971; "'Bus' Plan Legal, Broad Rulings of Court Say: Southerners Denounce Rulings as 'Tragic,'" *Arkansas Gazette,* 21 April 1971. Although Little Rock had also filed for a review of its school desegregation plan, the high court chose not to hear arguments in the Little Rock case along with the others under consideration in *Swann.* One of the newest justices on the Court, Harry A. Blackmun, sat on the 8th Circuit and signed onto the majority opinion in *Clark* a mere week before he was confirmed by the Senate (Peter Milius, "Blackmun Court Ruling Opposes Nixon," *Washington Post Times Herald,* 15 May 1970; "Supreme Court Agrees to Rule on Busing to Gain Integration," *Los Angeles Times,* 1 September 1970).
9. *Clark v. Board of Education of the Little Rock School District,* 449 F.2d 493 (8th Cir. 1971).
10. Statement of Hon. Elliot L. Richardson, Secretary, Department of Health, Education and Welfare, House Subcommittee No. 5 of the Committee on the Judiciary, *Hearings on the Proposed Amendments to the Constitution and Legislation Relating to Transportation and Assignment of Public School Pupils,* 92nd Cong., 2nd sess., 13 April 1972, 1206–7, 1227.
11. Roy Reed, "White Academies Thrive in the South: But Fewer Pupils Flee the Desegregated Schools," *New York Times,* 29 August 1971. Rector had long enjoyed a reputation as one of the first businessmen to publicly oppose Governor Faubus by supporting a moderate slate of school board members in 1958–59. However, his support for gradual desegregation in the 1950s may have been motivated by more than altruism. In the 1960s, Rector's real estate developments in the city's

West End boomed as whites fled integration in the central city. The historian Ben F. Johnson III has argued that Rector opened Pulaski Academy because district-wide desegregation "threatened the value" of the same suburban real estate years later (Johnson, "After 1957," 258–83). See also Roy Reed, "Resegregation"; Scudder, "Two Separate Societies"; James Scudder, "The Role of Real-Estate Dealers: Have They Influenced the Desegregation Case?," *Arkansas Democrat,* 21 April 1971; Anderson, *Little Rock,* 233.

12. Johnson, "After 1957," 281.
13. Richard Nixon, "Address to Congress, March 20, 1972," reprinted in *School Busing: Constitutional and Political Developments,* vol. 2: *The Public Debate over Busing and Attempts to Restrict Its Use,* ed. Davison M. Douglas (New York: Garland Publishing, 1994), 152–68; Orfield, *Must We Bus? Segregated Schools and National Policy* (Washington, DC: Brookings Institution, 1978), 104–5, 254; "Nixon Asks for Busing Block: Urges Moratorium on Federal Court Orders," *Arkansas Democrat,* 17 March 1972.
14. House Subcommittee No. 5 of the Committee on the Judiciary, *Hearings on the Proposed Amendments to the Constitution and Legislation Relating to Transportation and Assignment of Public School Pupils,* 92nd Cong., 2nd sess., 1972.
15. Statement of the US Commission on Civil Rights Concerning the President's Message to Congress and Proposed Legislation on Busing and Equal Educational Opportunities, House Subcommittee, *Hearings on the Proposed Amendments to the Constitution and Legislation Relating to Transportation and Assignment of Public School Pupils,* 29 March 1972, 1134.
16. Ibid. Jeanne Theoharis reminds us that historians have not been sensitive to the parallels civil rights organizations worked to make between earlier efforts to resist desegregation and antibusing movements. Antibusing advocates, particularly in the North, are not frequently labeled as "segregationists" in historical accounts but rather are described as part of a "white backlash." Theoharis contends that antibusing advocates were part of a "frontlash" designed to "block African-American educational, job, and housing opportunities." This is certainly the case in Little Rock, where antibusing sentiment surfaced before the implementation of federal court orders and undergirded the school district's legal petitions in favor of neighborhood zoning. See Jeanne Theoharis, "Hidden in Plain Sight: The Civil Rights Movement Outside the South," in *The Myth of Southern Exceptionalism,* ed. Matthew D. Lassiter and Joseph Crespino (New York: Oxford University Press, 2010), 51.
17. As quoted in Nathaniel R. Jones, "Boston and Little Rock: The Issue Is the Same," *Washington Post,* 3 January 1975.
18. Julian Bond, "The Media and the Movement: Looking Back from the Southern Front," in *Media, Culture and the Modern African American Freedom Struggle,* ed. Brian Ward (Gainesville: University Press of Florida, 2001), 28–29; Robert J. Norrell, "One Thing We Did Right: Reflections on the Movement," in *New Directions in Civil Rights Studies,* ed. Armstead L. Robinson and Patricia Sullivan (Charlottesville: University of Virginia Press, 1991), 75–77; Edward P. Morgan, "The Good, The Bad, and the Forgotten: Media Culture and the Public Memory of the Civil Rights

Movement," in *The Civil Rights Movement in American Memory*, ed. Renee Romano and Leigh Raiford (Athens: University of Georgia Press, 2006), 138–40. For more on coverage of the Little Rock school desegregation crisis in 1957 itself, see Gene Roberts and Hank Klibanoff, *The Race Beat: The Press, The Civil Rights Struggle, and The Awakening of a Nation* (New York: Vintage Books, 2006), 43–60, 143–83; and Allison Graham, "Remapping Dogpatch: Northern Media on the Southern Circuit," *Arkansas Historical Quarterly* 56, no. 3 (Autumn 1997): 334–40.

19. Jacquelyn Dowd Hall coined the term "narrative breach" in her essay "The Long Civil Rights Movement and the Political Uses of the Past," *Journal of American History* 91, no. 4 (March 2005): 1233–63. See also Peniel E. Joseph, "Introduction: Toward a Historiography of the Black Power Movement," in *The Black Power Movement: Rethinking the Civil Rights-Black Power Era*, ed. Peniel E. Joseph (New York: Routledge, 2006), 1–26; Clayborne Carson, "Civil Rights Reform and the Black Freedom Struggle," in *The Civil Rights Movement in America*, ed. Charles Eagles (Jackson: University Press of Mississippi, 2006), 28; George Lipsitz, *American Studies in a Moment of Danger* (Minneapolis: University of Minnesota Press, 2001), 78.

20. For example, see Henry S. Huntington, letter to the editor, "On Busing in Boston and Equal Opportunity," *New York Times*, 28 October 1974; William Raspberry, "The Differences between Little Rock and Boston," *Washington Post*, 18 December 1964.

21. Arnold R. Hirsch, *Making the Second Ghetto: Race and Housing in Chicago, 1940–1960* (Cambridge: Cambridge University Press, 1983); Kenneth T. Jackson, *Crabgrass Frontier: The Suburbanization of the United States* (New York: Oxford University Press, 1985); Thomas J. Sugrue, *The Origins of the Urban Crisis: Race and Inequality in Postwar Detroit* (Princeton, NJ: Princeton University Press, 1996); David M.P. Freund, *Colored Property: State Policy and White Racial Politics in Suburban America* (Chicago: University of Chicago Press, 2007). As Matthew Lassiter has recently noted, although historians have excavated the official state action underlying residential segregation throughout the United States, "civil rights advocates have always faced extreme difficulty in connecting the historical dots for white suburban audiences and for many federal jurists as well." See Matthew D. Lassiter, *The Silent Majority: Suburban Politics in the Sunbelt South* (Princeton, NJ: Princeton University Press, 2006), 134.

22. Lassiter, *The Silent Majority*, 14–15, 45–46, 122–23, 142.

23. For more on the working-class wing of the Boston antibusing movement, see Emmett H. Buell Jr. with Richard A. Brisbin Jr., *School Desegregation and Defended Neighborhoods: The Boston Controversy* (Lexington, MA: D. C. Heath and Company, 1982). According to Buell and Brisbin, public opinion polls revealed that a commitment to neighborhood schools, particularly in "defended neighborhoods" threatened by other unwanted social changes such as urban renewal or gentrification, fueled the antibusing movement.

24. Theoharis, "Hidden in Plain Sight," 51–54.

25. Sybil Stevenson, "Reflections on Little Rock," *Theory into Practice* 17, no. 2 (1978): 179–80.

26. Leo Collins, weekly columnist, "Ignorance Flairs in Boston," *Southern Mediator Journal*, 27 September 1974; Dr. J. F. Cooley, "Cooley Said It!" (weekly column), *Southern Mediator Journal*, 27 September 1974; "Racial Violence in Boston" (editorial), *Southern Mediator Journal*, 11 October 1974; "Little Rock Busing Must Continue" (editorial), *Southern Mediator Journal*, 29 June 1973; Leo Collins, "Textbooks Lie," *Southern Mediator Journal*, 8 September 1972.
27. Nathaniel R. Jones, "Boston and Little Rock: The Issue Is the Same," *Washington Post*, 3 January 1975; Tom Wicker, "A Tale of 2 Cities," *New York Times*, 3 November 1974.
28. Roger Wilkins, "Northern Justice," *New York Times*, 24 September 1974.
29. Peter Milius, "Apartheid in the City Schools: Boston Typifies Battle over Integration Goals," *Washington Post Times Herald*, 4 April 1971; see Matthews, "Why Just Us?"
30. These alternative student assignment plans are known as the Oregon Report and the Parsons Plan. See University of Oregon, School of Education, Bureau of Educational Research, "A Report to the Board of Directors of the Little Rock School District, Little Rock, Arkansas," May 1967, LRSB; and Parsons, "Desegregation Report: Little Rock School District," January 1968, LRSB. See also *Clark v. Board of Education* (8th Cir. 1970); Johnson, "After 1957," 258–83; Paul Fair, "Little Rock: Then and Now," *Theory into Practice* 17, no. 1 (February 1978): 40; Anderson, "The Little Rock School Desegregation Crisis: Moderation and Social Conflict," *Journal of Southern History* 70, no. 3 (August 2004): 620–31; "Little Rock Vetoes Integration Plan," *New York Times*, 13 March 1968.
31. Johnson, "After 1957," 277, 283.
32. "Anything Goes" (editorial), *Arkansas Democrat*, 21 April 1971; Karr Shannon, "Court Tracks Warren, Ignores Constitution," *Arkansas Democrat*, 23 April 1971; "Hardly Compatible" (editorial), *Arkansas Democrat*, 15 May 1970.
33. Johnson, "After 1957," 276.
34. Nixon, "Address to Congress, March 20, 1972," 152–68; Matthew D. Lassiter, "De Jure/De Facto Segregation: The Long Shadow of a National Myth," in *The Myth of Southern Exceptionalism*, ed. Matthew D. Lassiter and Joseph Crespino (New York: Oxford University Press, 2010), 39–41; Orfield, *Must We Bus?*, 104–5, 254; "Nixon Asks for Busing Block."
35. Eric Wentworth, "25 States Seen Hit by Nixon Bus Plan," *Washington Post Times Herald*, 30 April 1972.
36. Patsy McKown and Roger Armbrust, "Will Area Busing Stop? President's Proposed Moratorium Could Affect LR Schools," *Arkansas Democrat*, 17 March 1972.
37. "Little Effect in Arkansas: John W. Walker Evaluates Busing Moratorium," *Arkansas Democrat*, 18 March 1972.
38. Joseph Tilden Rhea, *Race Pride and the American Identity* (Cambridge, MA: Harvard University Press, 1997); Andrea A. Burns, *From Storefront to Monument: Tracing the Public History of the Black Museum Movement* (Amherst: University of Massachusetts Press, 2013); Martha Biondi, *The Black Revolution on Campus* (Berkley: University of California Press, 2012).

39. Tammy S. Gordon, *The Spirit of 1976: Commerce, Community, and the Politics of Commemoration* (Amherst: University of Massachusetts Press, 2013).
40. Manning Marable, *Living Black History: How Reimagining the African American Past Can Remake America's Racial Future* (New York: Basic Books, 2006), 58. W. E. B. DuBois's efforts to reshape and contest the public memory of the Civil War is one of the most frequently cited manifestations of this tradition. See David Blight, *Race and Reunion: The Civil War in American Memory* (Cambridge, MA: Belknap Press of Harvard University Press, 2001).
41. Roy Wilkins, memorandum to All Branches, Youth Councils, College Chapters, State Conferences, to Members of the National Board of Directors and to the Staff, 17 March 1972, folder 10, box 145, Part VII, NAACP Papers, Library of Congress, Washington, DC (NAACP Papers).
42. "NAACP Is Ready for Busing Fight, Counsel Asserts," *Arkansas Gazette,* 20 March 1972.
43. "NAACP Director Denounces Stand of Nixon on Busing," *Arkansas Gazette,* 19 March 1972.
44. Rik O'Neal, "Blacks Make Pilgrimage to Central High: NAACP Leaders Score Nixon's Antibusing Stand," *Arkansas Democrat,* 19 March 1972.
45. US Commission on Civil Rights, *School Desegregation in Little Rock, Arkansas: A Staff Report of the US Commission on Civil Rights* (Washington, DC: US Commission on Civil Rights: Government Printing Office, June 1977); US Commission on Civil Rights, *Your Child and Busing,* Clearinghouse Publication No. 36 (Washington, DC: Government Printing Office, May 1972).
46. US Commission on Civil Rights, *Your Child and Busing.* See also Statement of Mr. Theodore M. Hesburgh, Chairman, US Commission on Civil Rights, House Subcommittee, 1 March 1972, 186–236; Statement of Hon. Stephen Horn, Vice Chairman, US Commission of Civil Rights, House Subcommittee, 10 May 1972, 1589, 1597; Statement of US Commission on Civil Rights Concerning the President's Message to Congress and Proposed Legislation on Busing and Equal Educational Opportunities, House Subcommittee, 1134–35, in *Hearings on the Proposed Amendments to the Constitution and Legislation Relating to Transportation and Assignment of Public School Pupils,* 92nd Cong., 2nd sess., 13 April 1972.
47. "School Opening" (editorial), *Southern Mediator Journal,* 31 August 1973; "Busing off to a Fair, Faltering Start: Only Normal Confusion for First Day," *Arkansas Democrat,* 30 August 1971; Tucker Steinmetz, "Students Take Busing in Stride; Day 'Ordinary,'" *Arkansas Gazette,* 31 August 1971; "Blacks Praise Students and Parents for 'Standing Tall' at School Opening," *Arkansas Gazette,* 7 September 1971.
48. *Little Rock, 17 Years Later* (New York: NAACP Legal Defense and Educational Fund, 1974).
49. "Scene of '57 US Crisis Now Just a High School: Fully Integrated, Little Rock's Central High Recalls Crisis over First Black Students," *Los Angeles Times,* 3 November 1974.
50. Roy Reed, "Little Rock School Now Integration Model," *New York Times,* 8 September 1976; "Scene of '57 US Crisis Now Just a High School."

51. John Egerton, "Little Rock, 1976: 'Going Back Would be Unthinkable,'" *Southern Exposure* 1 (Summer 1979): 45–46. Also published in *School Desegregation: A Report Card from the South* (Atlanta: Southern Regional Council, 1976). See also "Scene of '57 US Crisis Now Just a High School"; Fair, "Little Rock: Then and Now," 39–42.
52. Jeff Prugh, "Little Rock 20 Years Later: Integration Violence a Bad Dream," *Los Angeles Times*, 25 September 1977; Roy Reed, "Little Rock School Now Integration Model."
53. James Merriweather, "Central High Commemorates '57," *Arkansas Gazette*, 29 September 1977; James Scudder, "Central Revisited: Cheers, Not Jeers," *Arkansas Democrat*, 29 September 1977.
54. "Little Rock School District Policy Statement," Little Rock School Board Special Meeting, January 4, 1977, LRSB; Fair, "Little Rock: Then and Now," 39–42; US Commission on Civil Rights, *School Desegregation in Little Rock, Arkansas*, 14.
55. US Commission on Civil Rights, *School Desegregation in Little Rock, Arkansas*, 10–16.
56. "Little Rock School District Policy Statement"; Fair, "Little Rock: Then and Now," 39–42; US Commission on Civil Rights, *School Desegregation in Little Rock, Arkansas*, 14.
57. US Commission on Civil Rights, *School Desegregation in Little Rock, Arkansas*, 12.
58. For a different interpretation of these developments see David Gene Vinzant, "Little Rock's Long Crisis: Schools and Race in Little Rock, Arkansas, 1863–2009" (PhD diss., University of Arkansas, 2010), particularly concluding remarks, 314–23. Vinzant's work provides excellent context for those interested in educational segregation in Little Rock before the 1957 school desegregation crisis, and he also provides extended discussion of developments between 1957 and 1976. However, his study is less attentive to and less critical of the turn away from the desegregation paradigm that developed during those years and the weakening of court oversight over the following three decades. Indeed, Vinzant questions whether "the struggle to integrate schools was the best way to help educationally disadvantaged black children" given the persistent achievement gap and suggests that African American students could achieve better educational outcomes in predominantly black schools. Vinzant also underscores the effect of "mandatory school assignments" on white flight. He argues that court-ordered desegregation effectively "drove whites out of Little Rock" and "made the metropolitan area more segregated than it would have otherwise been." In contrast, by taking a closer look at the way school desegregation policy has evolved in the Little Rock school district since the 1980s, the present book suggests that it is not court-ordered desegregation per se but rather the way the process of school desegregation has been implemented and evaded in the city that has produced white flight, disinvestment in public education, and persistent disparities in student achievement.

3. Recasting Moderation and Resistance

1. Paul Henderickson, "Orval Faubus and the Shadow of History; In the Era of a Another Arkansan, the Ailing Former Governor Strives to Stave Off a Segrega-

tionist Legacy," *Washington Post,* 25 January 1993; Roy Reed, *Faubus: The Life and Times of an American Prodigal* (Fayetteville: University of Arkansas Press, 1997), vii, 335–36; Harry S. Ashmore, "The Legacy of Orval Faubus" (book review), *New Crisis,* 104, no. 1 (October 1997): 20.

2. Orval Faubus, *Down from the Hills* (Little Rock: Democrat Lithographing & Printing Press, 1980), 431, 456, 500; Orval Eugene Faubus, *Down from the Hills II* (Little Rock: Democrat Printing & Lithographing Company, 1985), 483. See also "Innocent Victims," folder 2, box 13, series 2, Orval Eugene Faubus Addendum, Special Collections, University of Arkansas Libraries, Fayetteville (Faubus Addendum); "Questions to Former Governor Faubus by a Student on the Central High School Crisis," folder 5, box 14, series 2, Faubus Addendum.

3. Orval Eugene Faubus to O. R. Baldwin, Pastor, North Little Rock, 31 May 1973, folder 5, box 13, series 2, Faubus Addendum.

4. For example, see Perrin Jones, "Faubus Writes Remarkable Book" (citizen editor book review), *Searcy Daily Citizen,* 11 February 1981, folder 4, box 13, series 2, Faubus Addendum.

5. Leland Duvall, "'Down from the Hills': Scrapbook with Footnotes," *Arkansas Gazette,* 1 February 1981. News clipping and Faubus's handwritten note in folder 4, box 13, series 2, Faubus Addendum.

6. Walter L. Brown, "Down from the Hills" (book review), n.p., n.d., folder 4, box 13, series 2, Faubus Addendum.

7. Henderickson, "Orval Faubus and the Shadow of History"; Judith Colp, "Symbol of Era, Orval Faubus Writes, Reflects," *Washington Times,* 26 May 1992; Reed, *Faubus,* 336, 369; "Faubus at LR Promoting His Book on Earlier Years of His Political Career," *Arkansas Gazette,* 6 June 1980; Rex Nelson, "Orval E. Faubus, Selling His Book, Visits Arkadelphia," *Daily Siftings Herald,* Arkadelphia, Arkansas, 25 May 1981; Letter to O. E. Faubus from B. W. Hicks; and "Faubus Book Now Being Published," excerpt from the upcoming book and note from author, *England Democrat,* 20 August 1980, folder 4, box 3, series 2, Faubus Addendum.

8. Tee Dolphus, "The Little Rock Story Is Being Told without the Help of Major Participants," *Southern Mediator,* 27 June 1980, folder 13, box 12, subseries 5, series 5, Daisy Bates Papers, Special Collections, University of Arkansas Libraries, Fayetteville (Bates Papers, UAF).

9. James T. Baker, *Brooks Hays* (Macon, GA: Mercer University Press, 1989), 144–47.

10. John Kyle Day, "The Fall of a Southern Moderate: Congressman Brooks Hays and the Election of 1958," *Arkansas Historical Quarterly* 59, no. 3 (Autumn 2000): 242–43; Brooks Hays, *A Southern Moderate Speaks* (Chapel Hill: University of North Carolina Press, 1959), 19–20, 30–31, 48, 222–24.

11. Hays, *A Southern Moderate Speaks,* 94–96, 130, 162.

12. Ibid., 135–36, 141.

13. Ibid., 176, 181.

14. Dale Alford and L'Moore Alford, *The Case of the Sleeping People (Finally Awakened by Little Rock School Frustrations)* (Little Rock: Pioneer Press, 1959), 85–90, 94,

100–101. On the 1958 election see Day, "The Fall of a Southern Moderate," 254–58; "Arkansas: Victory without Hate?," *Time*, 23 June 1958; "By Telephone from Little Rock: Representative Brooks Hays, Democrat of Arkansas," *US News & World Report*, 14 November 1958.

15. Brooks Hays, *A Hotbed of Tranquility: My Life in Five Worlds* (New York: Macmillan, 1968), 45–46.
16. Brooks Hays, *Politics Is My Parish* (Baton Rouge: Louisiana State University Press, 1981), 193–94; Baker, *Brooks Hays*, 95.
17. Hays, *A Southern Moderate Speaks*, 94–96, 130, 137, 157, 174, 180–81, 217, 223–30.
18. Hays, *Politics Is My Parish*, 180. These kinds of statements led Hays's biographer, James T. Baker, to conclude that Hays was an unqualified "liberal" who merely masked his views while he was an elected official (Baker, *Brooks Hays*, 54–55).
19. Elizabeth Shores, "Producers Seek Morality Play in Hays Film Story," *Arkansas Democrat*, 16 September 1979; Roosevelt Thompson, "Television Crew to Visit for Film on Brooks Hays," *The Tiger* (Little Rock Central High School newspaper), 12 October 1979; Roosevelt Thompson, "Former Congressman Hays Visits to Gain Scenes for Documentary," *The Tiger*, 9 November 1979, folder 12, box 4, subseries 2, series 1, Brooks Hays Supplementary Papers, Special Collections, University of Arkansas, Fayetteville (Hays Supplement). See also *Brooks Hays: Return to Little Rock*, prod. David Solomon, Arkansas Region of the National Conference of Christians and Jews, 1980, videocassette.
20. David Solomon, proposal, "Moral Crises in Government" series, "Brooks Hays: The Moral Impulse," and David Solomon to Hon. Thomas O'Neill, Speaker of the House of Representatives, 7 November 1979, in folder 9, box 4; David Solomon, proposal, "Brooks Hays: Return to Little Rock," 1978, in folder 10, box 4, subseries 2, series 1, Hays Supplement. See also Linda Brinson, "A Star at 82: He's a Former Everything, And Now Subject of a Film," *The Sentinel* (Winston-Salem, NC), 10 September 1980; Elizabeth F. Shores, "Ex-Congressman Starring in Film on School Crisis," *Arkansas Democrat*, 25 July 1979.
21. Shores, "Ex-Congressman Starring in Film on School Crisis"; Elizabeth Shores, "Crisis Documentary Begins: Film on Brooks Hays to Show 'Moral Courage,'" *Arkansas Democrat*, 12 September 1979.
22. David Solomon to Dr. Schlesinger, 7 November 1979; and David Solomon to Hon. Thomas O'Neill, Speaker of the House of Representatives, 7 November 1979, in folder 9, box 4, subseries 2, series 1, Hays Supplement; Shores, "Ex-Congressman Starring in Film on School Crisis"; Brinson, "A Star at 82."
23. "Schmutz Speaks Out on Brooks Hays Documentary," *Arkansas Democrat*, 24 September 1979.
24. "AETN May Bar Film on LR Crisis," *Arkansas Gazette*, 20 September 1979. The Little Rock school desegregation crisis was one of the first events to be extensively broadcast on network news. In their history of the media coverage of the crisis, Gene Roberts and Hank Klibanoff observed that several reporters breached ethical boundaries, even urging the crowd gathered outside Central High School to

reenact events if they had not captured them on camera (Gene Roberts and Hank Klibanoff, *The Race Beat: The Press, The Civil Rights Struggle, and The Awakening of a Nation* [New York: Vintage Books, 2006], 160). Because of these incidents, some residents of Little Rock argue that the iconic images associated with the crisis were manufactured—not captured—on film. Schmutz's charge was less explosive—he was primarily concerned with the selection and editing of images filmed outside the school, not their historical authenticity.

25. Renee C. Romano, *Racial Reckoning: Prosecuting America's Civil Rights Murders* (Cambridge, MA: Harvard University Press, 2014), 16.

26. "Desegregation Film May Not Air in the State," *Arkansas Democrat*, 19 September 1979; "AETN May Bar Film on LR Crisis."

27. Unlike European networks, American public television is a decentralized system of loosely federated affiliates that tap into a national library of programs. Since 1975, PBS affiliates have agreed to support a "core schedule" of programs, but they may still decline to air nationally distributed programs that they do not believe suit the interests of local audiences. In the 1960s and 1970s, for example, Southern public television stations sometimes refused to broadcast nationally distributed programs that addressed civil rights and race relations. For more on the structure of public television and its effect on documentary film production see James Day, *The Vanishing Vision: The Inside Story of Public Television* (Berkeley: University of California Press, 1995), and B. J. Bullert, *Public Television: Politics and the Battle over Documentary Film* (New Brunswick, NJ: Rutgers University Press, 1997).

28. "AETN May Bar Film on LR Crisis"; Day, *The Vanishing Vision*, 121, 326–30.

29. Bullert, *Public Television*, 2–8, 13–14, 38, 188–89.

30. George Wells, "Hays Says Film 'Favorable' on LR," *Arkansas Gazette*, 28 October 1979; Elizabeth F. Shores, "Hays Predicts Favorable View of State in Film," *Arkansas Democrat*, 12 October 1979.

31. Paul Greenberg, "A Whiff of the Old Days" (opinion), *Tulsa World*, 26 September 1979.

32. "The Way It Was at Little Rock" (editorial), *Arkansas Gazette*, 22 September 1979. See also Richard E. Yates, "Show the Film—Contribution is Good for Our State Soul," *Arkansas Democrat*, 7 October 1979.

33. "The Arkansas Press: Educational Television and Citizenship," *Pine Bluff Commercial* and *Dumas Clarion* editorials reprinted in *Arkansas Gazette*, 21 October 1979. See also "Association Board is 'Concerned' about AETN's Censorship Policies," *Arkansas Gazette*, 10 September 1979; "The Way It Was at Little Rock"; Richard Stein, letter to the editor, "Screening Out Undesirable History," *Arkansas Gazette*, 30 September 1979.

34. Jim Allen, "Clinton blasts AETN for comments on Hays Film," *Arkansas Democrat*, 10 December 1979; "A Word from Clinton" (editorial), *Arkansas Gazette*, 19 December 1979; Governor Bill Clinton to Arkansas Endowment of Humanities, 7 August 1980, folder 11, box 4, subseries 2, series 1, Hays Supplement.

35. Governor Bill Clinton to Arkansas Endowment of Humanities; Susan Frantz,

"250 Attend LR Premiere of Film Detailing Hays's Role in School Crisis," *Arkansas Gazette*, 10 August 1980; "Return to Little Rock," newsletter, Arkansas Endowment for the Humanities, August 1980, folder 12, box 4, subseries 2, series 1, Hays Supplement.

36. Frantz, "250 Attend LR Premiere of Film Detailing Hays's Role in School Crisis"; Erwin L. McDonald to Brooks Hays, "When Duty Calls," typescript for *Daily Courier-Democrat*, 15 August 1980; Don McEvoy, Senior Vice President of the National Conference of Christians and Jews, "Keeping the Dream Alive," n.d., folder 12, box 4, subseries 2, series 1, Hays Supplement.
37. Thompson, "Former Congressman Hays Visits to Gain Scenes for Documentary."
38. Elizabeth F. Shores, "Brooks Hays Film Skims over Social Forces, Moral Dilemma of Career," *Arkansas Democrat*, 11 August 1980; Shores, "Producers Seek Morality Play in Hays Film Story"; William W. Stead, "Unfulfillment of the Brooks Hays Film" (letter to the editor), *Arkansas Gazette*, 17 August 1980.
39. *Brooks Hays: Return to Little Rock*.
40. Elizabeth Huckaby, *Crisis at Central High, Little Rock 1957–58* (Baton Rouge: Louisiana State University Press, 1980), 218.
41. Elizabeth Huckaby, "The Gun Cabinet and Chance on the Long Road to the Publication of CRISIS AT CENTRAL HIGH 1957–1958," n.d., folder 10, box 9, Elizabeth Huckaby Papers, Special Collections, University of Arkansas Libraries, Little Rock (Huckaby Papers, UALR).
42. Huckaby, *Crisis at Central High*, 2, 12–13, 48, 94–95.
43. Ibid., xvi, 48; Untitled document typed from notes written in Huckaby's hand, n.d., folder 1, box 10, Huckaby Papers, UALR.
44. Huckaby, *Crisis at Central High*, 109–10, 130.
45. Ibid., 85, 96.
46. Huckaby, "The Gun Cabinet"; Bob Wisehart, "A Reluctant, 'Little' Hero," *Times-Picayune*, 1 February 1981. For more on the "Lost Year" see Sondra Gordy, *Finding the Lost Year: What Happened When Little Rock Closed Its Public Schools* (Fayetteville: University of Arkansas Press, 2009), 24. Gordy chronicles Huckaby's activities during the "Lost Year" of 1958–59 extensively.
47. Huckaby, "The Gun Cabinet." For more on the teacher purge and the effort to recall the segregationist school board members responsible, see Sara Alderman Murphy, *Breaking the Silence: Little Rock's Women's Emergency Committee to Open Our Schools, 1958–1963* (Fayetteville: University of Arkansas Press, 1997); Vivion Lenon Brewer, *The Embattled Ladies of Little Rock. 1968–1963: The Struggle to Save Public Education at Central High* (Fort Bragg, CA: Lost Coast Press, 1999).
48. "Publishers' assessment of THAT YEAR AT CENTRAL HIGH by Elizabeth Paisley Huckaby," n.d., folder 3, box 7, Huckaby Papers, UALR; Huckaby, "The Gun Cabinet."
49. Huckaby, "The Gun Cabinet"; Elizabeth F. Shores, "Central High Teacher's Journal to Become Film," *Arkansas Democrat*, 10 October 1979. NBC drew up an option contract but ultimately decided not to produce the film. The lawyer who had drawn

up the contract then moved over to Time-Life Films and mentioned the option to her new boss, producer Freyda Rothstein. The resulting film was ultimately broadcast on CBS.
50. Richard Levinson and William Link, *Stay Tuned: An Inside Look at the Making of Prime-Time Television* (New York: St. Martin's Press, 1981), 27, 31, 105–6.
51. Jerry Buck, AP Television, *The State*, 30 January 1981, folder 6, box 4, Huckaby Papers, UALR; "VOICE asks the authors of 'Crisis at Central High': Is This the Way It Actually Happened?," *Scholastic Voice* 65, no. 9 (9 January 1981): 6–7.
52. Steven Lipkin, "US Docudrama and 'Movie of the Week," in *New Challenges for Documentary*, 2nd ed., ed. Alan Rosenthal and John Corner (Manchester: Manchester University Press, 2005), 457.
53. Allison Graham, *Framing the South: Hollywood, Television, and Race during the Civil Rights Struggle* (Baltimore: Johns Hopkins University Press, 2001), 13; Alison Graham, "Reclaiming the South: Civil Rights Films and the New Red Menace," in *Media, Culture, and the Modern African American Freedom Struggle*, ed. Brian Ward (Gainesville: University Press of Florida, 2001), 82–103; Edward P. Morgan, "The Good, The Bad, and the Forgotten: Media Culture and the Public Memory of the Civil Rights Movement," in *The Civil Rights Movement in American Memory*, ed. Renee Romano and Leigh Raiford (Athens: University of Georgia Press, 2006), 138. In her book, *Racial Reckoning*, Renee C. Romano examines the elevation of white moderates as heroes in the reopening and prosecution of civil rights cold cases in the 1990s. In popular narratives related to the trials, white prosecutors symbolically renounced the racism of segregationists who murdered civil rights activists by bringing them to justice. As Romano notes, the identification of white prosecutors as the heroes of these narratives rather than the slain activists cast movement participants as "passive martyrs" and "downplayed black activism both during the civil rights era and later in the efforts to bring civil rights murders back into court" (151). Here, I argue that this process was already underway even before popular narratives of white redemption rose to prominence. The rhetorical elisions that divorced the actions of civil rights activists from the changes that they produced in American society created the context in which stories that identified white moderates as "key agents[s] for racial change" resonated with public audiences.
54. Robert Rosenstone pointed to many of these conventions of history on film in *Visions of the Past: The Challenge of Film to Our Idea of History* (Cambridge, MA: Harvard University Press, 1995).
55. Huckaby, "The Gun Cabinet"; Elizabeth Huckaby to Johnny Heflin, February 1981, folder 5, box 2; Elizabeth Huckaby to Professor Stanley N. Katz, 8 January 1981, folder 3, box 2, Huckaby Papers, UALR. See also Shores, "Central High Teacher's Journal to Become Film"; Wisehart, "A Reluctant, 'Little' Hero"; Roosevelt Thompson, "CBS to Air Movie on 1957 Crisis: Based on Diary Kept by Vice Principal," *The Tiger*, 26 October 1979, folder 6, box 4; untitled document typed from notes written in Huckaby's hand, n.d. , folder 1, box 10, Huckaby Papers, UALR.
56. *Crisis at Central High*, produced by Robert A. Papazian, written by Richard Levin-

son and William Link, dir. Lamont Johnson, based on the book by Elizabeth P. Huckaby (HBO Videos, Time-Life Productions, Inc., 1980).

57. Huckaby, *Crisis at Central High*, 67–68, 77, 84, 113, 116, 124, 148–52. As one reviewer noted, "Mrs. Huckaby's handling of this student [in her narrative] is an exercise in blaming the victim" (Lee Lorch, book review of *Crisis at Central High*, by Elizabeth Huckaby, *Freedomways* 22, no. 4 [1982]: 261–63). As an adult, Minnijean Brown Trickey has refuted Huckaby's description of her as a "volatile" student, and believes she was targeted for harassment because she refused to conform to the racial expectations of white students and administrators (Elizabeth Jacoway and Minnijean Brown Trickey, "Not Anger but Sorrow: Minnijean Brown Trickey Remembers the Little Rock Crisis," *Arkansas Historical Quarterly* 64, no. 1 [Spring 2005]: 12, 21, 23–25).

58. Dolphus, "The Little Rock Story Is Being Told without the Help of Major Participants," *Southern Mediator*. See also "Crusader from Little Rock: The Quiet Courage of Daisy Bates," *Washington Post*, 31 March 1981; George Lipsitz, *Time Passages: Collective Memory and American Popular Culture* (Minneapolis: University of Minnesota Press, 1990), 11, 20.

59. Bill Lewis, "Like '57 Over Again: Television Version Had Its Own Hassles," *Arkansas Gazette*, 1 February 1981.

60. Huckaby, *Crisis at Central High*, xvi, 48, 222; Untitled document typed from notes written in Huckaby's hand, n.d., folder 1, box 10, Huckaby Papers, UALR.

61. Huckaby, *Crisis at Central High*, 219–22; "Reminiscences of Elizabeth Huckaby," interview by Eisenhower Administration Project, 1972, transcript, Oral History Research Office, Columbia University, New York, 6.

62. "VOICE asks," 6–7; Shores, "Central High Teacher's Journal to Become Film."

63. "Great Drama, and History Too," *Oak Ridger*, 11 February 1981, folder 6, box 4, Huckaby Papers, UALR; Martha Douglas, "33rd Emmy Awards Show Drops Streamlined Format, Brings on the Stars," *Arkansas Gazette*, 13 September 1981. For national reviews of the docudrama see John J. O'Connor, "TV: Little Rock, 1957: 'Crisis at Central High,'" *New York Times*, 4 February 1981; Tom Shales, "High Noon in Dixie: 'Crisis at Central High'; 'Crisis' in Little Rock," *Washington Post*, 4 February 1981.

64. Richard Maple to Elizabeth Huckaby, 5 February 1981; Elizabeth Huckaby to Richard Maple, 8 February 1981, folder 5, box 2, Huckaby Papers, UALR.

65. "Docu-drama Reflects Important 'Omission,' Ex-Student Leader Says," *Arkansas Gazette*, 1 February 1981.

66. When asked as a student whether he thought the Little Rock Nine should be admitted to Central, Brodie replied, "Sir, it's the law. We are going to have to face it sometime . . . If it's a court order, we have to follow it and abide by the law" (*Arkansas Gazette*, 10 September 1957, as quoted in David L. Chappell, "Diversity with a Racial Group: White People in Little Rock, 1957–1959," *Arkansas Historical Quarterly* 66, no. 2 [Summer 2007]: 188; more broadly, Chappell has argued that Central High school students expressed more moderate racial views than their parents).

67. Doug Smith, "What about the Others at Central High in 1957?," *Arkansas Gazette*, 1 February 1981; Doug Smith, "Class of '58 Vowed the Conflict Wouldn't Spoil Their Senior Year," *Arkansas Gazette*, n.d., folder 13, box 12, subseries 5, series 5, Bates Papers, UAF. Over the years, some white Central High alumni have elaborated on these themes. For example, see Ralph Brodie and Marvin Schwartz, *Central in Our Lives: Voices from Little Rock Central High School, 1957–1959* (Little Rock: Butler Center for Arkansas Studies, 2007).
68. Huckaby, "The Gun Cabinet."
69. *Crisis at Central High,* HBO Videos, Time Life Productions, Inc., 1980.
70. Thompson, "CBS to Air Movie on 1957 Crisis."
71. Smith, "What about the Others at Central High in 1957?"
72. Levinson and Link, *Stay Tuned,* 138–39.
73. Harry Ashmore, foreword to *Crisis at Central High: Little Rock, 1957–58,* written by Elizabeth Huckaby (Baton Rouge: Louisiana State University Press, 1980), xiv.
74. John A. Kirk, "The Little Rock Crisis and Postwar Black Activism in Arkansas," *Arkansas Historical Quarterly* 66, no. 2 (Summer 2007): 224–25.
75. *Clark v. Board of Education of the Little Rock School District,* 705 F.2d 265 (8th Cir. 1983); *Little Rock School District v. Pulaski County Special School District No. 1,* 778 F.2d 404 (8th Cir. 1985); US Commission on Civil Rights, *School Desegregation in Little Rock, Arkansas* (Washington, DC: The Commission, June 1977), 2, 9–11; Paul Masem, "Resegregation: A Case Study of an Urban School District" (EdD diss., Vanderbilt University, 1986), 104–6; Egerton, "Little Rock, 1976," 45–46; Prugh, "Little Rock 20 Years Later."
76. Masem, "Resegregation," 88–89, 242–44.
77. Ibid., 110, 112, 153, 228, 240.
78. Ibid., 91–92, 153; *Clark v. Board of Education* (8th Cir. 1983).
79. Masem, "Resegregation," 98–99 (citing Little Rock school board meeting minutes, 25 June 1981).
80. *Milliken v. Bradley,* 418 US 717 (1974).
81. Norman C. Amaker, "Milliken v. Bradley: The Meaning of the Constitution in School Desegregation Cases," conference report from the United States Commission on Civil Rights, *Milliken v. Bradley: The Implications for Metropolitan Desegregation* (Washington, DC: Government Printing Office, 1974).
82. *Clark v. Board of Education* (8th Cir. 1983); *Little Rock v. Pulaski County* (8th Cir. 1985); "Resolution Pertaining to District Boundary Lines," Regular Meeting, 21 June 1979, Little Rock School District Administration Building, Little Rock, Arkansas (LRSB); Masem, "Resegregation," 5; "School Districts Discuss Cooperation," *Arkansas Gazette,* 12 March 1980; "County Rejects Request to Cooperate," *Arkansas Democrat,* 13 March 1980.
83. "Walker to File Suit, Seek White Majority in LR School District," *Arkansas Gazette,* 4 September 1981.
84. Masem, "Resegregation," 145. In doing so, the Little Rock school board hired civil rights lawyers to represent the district, some of whom had worked with attorney John Walker, the longtime representative of African American students in the Little

Rock school litigation (Wiley A. Branton, "Little Rock Revisited: Desegregation to Resegregation," *Journal of Negro Education* 52, no. 3 [Summer 1983]: 269).

85. *Little Rock v. Pulaski County* (8th Cir. 1985).
86. Henry Woods and Beth Deere, "Reflections on the Little Rock School Case," *Arkansas Law Review* 44, no. 4 (1991): 982.
87. *Little Rock v. Pulaski County* (8th Cir. 1985); "Judge Says Others Added to Little Rock Bias," *New York Times*, 14 April 1984. Woods believed that the 61/39 white-black ratio of the consolidated districts would "stabilize the district, stop white flight, and end segregation in the LRSD" (Woods and Deere, "Reflections on the Little Rock School Case," 983).
88. Roy Reed, "Little Rock a Symbol Again: The Resegregation of Schools," *New York Times*, 23 March 1985; "Legislation for Forgetting" (editorial), *Arkansas Gazette*, 15 January 1985; James Scudder, "White, Kelly Give Opposite Views on Consolidation," *Arkansas Gazette*, 11 January 1985; "Leadership and Consolidation" (editorial), *Arkansas Gazette*, 1 January 1985.
89. Drew S. Days III, "Turning Back the Clock: The Reagan Administration and Civil Rights," *Civil Liberties Law Review* 19, no. 2 (1984): 468–72; Jim Bencivenga, "The Landmark Desegregation Ruling and Its 30-Year Legacy," *Christian Science Monitor*, 11 May 1984, 21; Gary Orfield, "Turning Back to Segregation," in *Dismantling Desegregation: The Quiet Reversal of* Brown v. Board of Education," ed. Gary Orfield, Susan Eaton, and the Harvard Project on School Desegregation (New York: New Press, 1996), 17–18.
90. "Justice Enters Rights Case," *Washington Post*, 5 March 1985; Reed, "Little Rock a Symbol Again;" editorial on Justice Department intervention in the case, *Arkansas Gazette*, 7 March 1985.
91. *Little Rock v. Pulaski County* (8th Cir. 1985). The appeals court judges who dissented from this decision were even more conservative in their assessment of the nature and scope of the interdistrict violations in this case and the extent of the remedy the courts should permit. See also *Little Rock School District v. Pulaski County Special School District No. 1*, 833 F.2d 112 (8th Cir. 1988).
92. *Little Rock v. Pulaski County* (8th Cir. 1985); *Little Rock v. Pulaski County* (8th Cir. 1988).
93. Ronald Smothers, "At Little Rock, 30 Years Later: Starting Over," *New York Times*, 27 September 1987; Robert L. Brown, *The Second Crisis of Little Rock: A Report on Desegregation within Little Rock Public Schools* (Little Rock: Winthrop Rockefeller Foundation, 1988), 9.
94. "Proposal for Balancing Children in Classroom By Race," Regular Meeting, 27 August 1981, LRSB; *Clark v. Board of Education* (8th Cir. 1983); Masem, "Resegregation," 99–106; Mark Oswald, "Racial Grouping Plan for LR School District Held Unconstitutional: Board Member Doesn't Plan to Try Appeal," *Arkansas Gazette*, 4 September 1981.
95. *Clark v. Board of Education* (8th Cir. 1983); Masem, "Resegregation," 114, 131, 136; Reginald Stuart "Schools Try to Attract Whites by Easing Integration Efforts," *New York Times*, 1 June 1982.

96. *Clark v. Board of Education* (8th Cir. 1983).
97. Ibid.
98. Brown, *The Second Crisis of Little Rock,* 13–14; Robert L. Brown, "The Third Little Rock Crisis," *Arkansas Historical Quarterly* 65, no. 1 (Spring 2006): 39–44.
99. *Little Rock v. Pulaski County* (8th Cir. 1988); Brown, *The Second Crisis of Little Rock,* 13–14.
100. *Little Rock School District v. Pulaski County Special School District No. 1,* 921 F.2d 1371 (8th Circ. 1990).
101. This decision troubled Judge Henry Woods who felt that the Eighth Circuit Court of Appeals was advancing a theory that "'constitutionality' is a floating concept, and that determination of the constitutionality of remedies depends on whether the case is settled or litigated" (Woods and Deere, "Reflection on the Little Rock School Case," 997–1002).
102. *Little Rock v. Pulaski County* (8th Circ. 1990).

4. Displacing Blame

1. Kevin Freking, "Huckabee Aim for Central Stirs Reaction: Legislators Ponder 'Reconciliation' Fete," *Arkansas Democrat-Gazette,* 23 January 1997.
2. Owen J. Dwyer, "Memorial Landscapes Dedicated to the Civil Rights Movement" (PhD diss., University of Kentucky, 2000), 83.
3. Renee C. Romano, *Racial Reckoning: Prosecuting America's Civil Rights Murders* (Cambridge, MA: Harvard University Press, 2014), 107, 138, 140, 167.
4. Paul Louis Street, *Segregated Schools: Educational Apartheid in Post-Civil Rights America* (New York: Routledge, 2005), 5–6, 36–37. See also Leonard Steinhorn and Barbara Diggs-Brown, *By the Color of Our Skin: The Illusion of Integration and the Reality of Race* (New York: Dutton, 1999); Jacquelyn Dowd Hall, "The Long Civil Rights Movement and the Political Uses of the Past," *Journal of American History* 91, no. 4 (March 2005): 1237.
5. Romano, *Racial Reckoning,* 147, 184–85. More broadly, this kind of rhetoric also provides convenient camouflage for the real consequences of neoliberal policies that have elevated the free market, laissez-faire economic policy, and privatization over democratic participation, government regulation, social justice, and public welfare (George Lipsitz, *American Studies in a Moment of Danger* [Minneapolis: University of Minnesota Press, 2001], 77–78).
6. Jim Auchmutey, "Tributes to a Cause: A Roundup of Museums and Monuments Commemorating the Movement that Changed the South—and the Nation," *Atlanta Journal-Constitution,* 24 August 1997.
7. Jake Sandlin, "Living in the Past: With Such a Long and Varied History, It's No Wonder that Little Rock Is Becoming a City of Museums. But Where Will We Get All the Financing?," *Arkansas Democrat-Gazette,* 16 November 1996.
8. W. Fitzhugh Brundage, *The Southern Past: A Clash of Race and Memory* (Cambridge, MA: Harvard University Press, 2005), 305; Dwyer, "Memorial Landscapes Dedicated to the Civil Rights Movement," 15.

9. Max Brantley, "Build a Museum and They Will Come" (editorial), *Arkansas Times*, 4 November 1993.
10. Max Brantley, "Why Not Little Rock?" (editorial), *Arkansas Times*, 18 August 1994.
11. Glenn Eskew, "The Birmingham Civil Rights Institute and the New Ideology of Tolerance," in *The Civil Rights Movement and American Memory*, ed. Renee C. Romano and Leigh Raiford (Athens: University of Georgia Press, 2006), 29–30, 52. See also Brundage, *The Southern Past*, 319.
12. Everett Tucker Jr. was executive secretary of the Chamber of Commerce in 1957 and was elected to the school board in the wake of the school desegregation crisis with the support of the Women's Emergency Committee to Open Our Schools (WEC). Tucker was a self-proclaimed segregationist who nonetheless supported keeping public schools open and opposed the attempted purge of forty-four public school teachers during the 1958–59 school year. Because of this position he was accused of being an "integrationist" and a "puppet of the federal government" by Governor Orval Faubus. When he became school board president, Tucker worked to keep integration to a minimum through the establishment of a pupil placement plan and the selection of school sites in racially homogeneous neighborhoods. Sara Alderman Murphy, *Breaking the Silence: Little Rock's Women's Emergency Committee to Open Our Schools, 1958–1963* (Fayetteville: University of Arkansas Press, 1997), 58, 107, 161, 171–72, 181, 186, 196–97, 225–26; David Gene Vinzant, "Little Rock's Long Crisis: Schools and Race in Little Rock, Arkansas, 1863–2009" (PhD diss., University of Arkansas, 2010), 121.
13. Elizabeth McFarland, "Central High Integration Observance Brings Call for Reconciliation," *Arkansas Democrat-Gazette*, 17 August 1997; Danny Shameer, "Clinton to Attend Central High Integration Anniversary," *Arkansas Democrat-Gazette*, 14 June 1997; Max Brantley, "40 Years and a Museum," *Arkansas Times*, 19 September 1997; Skip Rutherford, interview by author, 6 July 2016; Rett Tucker, interview by author, 25 July 2016. See also Cathy J. Collins, "Forgetting and Remembering: The Desegregation of Central High School in Little Rock, Arkansas: Race, Community Struggle, and Collective Memory" (PhD diss., Fielding Graduate Institute, 2004), 231–32; Elizabeth Darwin Grobmyer, "A History of the Commemoration of the Fortieth Anniversary of the Desegregation of Little Rock Central High School" (MA thesis, University of Arkansas at Little Rock, 1999), 21–22.
14. Dailey initially asked Tucker to serve as the chair of the commission, but agreed to appoint Dr. Gail Reede-Jones, a black physician and member of Central's PTA, to serve as co-chair at Tucker's request. Daisy Bates also served as an honorary chairman. Grobmyer, "A History of the Commemoration," 22–28, 35–36.
15. Eskew, "The Birmingham Civil Rights Institute and the New Ideology of Tolerance," 29–30, 45–46; Brundage, *The Southern Past*, 310–11; Owen J. Dwyer, "Interpreting the Civil Rights Movement: Place, Memory, and Conflict," *Professional Geographer* 52, no. 4 (2000): 666; Romano, *Racial Reckoning*, 83–84, 195–96.
16. Mark E. Abernathy, "A Little History behind the Central High Museum and Visitor

Center," *Arkansas State Press*, 2 October 1997; Johanna Miller Lewis, e-mail correspondence with author, 17 December 2009; Grobmyer, "A History of the Commemoration," 18–19; Collins, "Forgetting and Remembering," 230; Ethel Ambrose, interview by author, 28 July 2016.

17. Andrea A. Burns, *From Storefront to Monument: Tracing the Public History of the Black Museum Movement* (Amherst: University of Massachusetts Press, 2013), 73, 156–57; Dwyer, "Interpreting the Civil Rights Movement," 662; Brundage, *The Southern Past*, 273–74, 301–2; Owen J. Dwyer, "Memory on the Margins: *Alabama's Civil Rights Journey* as a Memorial Text," in *Mapping Tourism*, ed. Stephen P. Hanna and Vincent J. Del Casino Jr. (Minneapolis: University of Minnesota Press, 2003), 40.

18. Lewis e-mail correspondence; Grobmyer, "A History of the Commemoration," 21–22.

19. Collins, "Forgetting and Remembering," 232, 238–39; Brantley, "40 Years and a Museum," *Arkansas Times*, 19 September 1997; Grobmyer, "A History of the Commemoration," 24–25; Lewis e-mail correspondence; Ambrose interview.

20. Ambrose interview; Elizabeth Jacoway, "Understanding the Past: The Challenge of Little Rock," in *Understanding the Little Rock Crisis: An Exercise in Remembrance and Reconciliation*, ed. Elizabeth Jacoway and C. Fred Williams (Fayetteville: University of Arkansas Press, 1999), 2.

21. Tucker interview; Ronnie Nichols, interview by author, 6 July 2016; Sandlin, "Living in the Past"; John Brummett, " Flag Flap Settlement: Fight Was Ill-Advised," *Arkansas Democrat-Gazette*, 24 June 1997; Leslie Newell Peacock, "A Place to Learn: At Last, a Museum to Remember the Central Crisis," *Arkansas Times*, 19 September 1997; Max Brantley, "40 Years and a Museum"; Johanna Miller Lewis, " 'Build a Museum and They Will Come': The Creation of the Central High Museum and Visitor Center," *Public Historian* 22, no.4 (Autumn 2000): 30–31.

22. Tucker interview; Rutherford interview; Nichols interview; Danny Shameer, "Huckabee Endorses Central High Project: National Status Sought for Historic Site," *Arkansas Democrat-Gazette*, 18 February 1997; Frank Wolfe, "Fund Drive for Central in High Gear," *Arkansas Democrat-Gazette*, 20 April 1997; Michael Maddell, Superintendent, Little Rock Central High School National Historic Site, interview by author, 26 April 2007.

23. Tucker interview; Rutherford interview; Peacock, "A Place to Learn"; "Central High Museum: A History of the Site," *Arkansas State Press*, 9 October 1997; Collins, "Forgetting and Remembering," 233–34; Lewis, " 'Build a Museum and They Will Come,' " 31.

24. Ambrose interview.

25. Steven C. Dubin, *Displays of Power: Controversy in the American Museum from the Enola Gay to Sensation* (New York: New York University Press, 1999); *History Wars: The Enola Gay and Other Battles for the American Past*, ed. Edward T. Linenthal and Tom Engelhardt (New York: Henry Holt, 1996).

26. Erin Krutko, "Colonial Williamsburg's Slave Auction Re-enactment: Controversy,

African American History and Public Memory" (MA thesis, College of William and Mary, 2003); Patrick Hagiopan, "Race and Politics of Public History in the United States," in *Keep Your Head to the Sky: Interpreting African American Home Ground,* ed. Grey Gundaker (Charlottesville: University Press of Virginia, 1998); Burns, *From Storefront to Monument,* 72–105.

27. Dwyer, "Interpreting the Civil Rights Movement," 660–71; Dwyer, "Memory on the Margins," 38. See also *Civil Rights History from the Ground Up: Local Struggles, a National Movement* (Athens: University of Georgia Press, 2011).
28. Lewis, "'Build a Museum and They Will Come,'" 32–34.
29. Lewis, "'Build a Museum and They Will Come,'" 32–33n.3.
30. Jacoway, "Understanding the Past: The Challenge of Little Rock," 2–3.
31. A book was published as a result of this conference. See *Understanding the Little Rock Crisis: An Exercise in Remembrance and Reconciliation,* ed. Elizabeth Jacoway and C. Fred Williams (Fayetteville: University of Arkansas Press, 1999). Jacoway describes the impetus behind the conference's creation in her introduction.
32. Lewis, "'Build a Museum and They Will Come,'" 32–33n.3; Laura A. Miller, interview by author, 4 September 2009; Lewis e-mail correspondence.
33. Lewis e-mail correspondence; Nichols interview.
34. Lewis, "'Build a Museum and They Will Come,'" 33–35.
35. Collins, "Forgetting and Remembering," 243–44.
36. Ambrose interview.
37. From planning committee minutes excerpted in Collins, "Forgetting and Remembering," 244–45.
38. Jacoway, "Understanding the Past: The Challenge of Little Rock," 3–4.
39. For more see Roy Rosenzweig and David Thelen, *The Presence of the Past: Popular Uses of History in American Life* (New York: Columbia University Press, 1998), 105.
40. Lewis, "'Build a Museum and They Will Come,'" 34; Miller interview; Lewis e-mail correspondence; Tucker interview.
41. From planning committee minutes excerpted in Collins, "Forgetting and Remembering," 240–41.
42. Ambrose interview.
43. Tucker interview.
44. Collins, "Forgetting and Remembering," 243.
45. Tucker interview.
46. The following analysis is based on a visit to the exhibit in the Central High Museum and Visitor Center located in the refurbished Mobil gas station on 25 April 2007. All quotations from the exhibit unless otherwise specified are taken from the author's notes and photographs of the exhibit text. When it opened, the exhibit also featured a period television set that replayed news broadcasts from 1957—at the time of the author's visit, this part of the display was not functioning. Exhibit planner Abbie Chessler hoped that the use of the historic footage would "transport" visitors "back in time" (Peacock, "A Place to Learn").
47. Lewis, "'Build a Museum and They Will Come,'" 33–36; Nichols interview.

48. Lewis, "'Build a Museum and They Will Come,'" 30, 34; Nichols interview.
49. Lois Romano, "Civil Rights Symbol Slides into Decay; Little Rock's Historic Central High Needs $6 Million in Repairs," *Washington Post*, 28 September 1996.
50. Based on sealed comments held as part of the Central High Museum Historical Collections, now held by the National Park Service. Lewis, "'Build a Museum and They Will Come,'" 30–31, 41; Lewis e-mail correspondence; Miller interview.
51. Craig Rains to Rett Tucker, 14 April 1997, as quoted in Lewis, "'Build a Museum and They Will Come,'" 41–42; Max Brantley, "40 Years and a Museum."
52. Grobmyer, "A History of the Commemoration," 59–60.
53. Ralph Brodie and Craig Rains, "Show of Moderation Inside CHS" (editorial), *Arkansas Democrat-Gazette*, 17 October 1997. See also John Brummett, "Shedding Defensiveness: One of Central's Challenges" (editorial), *Arkansas Democrat-Gazette*, 25 October 1997.
54. Craig Rains to Rett Tucker, 14 April 1997, as quoted in Lewis, "'Build a Museum and They Will Come,'" 41.
55. Lewis, "'Build a Museum and They Will Come,'" 41; Lewis e-mail correspondence; Collins, "Forgetting and Remembering," 244–46.
56. Dwyer, "Interpreting the Civil Rights Movement," 666–67. See also Dwyer, "Memory on the Margins," 38.
57. Brantley, "40 Years and a Museum"; Collins, "Forgetting and Remembering," 245–46, 259.
58. The WEC has been lionized in several accounts and is frequently given credit for the reopening of the city's schools during the 1959–1960 school year. The elevation of the work of the WEC to center stage is another example of the work of white moderates being privileged over that of African American civil rights advocates. Despite the fact that the WEC took no principled stand on the school desegregation issue, and many of its members opposed desegregation, Elizabeth Jacoway has described their efforts as both a "moral and political movement" (Jacoway, "Down from the Pedestal: Gender and Regional Culture in a Ladylike Assault on the Southern Way of Life," *Arkansas Historical Quarterly* 56, no. 3 [Autumn 1997]: 345–52). In her account, Lorraine Gates notes that many of the organization's members preferred segregated education, but, she contends, "the women of the WEC publicly challenged the segregationists at every turn, and their actions were instrumental in the defeat of the extremists and the reopening of the city schools" (Gates, "Power from the Pedestal: The Women's Emergency Committee and the Little Rock School Crisis," *Arkansas Historical Quarterly* 66, no. 2 [Summer 2007]: 195). It would be more accurate to say that an equally important—and instrumental—role was played by the NAACP and the black plaintiffs who took their case to the federal courts, which found the school closing laws unconstitutional. Legal historian Tony Freyer has observed that there is a tendency to emphasize the importance of the school board recall over this court litigation. However, he asserts, "it is unlikely that the moderates would have acted when they did had not the Supreme Court finally closed the channels of political maneuver sanctified by appeals to constitutional

symbols of states' rights and interposition" (Tony A. Freyer, *Little Rock on Trial: Cooper v. Aaron and School Desegregation* [Lawrence: University Press of Kansas, 2007], 210). Moreover, it must be noted that without the bloc vote that the African American community supplied in the school board recall election, the moderate candidates would not have been elected over their segregationist counterparts (Irvine J. Spitzberg Jr., *Racial Politics in Little Rock, 1954–1965* [New York: Garland Publishing, 1987], 110; Karen Anderson, *Little Rock: Race and Resistance at Central High School* [Princeton, NJ: Princeton University Press, 2010], 191).

59. Lewis, "'Build a Museum and They Will Come,'" 43.
60. Rutherford interview.
61. Brundage, *The Southern Past*, 319.
62. Ambrose interview.
63. Jack Schnedler, "Sizing Up Our Newest Tourist Site," *Arkansas Democrat-Gazette*, 28 September 1997.
64. Danny Shameer, "Central High on '96 Endangered List: National Preservation Group Calls Attention to Historic Places That Need Fixing Up," *Arkansas Democrat-Gazette*, 18 June 1996; Wolfe, "Fund Drive for Central in High Gear"; Robbie Moreland-Adams, "Elizabeth Eckford Recalls Her Long Walk into Little Rock History," *Christian Science Monitor*, 24 September 1997; Richard Benedetto, "After 40 Years, A Return to Central High," *USA Today*, 25 September 1997; Kim Cobb, "Girl's Pain Has Lasted a Lifetime; Elizabeth Eckford Still Suffers from Her Battle for Desegregation," *Houston Chronicle*, 26 September 1997.
65. Jacoway, "Understanding the Past," 14.
66. Larry Copeland, "40 Years after School Desegregation, The Struggle Continues: Little Rock Still Gripped by Race Tension," *Philadelphia Inquirer*, 18 August 1997; Grobmeyer, 53–54.
67. Linda S. Caillouet, "It's Costly, but Central High Shaping Up," *Arkansas Democrat-Gazette*, 8 July 1997; John Brummett, "Central District Looks Past Thursday," *Arkansas Democrat-Gazette*, 21 September 1997; John Brummett, "Central: A Beginning, but of What?," *Arkansas Democrat-Gazette*, 26 October 1997; Collins "Forgetting and Remembering," 251–52; Ambrose interview. While visiting Little Rock for the fiftieth anniversary commemoration, the author witnessed new attempts to give the Central High historic district a facelift as lawns were resodded in preparation for the event.
68. John W. Walker, "No Reason to Celebrate: A Civil Rights Lawyer Sees Scant Progress," *Arkansas Times*, 19 September 1997; Scott Parks, "Past Relived: As the Little Rock Nine Enter the School House Door Four Decades Later, Residents Examine Their Segregated Past and Present, and Wonder How Far the City Has Advanced," *Tampa Tribune*, 20 September 1997.
69. "Magnet Interest Soaring: Suburban Kids Transferring to LR," *Arkansas Gazette*, 27 April 1991; Robert McCord, "Failing Scores Mean District Must Do More for Students," *Arkansas Gazette*, 14 May 1991; Cary Bradburn, "LR Schools Insensitive, Report Says: Intervenors See Racism," *Arkansas Gazette*, 26 July 1991; Cynthia

Howell, "Only 5 Whites Preregister for LR's Incentive Schools," *Arkansas Democrat-Gazette*, 9 March 1994; Cynthia Howell, "LRSD Tries to Redefine 'Balance': Short of Racial Goals, It Seeks to Relax Rules," *Arkansas Democrat-Gazette*, 28 March 1995.

70. Copeland, "40 Years after School Desegregation, The Struggle Continues"; Peter Baker, "40 Years Later, 9 Are Welcomed: Little Rock Marks Civil Rights Milestone," *Washington Post*, 26 September 1997.

71. For examples see Kevin Sack, "Civil Rights Anniversary Points to Unfinished Tasks," *New York Times*, 21 September 1997; Benedetto, "After 40 Years, a Return to Central High"; Peter Baker, "40 Years Later, 9 Are Welcomed: Little Rock Marks Civil Rights Milestone," *Washington Post*, 26 September 1997; Danny Shameer, "Leaders Look at Status of Integration Today," *Arkansas Democrat-Gazette*, 26 September 1997. Interest in student seating patterns in the cafeteria may have been prompted by the publication of Beverly Daniel Tatum's book *"Why Are All the Black Kids Sitting Together in the Cafeteria?" and Other Conversations about Race* (New York: Basic Books, 1997).

72. Brummett, "Central: A Beginning, but of What?" Brummett reacted to an article by Julian E. Barnes, "Segregation, Now," *US News & World Report*, 22 September 1997.

73. Cynthia Howell, "LRSD Tries to Redefine 'Balance': Short of Racial Goals, It Seeks to Relax Rules," *Arkansas Democrat-Gazette*, 28 March 1995; Cynthia Howell, "2 Experts Arm Schools for Motions: Districts Want Out of Court Supervision," *Arkansas Democrat-Gazette*, 16 May 1996.

74. *Board of Education of Oklahoma City v. Dowell*, 498 US 237 (1991); *Freeman v. Pitts*, 503 US 467 (1992); *Missouri v. Jenkins*, 515 US 79 (1995).

75. *Missouri v. Jenkins* (1995).

76. Cynthia Howell, "What Must LRSD Do? 2,097 Things: Desegregation Suit Spawns Obligations," *Arkansas Democrat-Gazette*, 20 July 1995; Cynthia Howell, "LRSD Works to Show Compliance: Officials Try to Prove They're Implementing Desegregation Plan," *Arkansas Democrat-Gazette*, 4 April 1996; Cynthia Howell, "LRSD 96.3% in Compliance, Williams Says," *Arkansas Democrat-Gazette*, 9 May 1996.

77. Cynthia Howell, "2 Experts Arm Schools for Motions"; Chris Reinolds, "Harvard Professor Rebuts 2 Other Segregation Experts," *Arkansas Democrat-Gazette*, 31 May 1996.

78. Scott Parks, "Past Relived"; Scott Parks, "Anniversary Also Marked with NAACP Demonstration," *Dallas Morning News*, 25 September 1997.

79. Cynthia Howell, "Desegregation Won't Close Black, White Gap, Expert Says," *Arkansas Democrat-Gazette*, 14 May 1996; *Little Rock School District v. Pulaski County Special School District No. 1* (Dist. Court, ED Arkansas, 2002), 146.

80. Cynthia Howell, "Strict Racial Standard Astounds School Expert," *Arkansas Democrat-Gazette*, 15 May 15 1996. For more of David J. Armor's views, see *Forced Justice: School Desegregation and the Law* (New York: Oxford University Press, 1995); *Little Rock v. Pulaski County* (Dist. Court, ED Arkansas, 2002), 146.

81. Reinolds, "Harvard Professor Rebuts 2 Other Segregation Experts." For more of Gary Orfield's views see Orfield, et al., *Dismantling Desegregation: The Quiet Reversal of Brown v. Board of Education* (New York: New Press, 1996).

82. Howell, "2 Experts Arm Schools for Motions"; Reinolds, "Harvard Professor Rebuts 2 Other Segregation Experts."
83. University Task Force on the Little Rock School District, *Plain Talk: The Future of Little Rock's Public Schools* (Little Rock: University of Arkansas at Little Rock, 1997).
84. Robert McCord, "Court Turns Corner on Busing," *Arkansas Gazette*, 24 January 1991. For McCord's views on the Little Rock school desegregation crisis of 1957 see his essay "An Unexpected Crisis," in *A Life Is More than a Moment: The Desegregation of Little Rock's Central High*, fiftieth anniversary ed. (Bloomington: Indiana University Press, 2007), 9–26. McCord asserts that Little Rock was relatively progressive, and that the crisis itself "stunned" the city. He minimizes the violence that gripped the city that September in comparison to "other school-integration crises around the country, several of them much more serious than Little Rock's." He concludes the eruption of a confrontation related to school desegregation had to happen somewhere.
85. John R. Starr, "Gloomy School News Performance Gap Widens," *Arkansas Democrat-Gazette*, 14 July 1995.
86. Fortieth anniversary commemorative ceremony, Little Rock, transcribed by author, 25 September 2007. Clinton and Huckabee's addresses are also transcribed in *Race, Politics, and Memory: A Documentary History of the Little Rock School Crisis*, ed. Catherine M. Lewis and J. Richard Lewis (Fayetteville: University of Arkansas Press, 2007).
87. Jim Lehrer, quoted in "Clinton, at Race Forum, Is Confronted on Affirmative Action," *New York Times*, 9 July 1998; Renee M. Smith, "The Public Presidency Hits the Wall: Clinton's Presidential Initiative on Race," *Presidential Studies Quarterly* 28, no. 4 (Fall 1998): 783; Hugh B. Price, "Actions Speak Louder," *Arkansas State Press*, 23 October 1997; Manning Marable, "A Conversation on Race," *Arkansas State Press*, 2 October 1997; Steven A. Holmes, "Clinton Panel on Race Urges Variety of Modest Measures," *New York Times*, 18 September 1998.
88. Jennifer Fuller, "Debating the Present through the Past: Representations of the Civil Rights Movement in the 1990s," in *Civil Rights and American Memory*, ed. Renee C. Romano and Leigh Raiford (Athens: University of Georgia Press, 2006), 168–72.
89. This change was made at the request of representatives of Little Rock's black community (Grobmeyer, "A History of the Commemoration," 44–45).
90. Romano, *Racial Reckoning*, 153–55.
91. Cynthia Howell, "Desegregation Plan Allows Slow Change," *Arkansas Democrat-Gazette*, 20 January 1998; Cynthia Howell, "Carnine: Desegregation Plan Stresses Achievement," *Arkansas Democrat-Gazette*, 27 January 1998; Cynthia Howell, "Plan Would Re-emphasize Neighborhood LR Schools," *Arkansas Democrat-Gazette*, 2 September 1998; Cynthia Howell, "School Board Oks Roberts' Revamp of Desegregation Plan: Judge's Approval Could Bring LR District Out of Federal Court Supervision by 2001," *Arkansas Democrat-Gazette*, 19 September 1997; Cynthia Howell, "Loosen Desegregation Reins, District Asks Judge," *Arkansas Democrat-Gazette*, 27 September 1997.

92. Cynthia Howell, "LR Schools to Submit Bid to Get Free of Monitoring: Board to Send Desegregation Report to US Judge," *Arkansas Democrat-Gazette*, 14 March 2001.
93. Cynthia Howell, "Falloff in Student Population Eating Hole in Districts' Desegregation Purse," *Arkansas Democrat-Gazette*, 6 March 2002.

5. Resisting Historical Erasure

1. An Act to Establish the Little Rock Central High School National Historic Site in the State of Arkansas, and for other purposes, Public Law 105–356 (S. 2232), 6 November 1998.
2. Elizabeth Eckford, public speech at Little Rock Central High School library, recorded by author, 28 April 2007; Elizabeth Eckford, public speech at the Central High School National Historic Site Visitor Center dedication ceremony, 24 September 2007, audio file, http://www.nps.gov/chsc/learn/news/visitor-center-dedication.htm.
3. Eckford, public speech at the Central High School National Historic Site Visitor Center dedication ceremony, 24 September 2007.
4. George Lipsitz, *Time Passages: Collective Memory and American Popular Culture* (Minneapolis: University of Minnesota Press, 1990), 11, 20. See also George Lipsitz, *Footsteps in the Dark: The Hidden Histories of Popular Music* (Minneapolis: University of Minnesota Press, 2007).
5. Quote translated in *Framing Public Memory*, ed. Kendell R. Phillips and John Lucaites (Tuscaloosa: University of Alabama Press, 2004), 2.
6. Eduardo Bonilla-Silva, *Racism without Racists: Color-Blind Racism and the Persistence of Racial Inequality in the United States* (Lanham, MD: Rowman & Littlefield, 2003), 178, 79.
7. *Board of Education of Oklahoma City v. Dowell*, 498 US 237 (1991) (emphasis added).
8. *Freeman v. Pitts*, 503 US 467 (1992).
9. Gary Orfield and Chungmei Lee, "Historic Reversals, Accelerating Resegregation, and the Need for New Integration Strategies" (UCLA: The Civil Rights Project/Proyecto Derechos Civiles, 2007), 5, 8–10, http://escholarship.org/uc/item/8h02n114.
10. Bonilla-Silva, *Racism without Racists*, 28.
11. *Board of Education of Oklahoma City v. Dowell* (1991).
12. Tim Wise, *Colorblind: The Rise of Post-Racial Politics and the Retreat from Racial Equity* (San Francisco: City Lights Books, 2010), 136–37.
13. Michael Omi and Howard Winant, *Racial Formation in the United States: From the 1960s to the 1990s*, 2nd ed. (New York: Routledge, 1994), 157.
14. Wise, *Colorblind*, 129–31.
15. *Missouri v. Jenkins*, 515 US 70 (1995).
16. Jacquelyn Dowd Hall, "The Long Civil Rights Movement and the Political Uses of the Past," *Journal of American History* 91, no. 4 (March 2005): 1235–38.

17. Omi and Winant, *Racial Formation in the United States*, 131.
18. Oral arguments in *Parents Involved in Community Schools v. Seattle School District No. 1, et al.* and *Crystal D. Meredith v. Jefferson County Board of Education, et al.*, 4 December 2006, as recorded by Alderson Reporting Company.
19. This history and the background of the Seattle case are outlined in Part I of Justice Breyer's dissent. Since Little Rock, like Louisville, was once found guilty of de jure violations, I have summarized the history of that district here. However, the pattern in Seattle is also very similar—with the distinction that Seattle settled its case out of court before being found guilty of de jure violations. Regardless, since all three districts were considered unitary in the area of student assignment in 2006, the Supreme Court's decision in this case was binding. *Parents Involved in Community Schools v. Seattle School Dist. No. 1*, 127 Sup .Ct. 2738 (2007).
20. As the deciding swing vote, Justice Kennedy concurred with the plurality and struck down the Seattle and Louisville plans, although he emphasized that the pursuit of diversity in the public schools was a "compelling interest." However, in Kennedy's view, the pursuit of this race-conscious objective did not justify the use of invidious racial classifications that systematically typed individuals by race. He urged the districts to pursue race-neutral means to achieve their race-conscious ends, by utilizing strategies such as the selection of new school sites, the redistribution of geographic attendance zones, and the establishment of special programs and magnet schools. Because these strategies did not utilize racial classifications, they would not be subjected to "strict scrutiny." Kennedy's approach to this question now governs the way school districts must formulate their student assignment plans. *Parents Involved v. Seattle* (2007).
21. Ibid.
22. See dissenting opinions ibid.
23. Leigh Raiford and Renee C. Romano, "Introduction: The Struggle over Memory," in *The Civil Rights Movement and American Memory*, ed. Renee C. Romano and Leigh Raiford (Athens: University of Georgia Press, 2006), xxi.
24. See special issue of *Arkansas Times*, 20 September 2008; Steven Brawner, "Little Rock Marks a Civil Rights Victory," *Christian Science Monitor*, 26 September 2007; Cynthia Howell, "LR Schools to Submit a Bid to Get Free of Monitoring: Board to Send Desegregation Report to US judge," *Arkansas Democrat-Gazette*, 14 March 2001. These conditions were also featured in *Little Rock Central: 50 Years Later*, prod. and dir. Brent Renaud and Craig Renaud, 70 min. (HBO Films, 2007), DVD.
25. "Joshua Intervenors' Proposed Findings of Fact and Conclusions of Law in Opposition to the LRSD's Request for Unitary Status Regarding the Plan Sections," *Little Rock School District v. Pulaski County Special School District No. 1* (Dist. Court, ED Arkansas, 2002), 3–6, 23, 26, 28–29, 32, 39–41.
26. Terrence Roberts, telephone interview by author, 29 March 2010; Terrence Roberts, *Lessons from Little Rock* (Little Rock: Butler Center Books, 2009), 146–50; Cynthia Howell, "Member of Little Rock Nine to Serve District as Consultant: Roberts 1 of 2 to Help Implement Revamped Desegregation, Education Plan," *Arkansas*

Democrat-Gazette, 28 July 1998; Cynthia Howell and Kimberly Dishongh, "Testimony Ends in Case Regarding School Integration: LR Nine Member Says District Focused on Court Release Instead of Students," *Arkansas Democrat-Gazette*, 25 July 2002; "Judge Asks for Briefs in Desegregation Case, Testimony Ends," Associated Press State & Local Wire, 25 July 2002.

27. Roberts, *Lessons from Little Rock*, 150–52.
28. *Little Rock v. Pulaski County* (Dist. Court, ED Arkansas, 2002), 90–92. This was an interesting reading of the history of the school desegregation litigation. While it was true that the district had filed the case as a plaintiff, it had never previously been declared unitary and was under court supervision precisely because it had violated the constitutional rights of African American students by maintaining a system of segregated education. As a plaintiff, the district made the case that the state of Arkansas, and the school systems of North Little Rock and Pulaski County, had contributed to the segregation of Little Rock schools, but Little Rock officials were also involved in the boundary changes and student transfers that produced the interdistrict violations that prompted the original settlement agreements and their subsequent revisions.
29. *Little Rock v. Pulaski County* (Dist. Court, ED Arkansas, 2002), 12–20, 51, 74, 93–94.
30. Cynthia Howell, "Desegregated One Year, LR District Plan Ignores Race in Assigning Pupils," *Arkansas Democrat-Gazette*, 19 September 2003.
31. Cynthia Howell, "Pulaski County Schools Facing Time of Decision over Desegregation Plans," *Arkansas Democrat-Gazette*, 17 February 2008; Cynthia Howell, "LR Specialty Schools Letting in More Blacks: Race Is Less of a Factor for Attendance," *Arkansas Democrat-Gazette*, 3 January 2005.
32. James Jefferson, "Judge Ends School Desegregation Plan," Associated Press Online, 13 September 2002.
33. Cynthia Howell, "NAACP Calls LR District's Court Release 'Second Crisis,'" *Arkansas Democrat-Gazette*, 18 September 2002.
34. Cynthia Howell, "LR Schools Seek Attorney's Disqualification," *Arkansas Democrat-Gazette*, 13 December 2006.
35. Andrew DeMillo, "Little Rock School Board Mostly Black," *Arkansas Democrat-Gazette*, 12 December 2006.
36. *Gratz et al. v. Bollinger et al*, 539 US 244 (2003); *Grutter v. Bollinger et al.*, 539 US 306 (2003); *Parents Involved v. Seattle* (2007).
37. "Order Declaring the Little Rock School District Unitary," *Little Rock School District v. Pulaski County Special School District et al.* (Dist. Court, ED Arkansas, 2006), 47–48.
38. "Out of the Court at Last, Little Rock's Schools Get Their Chance" (editorial), *Arkansas Democrat-Gazette*, 27 February 2007.
39. "Order Declaring the Little Rock School District Unitary," 49.
40. Statement on Expansion of Charter Schools within LRSD Boundary, Little Rock School District Civic Advisory Committee, 11 February 2016, http://www.lrsd.org/sites/default/files/civic%20advisory%20committee/2016/CAC%20SBE%20Written%20Response%2002%2011%202016.pdf; Alana Semeuls, "How Segregation Has Persisted

in Little Rock," *The Atlantic*, 27 April 2016; Jeff Bryant, "Charter Schools and the Waltons Take Little Rock Back to Its Segregated Past," 20 July 2016, http://www.alternet.org/education/charter-schools-and-waltons-take-little-rock-back-its-segregated-past.

41. Roberts, *Lessons from Little Rock*, 162–63. See also Dr. Terrence J. Roberts, "The Ongoing Battle for Equality," *Arkansas Democrat-Gazette*, 25 September 1997; Terrence Roberts, public comments at Little Rock Central High School fiftieth anniversary commemorative ceremony, 25 September 2007, transcription from videotape of television broadcast in author's files.

42. In December 1957, Bates herself told reporters that the nine students were "comparatively happy" and only had to deflect the "scattered" insults of fifty to one hundred "agitators" inside Central. Rather than interpret this statement and others like it as evidence of Bates's desire to undercut Faubus's position, some citizens and scholars have suggested that conditions at Central High School were not as difficult as the Little Rock Nine have described them in later years. For example, see David L. Chappell, "Diversity with a Racial Group: White People in Little Rock, 1957–1959," *Arkansas Historical Quarterly* 66, no. 2 (Summer 2007): 188.

43. Melba Pattillo Beals, *Warriors Don't Cry: A Searing Memoir of the Battle to Integrate Little Rock's Central High* (New York: Washington Square Press, 1994), 123; Carlotta Walls LaNier with Lisa Frazier Page, *A Mighty Long Way: My Journey to Justice at Little Rock Central High School* (New York: One World Books, 2009), 108.

44. Elizabeth Eckford, public speech at Little Rock Central High School library, recorded by author, 28 April 2007; Roberts, *Lessons from Little Rock*, 115.

45. Jacoway and Trickey, "Not Anger but Sorrow," 2.

46. Spirit Trickey, "Guiding My Mother's Place in History," *The Crisis* 114, no. 4 (July/August 2005), 52.

47. LaNier with Page, *A Mighty Long Way*, xi, 235, 240. Trickey also discussed the crisis with one of her children for the first time when *Crisis at Central High* aired (Jacoway and Trickey, "Not Anger but Sorrow," 2).

48. Elizabeth Eckford, public speech at Little Rock Central High School library.

49. David Margolick, "Through a Lens, Darkly," *Vanity Fair*, 24 September 2007. See David Margolick, *Elizabeth and Hazel: Two Women of Little Rock* (New Haven, CT: Yale University Press, 2011).

50. Beals, *Warriors Don't Cry*, xvii. See also Roberts, *Lessons from Little Rock*, 10–11.

51. LaNier with Page, *A Mighty Long Way*, 247–48. Minnijean Trickey also mentions this meeting in a published interview (Elizabeth Jacoway and Minnijean Brown Trickey, "Not Anger but Sorrow: Minnijean Brown Trickey Remembers the Little Rock Crisis," *Arkansas Historical Quarterly* 64, no. 1 [Spring 2005]: 13).

52. Karen Anderson, *Little Rock: Race and Resistance at Central High School* (Princeton, NJ: Princeton University Press, 2010), 6.

53. Roberts, *Lessons from Little Rock* 21, 23, 43, 78–80; Roberts interview. This interpretation of race relations in Little Rock stands in contrast to arguments advanced by scholars like C. Fred Williams who have argued that class, specifically working-class resentment of middle-class insulation from the full impact of desegregation,

rather than rampant racism was the animating cause of the school desegregation crisis (C. Fred Williams, "Class: The Central Issue in the 1957 Little Rock School Crisis," *Arkansas Historical Quarterly* 56, no. 3 [Autumn 1997]: 341–44). Here, although Roberts also underscores the privileged position of Little Rock's wealthy and upper-middle-class whites and their ability to insulate themselves from racial change, he suggests that this is an indication that the large crowds that gathered outside of Central High School were expressing common racial sentiments that shaped Little Rock society from top to bottom regardless of class divisions.

54. LaNier with Page, *A Mighty Long Way*, 16–17.
55. John A. Kirk, "The Little Rock Crisis and Postwar Black Activism in Arkansas," *Arkansas Historical Quarterly* 66, no. 2 (Summer 2007): 231; John A. Kirk, *Redefining the Color Line: Black Activism in Little Rock, Arkansas, 1940–1973* (Gainesville: University Press of Florida, 2002), 63–64.
56. Roberts, "The Ongoing Battle for Equality"; Roberts, *Lessons from Little Rock*, 88, 144–45.
57. LaNier with Page, *A Mighty Long Way*, 99.
58. Melba Pattillo Beals develops this analogy the furthest in her memoir *Warriors Don't Cry*.
59. Roberts, *Lessons from Little Rock*, 110.
60. Beth Roy, *Bitters in the Honey: Tales of Hope and Disappointment across Divides of Race and Time* (Fayetteville: University of Arkansas Press, 1999), 243–69.
61. Ralph Brodie and Marvin Schwartz, *Central in Our Lives: Voices from Little Rock Central High School, 1957–1959* (Little Rock: Butler Center for Arkansas Studies, 2007).
62. LaNier with Page, *A Mighty Long Way*, 66, 181.
63. Ibid., 34, 36; Faustine C. Jones, *A Traditional Model of Excellence: Dunbar High School of Little Rock Arkansas* (Washington, DC: Howard University Press, 1981); Kirk, *Redefining the Color Line*, 108–12; Margolick, "Through a Lens, Darkly."
64. Gloria Ray Karlmark, public comments at Little Rock Central High School fiftieth anniversary commemorative ceremony, 25 September 2007, transcription from videotape of television broadcast in author's files.
65. Elizabeth Eckford, public speech at Little Rock Central High School library; LaNier with Page, *A Mighty Long Way*, 45; Roberts, *Lessons from Little Rock*, 24–25, 29, 31, 33; Margolick, "Through a Lens, Darkly."
66. Roberts, *Lessons from Little Rock*, 30.
67. LaNier with Page, *A Mighty Long Way*, 57. These comments reflect the ambiguity that surrounds discussion of school desegregation in some African American communities. The closure of historically black institutions, the loss of African American faculty and educational traditions, and the hostile environment black students encountered in formerly white institutions has generated its own narrative of nostalgia and loss (Adam Fairclough, "The Little Rock Crisis: Success or Failure for the NAACP?," *Arkansas Historical Quarterly* 56, no. 3 [Autumn 1997]: 372).
68. "Clintons Pray with Little Rock Nine," *United Press International*, 27 September 1997.

69. James Jefferson, "Group Says Struggle for Access to Equal Opportunity Continues," *Associated Press*, 24 September 1997; Kevin Sack, "Civil Rights Anniversary Points to Unfinished Tasks," *New York Times*, 21 September 1997.
70. Omi and Winant, *Racial Formation in the United States*, 131.
71. *Little Rock Central: 50 Years Later*; Felicia R. Lee, "Return to a Showdown at Little Rock," *New York Times*, 25 September 2007.
72. Board of Directors of the Little Rock School District (4–2) to Dr. W-H Townsend, President of the Council on Community Affairs, November 1963, as transcribed in the board's minutes, Executive Meeting, 21 November 1963, Little Rock School District Administration Building, Little Rock, Arkansas (LRSB).
73. *Little Rock Central: 50 Years Later*.
74. Lee, "Return to a Showdown at Little Rock"; Colleen Walsh, "Little Rock Central: 50 Years Later; Documentary Film and Panel Discussion Mark Pivotal Civil Rights Moment," *Harvard Gazette*, 20 September 2007.
75. Roberts, *Lessons from Little Rock*, 162–63.
76. Ibid., 144–45.
77. Ibid., 144–45, 164–65.
78. Ibid., 131, 160.
79. Minnijean Brown Trickey, public comments at Little Rock Central High School fiftieth anniversary commemorative ceremony, transcribed by author, 25 September 2007.

Conclusion

1. Superintendent Robin White, interview by author, 28 October 2015.
2. The emphasis of these tours varies substantially and can be shaped by rangers' own personal relationships to the site's history and the experiences and interests of the visitors themselves. For example, Minnijean Brown Trickey's daughter Spirit Trickey worked as a park ranger at the site for a number of years and shared her mother's experience with site visitors. See Spirit Trickey, "Guiding My Mother's Place in History," *Crisis* 112, no. 4 (2005): 52. However, park rangers come from a variety of backgrounds. On 27 March 2015, the author took a tour with a park ranger who was the daughter of one of the National Guardsmen on site. The ranger placed an emphasis on the difficulty experienced by guardsmen and their families when they had to remain at Central during the 1957–58 school year and enforce the desegregation decree after the Guard was federalized.
3. Little Rock Central High School National Historic Site General Management Plan (US Department of Interior: National Park Service, 2002); Little Rock Central High School National Historic Site Long-Range Interpretive Plan (US Department of Interior: National Park Service, 2004).
4. Leigh Raiford and Renee C. Romano, "Introduction: The Struggle over Memory," in *The Civil Rights Movement and American Memory*, ed. Renee C. Romano and Leigh Raiford (Athens: University of Georgia Press, 2006), xvii.

5. Azza Salama Layton, *International Politics and Civil Rights Policies, 1941–1960* (New York: Cambridge University Press, 2000), 27, 82–83, 108; Paul Gordon Lauren, *Power and Prejudice: The Politics of Diplomacy and Racial Discrimination*, 2nd ed. (Boulder, CO: Westview Press, 1996), 202; Robert Frederick Burk, *The Eisenhower Administration and Black Civil Rights* (Knoxville: University of Tennessee Press, 1984), 11–12; Mary L. Dudziak, *Cold War Civil Rights: Race and the Image of American Democracy* (Princeton, NJ: Princeton University Press, 2001), 23–24. Symbolic gestures and tokenism frequently stood in for more substantive reforms in American informational campaigns and diplomatic efforts. See Penny M. Von Eschen, *Satchmo Blows Up the World: Jazz Ambassadors Play the Cold War* (Cambridge, MA: Harvard University Press, 2004). Moreover, the desire to leverage change within this Cold War climate also led to the purge of leftists from some civil rights organizations. See Martha Biondi, *To Stand and Fight: The Struggle for Civil Rights in Postwar New York City* (Cambridge, MA: Harvard University Press, 2003).
6. For further discussion about Eisenhower's action in response to international criticism, see Layton, *International Politics and Civil Rights Policies*, 109; Cary Fraser, "Crossing the Color Line in Little Rock: The Eisenhower Administration and the Dilemma of Race for US Foreign Policy," *Diplomatic History* 24, no. 2 (Spring 2000): 247; Harold R. Isaacs, "World Affairs and US Race Relations: A Note on Little Rock," *Public Opinion Quarterly* 22, no. 3 (Autumn 1958): 366.
7. As quoted in Layton, *International Politics and Civil Rights Policies*, 130. See also USIA Research and Reference Service, "Public Reactions to Little Rock in Major World Capitals," 29 October 1957, box 1, entry 1012, Record Group 306, United States Information Agency Papers, National Archives, College Park, MD (USIA Papers); "Post Little Rock Opinion on the Treatment of Negroes in the US," January 1958, box 1, entry 1011, USIA Papers; Michael Krenn, *Black Diplomacy: African Americans and the State Department, 1945–1969* (Armonk, NY: M. E. Sharpe, 1999), 105; Azza Salama Layton, "International Pressure and the US Government's Response to Little Rock," *Arkansas Historical Quarterly* 56, no. 3 (Autumn 1997): 263; Thomas Borstelmann, *The Cold War and the Color Line: American Race Relations in the Global Arena* (Cambridge, MA: Harvard University Press, 2001), 104; Dudziak, *Cold War Civil Rights*, 131; Fraser, "Crossing the Color Line in Little Rock," 253, 258.
8. Wilson P. Dizard, *Inventing Public Diplomacy: The Story of the U.S. Information Agency* (Boulder, CO: Lynne Rienner, 2004), 93.
9. Dudziak, *Cold War Civil Rights*, 216, 49–54. See also Krenn, *Black Diplomacy*, 41–42, 92–93; Kenneth Osgood, *Total Cold War: Eisenhower's Secret Propaganda Battle Home and Abroad* (Lawrence: University Press of Kansas, 2006), 255; Laura Belmonte, *Selling the American Way: U.S. Propaganda and the Cold War* (Philadelphia: University Press of Pennsylvania, 2008), 164.
10. Technical Specifications for "Nine From Little Rock," Project Number Du 4-2605, Guggenheim Papers, in the possession of Grace Guggenheim, Guggenheim Productions, Inc.; Krenn, *Black Diplomacy*, 104–5; Mary L. Dudziak, "The Little Rock Crisis and Foreign Affairs: Race, Resistance, and the Image of American Democ-

racy," *Southern California Law Review* 70, no. 6 (September 1997): 1698–99; Dudziak, *Cold War Civil Rights*, 142–44, 216; Fraser, "Crossing the Color Line in Little Rock," 252; Osgood, *Total Cold War*, 282–83; MacCann, *The People's Films*, 199–200.

11. Shelby W. Storck, "9 From Little Rock," pamphlet, box 12, entry 1063, USIA Papers.
12. The impact of the Little Rock school desegregation crisis on international public opinion was lasting. Little Rock was still referenced with regularity in USIA public opinion polls, and served as a marker against which subsequent events were measured. USIA Research and Reference Service, "Public Reactions to Little Rock in Major World Capitals," SR-8, 29 October 1957; "Post-Little Rock Opinion on the Treatment of Negroes in the US," PMS-23, January 1958, box 1, entry 1011, USIA Papers; USIA Research and Reference Service, "Racial Prejudice Mars the American Image," 17 October 1962, box 10, entry 1013A, USIA Papers. See also Layton, *International Politics and Civil Rights Policies*, 130.
13. See Notes on "The Nine," background, and early film treatment for "Ordeal in Little Rock / Recovery in Little Rock / Nine of Little Rock," n.d.; "Nine From Little Rock: A Film Treatment for the United States Information Agency," Guggenheim Papers. See also "Nine from Little Rock" English script (17 July 1964) showing changes for foreign versions (30 October 1964), box 28, entry 1098, USIA Papers; Melinda M. Schwenk, "Reforming the Negative through History: The U.S. Information Agency and the 1957 Little Rock Integration Crisis," *Journal of Communication Inquiry* 23, no. 3 (July 1999): 295–96.
14. Richard Dyer MacCann, *The People's Films: A Political History of US Government Motion Pictures* (New York: Hastings House, 1973), 199–200. For detailed statistics provided by the Southern Education Reporting Service on school desegregation in 1964 see Reed Sarratt, *The Ordeal of Desegregation: The First Decade* (New York: Harper & Row, 1966), table 1, 359.
15. Based on author's visit to Little Rock Central High School Historic Site with more than 100 students from the University of Wisconsin–Eau Claire, 27 March 2015.
16. Little Rock Central High School National Historic Site Long-Range Interpretive Plan.
17. An Act to Establish the Little Rock Central High School National Historic Site in the State of Arkansas, and for other purposes, Public Law 105–356 (S. 2232), 6 November 1998.
18. Elizabeth Eckford, public speech at Little Rock Central High School library, recorded by author, 28 April 2007.
19. Carlotta Walls LaNier with Lisa Frazier Page, *A Mighty Long Way: My Journey to Justice at Little Rock Central High School* (New York: One World Books, 2009), xi–xii.
20. Minnijean Brown Trickey, public comments at Little Rock Central High School's fiftieth anniversary commemorative ceremony, 25 September 2007, transcription from videotape of the television broadcast in author's files.
21. All quotations from the exhibit based on author's photographs and field notes taken at the opening of the new Little Rock Central High School National Historic Site Visitor Center, 24 September 2007.

22. Terrence Roberts, *Lessons from Little Rock* (Little Rock: Butler Center Books, 2009), 15.
23. Minnijean Brown Trickey, public comments at Little Rock Central High School's fiftieth anniversary commemorative ceremony. See also LaNier with Page, *A Mighty Long Way*, 103, 119–21.

INDEX

Aaron v. Cooper, 19–22, 26–28, 96, 132, 219–20n58
Abernathy, Mark, 115, 118
Abrams, Annie, 118, 125, 127, 133–34
academic achievement: assessment of, 147, 153, 155–56; racial disparities in, 7, 64–68, 101, 107, 114, 132, 136–43, 154, 160–61; racial disparities, naturalization of, 141–42, 144–45, 155, 176, 187 (*see also* colorblind jurisprudence). *See also* tracking, academic
Adcock, Joan, 134
Alford, Dale, 77
Alito, Samuel, 158–59
Ambrose, Ethel, 118–19, 121, 125, 127, 133–34
Anderson, Karen, 42, 170–71
anniversary commemoration: twentieth, 63–66; thirtieth, 168; fortieth, 111–21, 130, 134–48, 174–75; fiftieth, 149–50, 178, 181; sixtieth, 166
Arkansas Democrat, 56–57, 60, 75, 82
Arkansas Democrat-Gazette, 115, 133, 140–41, 165
Arkansas Educational Television Commission. *See* Arkansas Educational Television Network
Arkansas Educational Television Network (AETN), 79–86
Arkansas Endowment of Humanities. *See* Arkansas Humanities Council
Arkansas Gazette, 15, 65, 72, 82–84, 141

Arkansas General Assembly, 23, 117, 128
Arkansas Historical Quarterly, 72
Arkansas Humanities Council, 80–82, 119, 122
Arkansas State Board of Education, 103; hostile takeover of Little Rock school district, 166
Arkansas State Capitol Building, 151
Arkansas State Police, 24, 86
Arkansas State Press, 118, 195n5
Arkansas Times, 116
Armor, David J., 140–41
Ashmore, Harry, 98
attendance zones: gerrymandering, 19, 31–33, 216n12; impact on residential segregation, 46, 66, 202n11 (*see also* residential segregation: impact on schools); legal challenges to, 41, 46. *See also* housing, discrimination; minimal compliance; neighborhood schools; residential segregation

Bates, Daisy: and Little Rock Nine, 37–38, 168, 226n42; and public memory, 35–36, 41, 59–61, 73, 92–93, 116, 216n14 (see also *Long Shadow of Little Rock*; public memory); and race relations in Little Rock, 30–31, 34–38 (*see also* Little Rock, race relations); and school desegregation, views on, 14–16, 28–35, 38–40, 59–61; segregationist criticism of, 13–14, 21, 75, 195n25

Beals, Melba Pattillo, 167–69, 173, 175. See also Little Rock Nine; *Warriors Don't Cry*
Bethune, Edwin, Jr., 85
Biracial Advisory Committee, 101, 106
black nationalism, 5, 35
black students, 67; and constitutional rights, denial of, 13–15, 31–35, 39–41; and historically black schools, 19, 67, 173–74, 227n67; and persistent inequity, attributed to purported culture of poverty, 12, 68, 113, 137, 139, 142, 148, 155–56, 174–77 (*see also* academic achievement; colorblind jurisprudence: and racial inequity, naturalization of; discipline: disparities in treatment of white and black students, resegregation: and racial stigma associated with; tracking, academic); and screening to limit desegregation, 9, 14, 19–20, 30–33; and transfer requests, denial of, 16–19, 29–30, 198n58. *See also* Little Rock Nine; *individual entries for students*
Blackmun, Harry A., 201n8
Blossom, Virgil, 93; and *Brown v. Board*, interpretation of, 16–18, 20, 24–25, 27–28, 39, 41–42; and Faubus, Orval, 23–27, 197n48; NAACP criticism of, 17, 21–22, 30–34; professional reputation of, 16–19, 100, 195n7; segregationist criticism and harassment of, 13–15, 17, 22–23. *See also* Blossom Plan; *It HAS Happened Here*
Blossom Plan: as model of minimal compliance, 15–16, 19–20, 24, 28, 76–77 (*see also* minimal compliance); civil rights opposition to, 18, 21–22, 26–27, 30–34; community support for, 20–21, 23; legacy of, 17–18, 34, 38–42, 44–45, 100–101; petition for delay of, 27–28, 33; segregationist opposition to, 20, 22–28, 77 (*see also* Thomason suit). *See also* Blossom, Virgil; *It HAS Happened Here*

Board of Education of Oklahoma City v. Dowell, 12, 137–38, 152–54
Bonilla-Silva, Eduardo, 152, 154
Brantley, Max, 116, 118
Branton, Wiley, 21
Breyer, Stephen, 158–59
Brodie, Ralph, 65, 95–96, 130, 173, 212n57
Brooks Hays: Return to Little Rock, 79–86. *See also* Hays, Brooks; *A Southern Moderate Speaks*
Brown, Minnijean. *See* Trickey, Minnijean Brown
Brown, Robert L., 108
Brown v. Board of Education, 4–5, 174; current interpretation of, 158–60 (*see also* colorblind jurisprudence; *Parents Involved v. Seattle*); federal enforcement of in Little Rock, 1–2, 6–7, 17, 25, 77, 180–86 (*see also* 101st Airborne; Eisenhower, Dwight D.); public opinion in Little Rock, 26, 32, 96, 123, 128, 170–71, 212n57; reaction to (*see* massive resistance; minimal compliance)
Brummett, John, 137
Bullert, B.J., 82
Bumpers, Dale, 85, 120
busing: in Boston, 10, 50–56, 64, 90; as desegregation remedy, 10, 44, 46, 49–52, 54–59, 157; elimination of, 146–47, 160; in Little Rock, 7, 42–44, 46–48, 56–70, 94, 202n16; media coverage of, 50–52, 54–55; national opposition to, 10, 44, 48, 54–55, 62–63, 187; redefined as problem, 11, 48, 66–70, 99, 101, 105, 187

Capital Citizens' Council, 7–9, 13, 33–34, 75. *See also* White Citizens' Council
Carmichael, Stokely, 35
Carter, James Earl, Jr., 85
CBS, 90, 210–11n49
Central High Museum, Inc.: conflict within, 119–22, 126–27; organization of, 114–15, 118–21; planning committee, deliberations of, 122–27.

See also Little Rock Central High Museum and Visitor Center

Central High School: academic reputation of, 20, 116–17, 132–33, 174–75; administration of, 13, 21, 25, 27–28, 33–34, 86–89, 92 (*see also* discipline); as historic site, 116, 128, 179–80, 184, 188–89 (*see also* Little Rock Central High Museum and Visitor Center; Little Rock Central High School National Historic Site); symbolism of, 50–51, 59–65, 94, 112–13, 146–47 (*see also* anniversary commemoration)

Central High School Neighborhood Association, 112, 118–19, 134–35

Central in Our Lives, 173. *See also* Brodie, Ralph

Charles, Dale, 118, 134, 164

charter schools, 7, 166

Civil Rights Act (1964), 3, 5, 40, 45, 59–60, 187

civil rights activists: in Little Rock, 30, 36, 47, 69, 180, 219–21n58; marginalization of, 11, 65, 73, 91, 93, 99, 110, 150, 211n53, 219–21n58; and public memory, 12, 69, 112, 118, 152, 159–60 (*see also* public memory). *See also individual entries for civil rights organizations and activists*

Clark, Delores, 40

Clark v. Board of Education, 40–41, 43–47, 78, 106–8

Clinton, William Jefferson: and fortieth anniversary commemoration, 134, 142–43, 146, 148; as governor, 83, 104; and national historic site, 116, 120

Cold War, 6, 182–85

Collins, Cathy, 125, 127

Collins, Leo, 54

colorblind jurisprudence, 3, 11, 42, 151–160; minimal compliance, connections to, 42, 69, 152, 155, 161–63; and race-conscious remedies, rejection of, 52–53, 56–57, 69, 152–60; and race-neutral rhetoric, 18, 42, 45, 48, 143; and racial inequity,

naturalization of, 150–56, 174–77. *See also* resegregation; unitary status

compensatory education programs, 7, 58, 105, 109–10, 136, 140, 155–56. *See also* neighborhood schools: and racial isolation; resegregation

Cooper v. Aaron. See Aaron v. Cooper

Crenshaw, J. C., 21

Crisis at Central High: film, adaptation as, 86–87, 90–98, 168, 210–11n49; manuscript, reactions to, 89–90; white students, depiction of, 86–87. *See also* Huckaby, Elizabeth

Dailey, Jim, 117, 133, 134, 143

Daughtery, Robert, 164

Davies, Ronald N., 27

Davis, C. Anderson, 61

desegregation: reaction to, 102 (*see also* busing; resegregation); resistance to (*see* massive resistance; minimal compliance); systemic, 41, 45–48, 74. *See also* racial balance

Desegregation Settlement Agreement (1989), 117; compliance, definition of, 113–14, 137–42; implementation and assessment, 137, 139–41. *See also* incentive schools; interdistrict consolidation

discipline: disparities in treatment of black and white students, 7, 132, 136–37, 147; procedures during 1957–59 desegregation crisis, 17, 33, 88–89, 92, 130–31

Down from the Hills, 71–73. *See also* Faubus, Orval

Dudziak, Mary L., 183

Duvall, Leland, 72

Eckford, Elizabeth, 93, 167–69; first day of classes, 50–51, 61, 96–98, 129, 169 (*see also* massive resistance; media coverage); reflections of, 131, 133–34, 149–50, 185. *See also* Little Rock Nine

Education First, 56

Eisenhower, Dwight D., 1–2, 78, 91, 129; and *Brown v. Board,* enforcement of,

Eisenhower, Dwight D. (*continued*)
  25, 55, 77 (*see also* 101st Airborne);
  framing of school desegregation
  crisis, 6, 80–85, 123
Elementary and Secondary School
  Education Act (1965), 40
Ernest Green Story, 169. *See also* Green,
  Ernest

Fabre, Genevieve, 36, 118, 151
Fair, Paul R., 63–64
Faubus, Orval, 6, 15, 33, 77, 129;
  executive power of, 23–24; legacy
  of, 71–73, 91, 111, 128, 151; massive
  resistance, influence on, 24–26, 110,
  170, 172, 186; opponents, views on,
  72, 197n48, 216n12. *See also Down
  from the Hills*
Federal Communications Commission,
  81
Fisher, George, 84
Flemmings, George D., 59
Ford, Gerald R., 55
freedom-of-choice plans, 10, 7, 17, 157;
  constitutionality of, 40–41, 56. *See
  also* minimal compliance
Freeman v. Pitts, 12, 137–38, 153, 155
Friday, Herschel, 102
Fuller, Jennifer, 143

Garrity, W. Arthur, Jr., 50
geographic segregation. *See* residential
  segregation
Gillis, John, 3
Gordon, Tammy S., 59
gradualism, 8–9, 11, 18–19; as a
  mechanism of delay, 35, 69–70. *See
  also* minimal compliance
Graham, Allison, 91
Gratz v. Bollinger, 165
Green, Ernest, 129–30, 168–
  69; and fortieth anniversary
  commemoration, 142, 144–45, 148.
  See also *The Ernest Green Story*;
  Little Rock Nine
Green v. New Kent County, 41–43, 46,
  69, 110, 187

Griffin, Rev. Wendell, 118
Grutter v. Bollinger, 165
Guggenheim, Charles, 184

Hall, Jacquelyn Dowd, 3
Hall High School, 19, 68, 160
Hays, Brooks, 74–86, 98–99; and *Brown
  v. Board*, interpretation of, 75–79, 85,
  105; and Little Rock, representations
  of, 77, 82, 84; as martyr, 77–80,
  83, 85–86, 98–99 (*see also* white
  moderates: heroization of); and
  states' rights, 74–77, 85. See also
  *Brooks Hays: Return to Little Rock;
  Politics Is My Parish; A Southern
  Moderate Speaks*
Health, Education, and Welfare,
  Department of (HEW), 40, 47
history: passive construction of, 11–12,
  47–48, 63–70, 94, 137, 152, 177–78,
  180, 185; and historicization of civil
  rights movement, 9–12, 143, 152–53,
  177–78, 187–89; and historicization
  of Little Rock school desegregation
  crisis, 8–12, 56, 64–66, 112, 125,
  145–46, 149–50, 171. *See also* public
  history; reverse discrimination:
  and co-optation of civil rights
  movement
Holmes, Morris, 63
Horace Mann High School, 19, 174
Housing and Urban Development,
  Department of (HUD), 45. *See also*
  housing, discrimination
housing, discrimination, 19, 45, 52–53,
  66, 103
Huckabee, Mike, 111, 120, 133;
  and fortieth anniversary
  commemoration, 142–44, 146, 148
Huckaby, Elizabeth, 73, 93–94, 108,
  110; *Brown v. Board*, interpretation
  of, 87–88; heroization of, 91–95,
  98–99 (*see also* white moderates:
  heroization of); as vice principal of
  girls, 86–92, 212n57. See also *Crisis at
  Central High*

incentive schools, 7, 109–10, 135–36, 147–48

injunctions, responsibility for, 25–26, 33

integration. *See* desegregation

interdistrict consolidation: as desegregation remedy, 68, 74, 101–2, 157; limitations applied, 7, 105–6, 108–10; opposition to, 104–5. See also *Little Rock v. Pulaski County*

It HAS Happened Here, 10, 14–28; and desegregation litigation, 14–15, 39, 41–42, 100; reactions to, 23, 28, 34, 100, 170; title, source of, 24–25. *See also* Blossom Plan; Blossom, Virgil

Jacoway, Elizabeth, 26, 119–20, 122–25
Johnson, Ben F., III, 56–57
Johnson, Lyndon B., 55, 78
Jones, Nathaniel R., 54
Journal of Arkansas Education, 89
Journey to Little Rock, 169. *See also* Trickey, Minnijean Brown
Justice, Department of (DOJ), 25, 43, 58, 104–5

Karlmark, Gloria Ray, 168, 173–74. *See also* Little Rock Nine
Kearney, Janetta, 118, 127
Kennedy, John F., 78
King, Martin Luther, Jr., 5, 144, 192n10
Kirk, John A., 15, 18, 35–36, 99, 171–72

Lamb, Ted, 29
LaNier, Carlotta Walls, 168–74, 185. *See also* Little Rock Nine
Lessons from Little Rock, 166–67, 170–72, 177–78, 188. *See also* Roberts, Terrence
Levinson, Richard, 90, 92–94
Lewis, Johanna Miller, 122–32
Lewis, Sinclair, 23–24. See also *It HAS Happened Here*: and title
Link, William, 90, 92–93
Lipsitz, George, 93
Little Rock, 17 Years After, 62–63
Little Rock, race relations: Jim Crow segregation, 7, 9, 34, 36, 171–74; and persistence of inequity, 7, 39–41, 107–8, 113–14, 132–37, 148, 160–66, 176–78 (*see also* resegregation); progress over time, 47–48, 61–66, 69–70, 82, 87, 94–95, 110–12, 116, 132, 145–46, 171 (*see also* unitary status: as symbol of progress); progressive reputation, 20–21, 34, 36, 48, 65–66, 82–83, 87, 98–99, 110, 170–172, 186

Little Rock Central: 50 Years Later, 176–77

Little Rock Central High Museum and Visitor Center, 144; creation of, 114–127; dedication of, 133–34; exhibit within, 115, 121–22, 127–32; mission of, 125, 134. *See also* Central High Museum, Inc.

Little Rock Central High School National Historic Site: dedication of, 148–49, 180; education, discussion of, 180, 187–89; exhibits within, 179–182, 184–188; park rangers, 168, 180, 228n2; political support for, 116, 119–21

Little Rock Chamber of Commerce, 115–16, 216n12

Little Rock Housing Authority, 19, 45. *See also* housing, discrimination

Little Rock Nine: and anniversary commemorations, 65, 113, 133–34, 144–46; education, views on, 142, 144–45, 148, 175–78; harassment of, 13–14, 33, 88–89, 92, 129–31, 170, 172–73, 186, 226n42; parents of, 37, 93, 144–45, 168–69; as pioneers, 16, 35, 47, 53–54, 93, 144–45, 150–51, 180–81, 185; and public memory, 12, 130, 150–51, 184–86, 166–70, 177–78 (*see also* public memory); self-determination of, 37–38, 173–74, 185–86; silence of, 167–69, 184, 226n42; trademark, 170. *See also entries for individual students*

Little Rock Nine Foundation, 170
Little Rock Racial and Cultural Diversity Commission, 125
Little Rock v. Pulaski County, 101–6;

Little Rock v. Pulaski County (continued)
  LRSD as plaintiff, 103–14, 109–10, 162–63, 225n28; unitary status, petition for, 139–41, 160–65
Long Shadow of Little Rock, 14, 28–42, 195n5; reactions to, 15, 35–36, 73, 99. *See also* Bates, Daisy
Louisiana State University Press, 90
Love, Brandon, 160

magnet schools, 7, 99, 104–5, 140, 157; interdistrict, 105, 108, 147
Marable, Manning, 59
Margolick, David, 169
Marshall, Thurgood, 93, 102–3
marshals, United States, 25
Masem, Paul, 100–102, 106
massive resistance, 7–8, 22, 34–35, 76; and class, 170–71, 226–27n53; local sources of, 33–34, 172, 186; outside influence on, 15, 21, 23, 65–66, 77, 110, 170; v. minimal compliance, 15–17, 20, 28, 75–77, 171, 174 (*see also* minimal compliance); and school board recall, 34, 132, 201n11, 216n12; and school closure, 7, 17, 64–65, 89, 131–32; and states' rights, 22, 26, 128. *See also* Capital Citizens' Council; Eckford, Elizabeth: first day of classes; Faubus, Orval; media coverage; Mothers League of Central High School; National Guard; White Citizens' Council
Matthews, Jess, 92–93
Mayo, Ross, 138–39
McClellan, John L., 43–44
McCord, Robert, 141
McGee, Frank, 80
Means, Greg, 64
media coverage, 80–81, 172–73, 208–209n24, 226n42; and public memory, 50–52, 54–55, 80–86, 91, 96–98, 116, 129 (*see also* public memory); of Little Rock schools, 136–37. *See also entries for individual newspapers, film productions, and broadcast outlets*

A Mighty Long Way, 168–74. *See also* LaNier, Carlotta Walls
Miller, Laura, 125
Milliken v. Bradley, 102–3
minimal compliance, 15–20, 28, 30–33, 76–79; constitutionality of, 13–15, 17–18, 21–22, 28–35, 39–41; legacy of, 3, 42, 69, 152, 155, 161–63, 171 (*see also* colorblind jurisprudence); v. massive resistance, 9–10, 15–17, 20, 28, 75, 171, 174 (*see also* massive resistance). *See also* attendance zones; Blossom Plan; freedom-of-choice plans; gradualism; pupil placement plans; token integration; transfers, of students; white moderates
Missouri v. Jenkins, 12, 137–38, 155–56
Mitchell, John H., 43
moderates, white. *See* white moderates
Morgan, Edward P., 91
Mosaic Templars Cultural Center, 115–16, 118
Mothershed, Thelma. *See* Wair, Thelma Mothershed
Mothers League of Central High School, 13
museums, 111–12, 114–18, 122–23, 128, 131; relevance of, 125–26, 132–34. *See also* public history; *entries for individual institutions*

NAACP, 35: Arkansas State Conference 13, 36–38; and Blossom Plan, challenge to, 21–23, 27–28, 30–33 (*see also* Blossom Plan); Little Rock branch and national office, 21, 36–38, 170, 196n25, 199n82; and public memory, 59–61, 113–14, 132, 134, 148, 168, 219–20n58 (*see also* public memory); and school desegregation litigation, 4, 14–16, 30, 36, 132, 158, 164, 219–20n58. *See also* Bates, Daisy
NAACP Legal Defense Fund (LDF), 62–63
National Broadcasting Company, (NBC), 80–81, 90, 98
National Guard: federalized, 88, 129;

and segregation, enforcement of, 6, 24, 27, 33, 88, 96 (*see also* Faubus, Orval; massive resistance)
National Park Service, 120, 184, 186. *See also* Little Rock Central High School National Historic Site
Negro Council on Community Affairs, Little Rock (COCA), 38–40
neighborhood schools: as constitutionally faultless, 39, 45, 56–57 (*see also* colorblind jurisprudence); and racial isolation of, 48, 66, 103, 106, 114, 147–48; as remedy for white flight, 101, 103, 106, 140–41 (*see also* white flight); *See also* attendance zones; housing, discrimination; resegregation; residential segregation
Nichols, Ronnie, 125
Nine from Little Rock, 183–84. *See also* Eisenhower, Dwight D.
Nixon, Richard M.: busing moratorium, 49, 57–59; Faubus, Orval, comparison to, 60–61 (*see also* Faubus, Orval); federal law, enforcement of, 55, 59–61; Supreme Court, impact on, 58, 70, 102–3, 137–38, 187
Nora, Pierre, 150
North Little Rock School District (NLRSD), 100, 103, 109
Norwood v. Tucker, 29

Office of Desegregation Monitoring, 140
Omi, Michael, 155–56
101st Airborne: deployment of, 1–2, 6–7, 25, 129, 183; resentment of, 6–8, 17, 20, 25, 186; withdrawal of, 13, 86, 88
Oregon Report, 56
Orfield, Gary, 140–41, 153–54

Parents Involved v. Seattle, 156–60, 165, 224nn19–20
passive resistance. *See* minimal compliance
Parkview High School, 68
Parsons, Floyd W., 56, 58

Parsons Plan, 56
Partial K-6 Plan, 106–8
Patrons Organization Committee, 101
Patterson, T.E., 45
Pattillo, Melba. *See* Beals, Melba Pattillo
Philander Smith College, 175
Plessy v. Ferguson, 3
Politics Is My Parish, 76. *See also* Hays, Brooks
Pondexter, Linda, 138–39
Public Broadcasting Act (1967), 81
public history, 116, 118, 122–126. *See also* history museums; public memory
public memory: African American, 36, 58–59, 118, 122–23, 126; of civil rights movement, 3–6; contested, 3–4, 8, 12, 149–51, 159–60; in courts of law, 8, 11, 14–16, 28, 42, 48, 112–13, 157–60; and social change, 12, 36, 118, 150–52, 159–60, 167, 177–80, 184–89. *See also* history; public history
public television, 79–84, 209n27
Pulaski Academy, 47, 202n11
Pulaski County Special School District (PCSSD): and boundary adjustments, 100, 105–6; interdistrict consolidation, appeal of, 105–6 (see also interdistrict consolidation; *Little Rock v. Pulaski County*); merger, rejection of, 102–3; settlement plans, 108–9 (*see also* Desegregation Settlement Agreement (1989); Revised Desegregation Plan)
pupil placement plans, 7, 9–10, 17–18, 35, 216n12; complaints about, 38–40; constitutionality of, 29, 40, 43. *See also* minimal compliance
Pryor, David, 85, 117

racial balance: attainment of, 63, 94, 157; and demographic shifts, 140, 147–48, 153, 187 (*see also* resegregation); and race-conscious student assignment, 45, 109. *See also* desegregation
racism, redefinition of, 112, 144, 151–52, 155–59, 175. *See also* reverse discrimination

Raiford, Leigh, 159, 182
Rains, Craig, 130
Ray, Gloria. *See* Karlmark, Gloria Ray
Reagan, Ronald W., 104–5
Reaves, Lee, 81–83
reconciliation, racial, 111–13, 128, 136, 143; and symbolic renunciation of racial violence, 112, 117, 211n53 (*see also* anniversary commemoration: fortieth; segregationists: mob violence)
Rector, William, 47, 201n11
resegregation, 1–2, 101, 141, 153–54; and racially identifiable schools, 101, 105–9, 147–48, 160, 163–66; and racial stigma associated with, 147–48, 177. *See also* colorblind jurisprudence; neighborhood schools; residential segregation; white flight
residential segregation: impact on schools, 7, 19, 148, 160, 195n18 (*see also* attendance zones: impact on residential segregation); naturalization of, 48, 57–58, 66, 69, 154 (*see also* colorblind jurisprudence); prevalence of, 19, 45, 187. *See also* housing, discrimination; white fight
reverse discrimination, 9, 45, 152, 156–60; and co-optation of civil rights movement, 69–70, 142, 152, 15, 158–60, 165, 167. *See also* colorblind jurisprudence; *Parents Involved v. Seattle*
Revised Desegregation Plan, 113, 145–48, 161–63. See also *Little Rock v. Pulaski County;* unitary status
Renaud, Brent, 176–77
Renaud, Craig, 176
Reynolds, William Bradford, 104–5
Riggs, Cliff, 135
Roberts, John, 158–9
Roberts, Terrence: reflections of, 166–68, 170–74, 177–78, 188; testimony in court, 160–163. See also *Lessons from Little Rock;* Little Rock Nine
Robinson, Tommy F., 104

Romano, Renee C., 8, 81, 91, 144, 159, 182
Roosevelt, Eleanor, 35
Rothstein, Fryeda, 94, 211n49
Rousseau, Nancy, 176
Roy, Beth, 173
Rutherford, Skip, 117–18, 130, 132, 139, 148

Samuels, Gertrude, 30
Scalia, Antonin, 158–59
Schmutz, Fred, 80–83
segregation: de facto v. de jure, 5, 10, 49, 52–56 , 203n21; regional distinctions, 10, 43, 49–56, 202n16; vestiges of, 70, 103, 137, 153, 155. *See also* Little Rock, race relations: segregation
segregationists: and Faubus, Orval, 24–26, 110, 170, 172, 186; harassment of Little Rock Nine, 13–14, 33, 88–89, 92, 129–31, 170, 172–73, 186, 226n42; intimidation of white moderates, 22–24, 33, 74, 88, 170; local support for, 33–34, 172, 186; and mob violence, 22–25, 27–28, 50, 54–55, 80, 82–84, 96–98, 129; outside influence on, 15, 21, 23, 65–66, 77, 110, 170; students, 13–14, 88–89, 92, 129–31, 174. *See also* massive resistance; Thomason suit; *individual entries for segregationist organizations*
Sherrill, Peter, 106
Shores, Elizabeth, 85
Snyder, Vic, 120
Solomon, David, 79–81, 83, 85
Southern Christian Leadership Conference (SCLC), 5
Southern Mediator Journal, 54, 93
A Southern Moderate Speaks, 76–79. *See also* Hays, Brooks
Southern Regional Council, 34
Springer, Joy, 136
Starr, John R., 141
State Department, United States, 183
State Sovereignty Commission, Arkansas, 23–24
states' rights. *See* Hays, Brooks: and states' rights; massive resistance: and states' rights

Stevens, John Paul, 159
Stevenson, Sybil, 53–54
Street, Paul, 113
Student Nonviolent Coordinating Committee (SNCC), 5
Supreme Court, 9, 11, 58, 102, 137–38. *See also* massive resistance; minimal compliance; *entries for individual cases*
Swann v. Charlotte-Mecklenburg Board of Education, 46, 69, 201n8

Tate, U. Simpson, 21, 199n82
Testament monument, 151
Testing, standardized. *See* academic achievement: assessment of
Theoharis, Jeanne, 53, 202n16
Thomas, Clarence, 158–59
Thomas, Jefferson, 168. *See also* Little Rock Nine
Thomason suit, 26–27, 197n48. *See also* Blossom Plan: segregationist opposition to; Faubus, Orval: massive resistance, influence on
Time-Life Films, 90–93, 211n49
token integration, 8–9, 11, 13, 78–79; constitutional rights, denial of, 13–15, 31–35, 39–41; legacy of, 176. *See also* minimal compliance
tourism, 115, 117, 131–32, 136
tracking, academic, 7, 132, 136–37, 143, 160–61, 176. *See also* academic achievement
transfers, of students, 9; black students, denial of requests, 16–19, 29–30, 198n58 (*see also* black students); majority-to-minority interdistrict, 105, 147–48 (*see also* interdistrict consolidation; *Little Rock v. Pulaski County*); white students, leaving integrated institutions, 29–30, 33, 104 (*see also* white students). *See also* minimal compliance; pupil placement plans
transportation, student. *See* busing
Trickey, Minnijean Brown: expulsion of, 17, 33–34, 92, 212n57; reflections of, 168–69, 176–78, 188. *See also* Little Rock Nine
Trickey, Spirit, 168, 228n2
Trouillot, Michel-Rolph, 4
Tucker, Everett, Jr., 116–17, 216n12. *See also Norwood v. Tucker*
Tucker, Everett, III, 116–21, 127, 130

unitary status, 7, 145–46, 160–66 (see also *Little Rock v. Pulaski County*); and persistence of inequality, 9, 165–66 (*see also* resegregation); and racial innocence, 154–55, 158–60, 163, 165 (*see also* Little Rock, race relations: progressive reputation); as symbol of progress, 7, 145, 153–55, 157 (*see also* Little Rock, race relations: progress over time); and unconstitutionality of race-conscious student assignment, 158–60, 163–65 (*see also* colorblind jurisprudence; *Parents Involved v. Seattle*)
United States Information Agency, 183–84
University of Arkansas at Little Rock, 122, 124–25, 141
Upton, Wayne, 26
urban redevelopment, 45, 52, 115, 154. *See also* housing, discrimination; residential segregation
US Commission on Civil Rights, 49; and busing, 61–63, 67–68

Vann, David, 117–18, 148
Voting Rights Act (1965), 3, 5

Wair, Thelma Mothershed, 41, 168. *See also* Little Rock Nine
Walberg, Herbert, 139–41
Walker, John W., 58, 62, 103, 106, 135, 137, 164–66
Walls, Carlotta. *See* LaNier, Carlotta Walls
Warriors Don't Cry, 168–69, 173. *See also* Beals, Melba Pattillo
West End, of Little Rock, 19, 56, 202n11;

West End (continued)
opposition to busing, 56–57, 68, 74. See also attendance zones; neighborhood schools; residential segregation

White Citizens' Council, 8, 22, 170. See also Capital Citizens' Council

white flight, 11, 68, 132, 141; acceleration of, 99–100, 106; planned response to, 101–10, 147; to private schools, 47, 74, 99–101, 108, 160; as response to litigation, 141, 147, 195n18, 206n58 (see also busing: redefined as problem); to suburbs, 74, 100–101, 104–5, 201–2n11. See also housing, discrimination; *Little Rock v. Pulaski County;* residential segregation

White, Frank, 104

White, Robin, 180

white moderates, 9, 73–75, 78–79, 171; heroization of, 11, 65–66, 73, 78, 91, 94, 99, 110, 211n53, 219n58; intimidation of, 22–24, 33, 74, 88, 170; prevalence of, 82–83, 85–87, 98–99, 110, 131–32; relatability of, 72–73, 91–93, 98, 110; revival of policies, 73, 86, 99, 104–10; scholarship related to, 99. See also individual entries for white moderates and moderate organizations

white students: as bystanders, 87, 95–98, 130–31, 173, 212n66; declining enrollment of, 47, 100, 136 (see also white flight); discrimination against, 9, 45, 156–60 (see *Parents Involved v. Seattle;* reverse discrimination); preferential treatment of, 108, 160–61; as segregationists, 13–14, 88–89, 92, 129–31, 174 (see also segregationists). See also individual entries for students

Williams, Henry, 138, 141

Wilson, William, 162–63, 165

Winant, Howard, 155–56

Wise, Tim, 155

Women's Emergency Committee to Open Our Schools (WEC), 132, 216n12, 219n58. See also massive resistance: and school board recall; massive resistance: and school closure; white moderates

Woods, Henry, 103–04

Woodward, Joanne, 90, 94

Wright, Susan Webber, 146

X, Malcolm, 192n10

ERIN KRUTKO DEVLIN was raised in Cleveland, Ohio, a city that has also struggled with a history of racial segregation. She received her PhD in American studies in 2011 from the College of William and Mary, where her work on the public memory of the Little Rock school desegregation crisis received the Distinguished Dissertation Award in Humanities and Social Sciences. While completing her degree, she also wrote a National Park Service cultural resource study focused on segregation and African American visitation in Shenandoah National Park. Devlin has been a visiting instructor at Washington and Lee University and the Virginia Military Institute and assistant professor of American and public history at the University of Wisconsin–Eau Claire. She is currently assistant professor of history and American studies at the University of Mary Washington.